Russian Tutor
Grammar and Vocabulary Workbook

Michael Ransome and Marta Tomaszewski

First published in Great Britain in 2016 by John Murray Learning. An Hachette UK company.

Database right: Hodder & Stoughton (makers)

The *Teach Yourself* name is a registered trademark of Hachette UK.

British Library Cataloguing in Publication Data: a catalogue record for this title is available from the British Library.

Library of Congress Catalog Card Number: on file.

9781473623484

6

The publisher has used its best endeavours to ensure that any website addresses referred to in this book are correct and active at the time of going to press. However, the publisher and the author have no responsibility for the websites and can make no guarantee that a site will remain live or that the content will remain relevant, decent or appropriate.

The publisher has made every effort to mark as such all words which it believes to be trademarks. The publisher should also like to make it clear that the presence of a word in the book, whether marked or unmarked, in no way affects its legal status as a trademark.

Every reasonable effort has been made by the publisher to trace the copyright holders of material in this book. Any errors or omissions should be notified in writing to the publisher, who will endeavour to rectify the situation for any reprints and future editions.

Typeset by Cenveo© Publisher Services.

Printed and bound in Great Britain by CPI Group (UK) Ltd., Croydon, CR0 4YY.

John Murray Learning policy is to use papers that are natural, renewable and recyclable products and made from wood grown in sustainable forests. The logging and manufacturing processes are expected to conform to the environmental regulations of the country of origin.

Carmelite House
50 Victoria Embankment
London EC4Y 0DZ
www.hodder.co.uk

CONTENTS

Scope & sequence of units vi

Meet the authors x

How to use this book xi

The Russian alphabet xii

The Discovery Method xiii

Become a successful language learner xiv

UNIT 1
Я ищу 1
I'm looking for

UNIT 2
Приятного аппетита! 11
Enjoy your meal!

UNIT 3
Кто на фотографии? 20
Who is in the photograph?

UNIT 4
Это тебе очень идёт! 30
It really suits you!

UNIT 5
Вам понравилось? 38
Did you like it?

UNIT 6
Что ты делаешь в свободное время? 46
What do you do in your free time?

UNIT 7
Мой день 55
My day

UNIT 8
Какие у тебя планы? 61
What are your plans?

UNIT 9
Как**о**й у теб**я** реж**и**м? 70
What is your fitness regime?

UNIT 10
В зав**и**симости от пог**о**ды 78
It depends on the weather

UNIT 11
Куд**а**? 86
Where are you going?

UNIT 12
С пр**а**здником! 98
Let's celebrate!

UNIT 13
Если бы! 106
If only!

UNIT 14
Что случ**и**лось? 115
What happened?

UNIT 15
Ск**о**лько? 122
How many?

UNIT 16
Где жить? 132
Where should we stay?

UNIT 17
М**о**жно? 140
May I …?

UNIT 18
Скаж**и**те, пож**а**луйста! 147
Can you tell me, please?

UNIT **19**

Сег**о**дня на раб**о**те 155
Today at work

UNIT **20**

В сл**е**дующий раз 162
Next time …

Answer key 171

Glossary of grammatical terms. 229

Russian–English glossary 233

SCOPE AND SEQUENCE OF UNITS

Unit	CEFR	Topic	Learning outcome
UNIT 1 **Я ищу** pages 1–10	A1–B2	*Shopping*	• Describe what you are buying • Discuss quantities
UNIT 2 **Приятного аппетита!** pages 11–19	A2–B2	*Eating out*	• State likes and dislikes • Give reasons for opinions
UNIT 3 **Кто на фотографии?** pages 20–29	B1	*Family*	• Describe family in detail
UNIT 4 **Это тебе очень идёт!** pages 30–37	A2–B1	*Fashion*	• Describe clothes in detail
UNIT 5 **Вам понравилось?** pages 38–45	B1	*Media and culture*	• Give opinions about media
UNIT 6 **Что ты делаешь в свободное время?** pages 46–54	B1	*Hobbies and pastimes*	• Describe free-time activities and the reasons for choosing them
UNIT 7 **Мой день** pages 55–60	A2–B1	*Daily routine*	• Describe your own daily routine • Compare daily routines
UNIT 8 **Какие у тебя планы?** pages 61–69	B1–B2	*Holidays*	• Describe past holidays • Discuss future holiday plans
UNIT 9 **Какой у тебя режим?** pages 70–77	A1–B2	*Healthy living*	• Tell the time • Discuss healthy living
UNIT 10 **В зависимости от погоды** pages 78–85	A1–B1	*Weather*	• Discuss the weather • Explain what does *not* happen

Language		Skills	
GRAMMAR	**VOCABULARY**	**READING**	**WRITING**
Nominative, accusative and genitive cases	Food; clothes	A shopping trip	Describe your shopping trip in tweets™
Dative, instrumental and prepositional cases	Eating out; opinions	Restaurant reviews	Restaurant review
Pronouns	Family; people	A biography	An autobiography online
Adjectives	Clothes; colours	A fashion show blog	Survey about fashion
Comparative and superlative adjectives and adverbs	Media	A history of censorship	Viewing habits on a registration page
Verbs in the present tense	Free-time activities	Online survey about free time	Messaging about family free time
Reflexive verbs The passive voice	Daily routine	An email comparing typical days at work	A report on your working lifestyle
Past tense Future tense Aspect in Russian	Holiday activities	Online holiday home advert with reviews	A holiday blog
Telling the time Temporal phrases and prepositions	Sport and fitness	Article about healthy lifestyles	An online fitness survey
Negative expressions	Weather	Article on climate change	Holiday weather updates

UNIT 11 Куда? pages 86–97	A2–B1	Journeys	• Describe journeys in detail • Give instructions
UNIT 12 С праздником! pages 98–105	B1	Celebrations	• Form more complex sentences
UNIT 13 Если бы! pages 106–114	B2	Illnesses	• Discuss real and hypothetical situations
UNIT 14 Что случилось? pages 115–121	B1	Accidents	• Report what has been said or asked
UNIT 15 Сколько? pages 122–131	A2–B1	Long-haul travel	• Use numbers in a variety of ways
UNIT 16 Где жить? pages 132–139	B1	Accommodation	• Give detailed reasons and justifications for choices
UNIT 17 Можно? pages 140–146	B2	Customs and traditions	• Ask for permission and say what should or should not be done
UNIT 18 Скажите, пожалуйста! pages 147–154	A1–A2	Interviews	• Ask a range of questions • Give precise answers
UNIT 19 Сегодня на работе pages 155–161	B2	The world of work	• Understand a range of professional vocabulary
UNIT 20 Следующий раз … pages 162–170	B1	Living abroad	• Give nuanced answers to questions

Verbs of motion Imperatives	Trips	Office memo about travel abroad	A memo giving advice for a business trip to Moscow
The relative pronoun Verbs followed by specific prepositions	Celebrations and festivals	Blog entry about a Russian national holiday	Describing a photo from a celebration
The conditional and subjunctive moods	Illnesses	Magazine article about common illnesses	A diary entry about a trip affected by illness
Indirect statements and questions	Accidents	Accident reports	A report to support an insurance claim
Cardinal and ordinal numbers	Travel	A travelogue about the Trans-Siberian railway	A blog about a car journey across Russia
Compound conjunctions	Accommodation; furniture	Online adverts from an estate agent	An email describing your ideal home
Modal verbs and expressions	Traditions	A blog about superstitions	An account of superstitions in a letter
Interrogatives	Personal information	An interview with a Russian singer	A magazine interview with a celebrity
Adjectival and other pronouns	Business	An annual performance review	An appraisal of your Russian studies so far
Gerunds, reflexive pronouns	Living abroad	An article about living abroad	A blog about the experience of living abroad

Michael Ransome

I have taught Russian O level, GCSE and A level for some 35 years and throughout that time have been the co-author of many Russian courses widely used in UK schools at all levels, from beginners to university entrance. Having always sought to embrace the possibilities offered by new technologies in producing new materials and teaching, recently I have been developing materials to enable the secondary-school Russian classroom to benefit from rapidly evolving online opportunities, as well as student use of personal devices in their routine learning.

Marta Tomaszewski

I have taught Russian in schools for over ten years and have delivered INSET nationally on teaching Russian. I am also the co-editor and co-author of *Na Start*, *Vnimanie*, *Marsh*, the leading GCSE Russian course in schools. Having been brought up bilingual in Polish and English and then having studied French, Russian, German, Spanish and Romanian to differing levels and at different stages of my life, I hugely enjoy not just learning languages but also comparing their similarities and differences and finding out about new cultures. I am a strong believer in the notion that language is the key to any culture and that anyone can learn a second language if they have the motivation to do so.

If you have studied Russian before but would like to brush up on or improve your grammar, vocabulary, reading and writing skills, this is the book for you. *Russian Tutor* is a grammar workbook which contains a comprehensive grammar syllabus from high beginner to upper intermediate and combines grammar and vocabulary presentations with over 200 practice exercises.

The language you will learn is presented through concise explanations, engaging exercises, simple infographics, and personal tutor tips. The infographics present complex grammar points in an accessible format while the personal tutor tips offer advice on correct usage, colloquial alternatives, exceptions to rules, etc. Each unit contains reading comprehension activities incorporating the grammar and vocabulary taught, as well as free writing and real-life tasks. The focus is on building up your skills while reinforcing the target language. The reading stimuli include emails, blogs, social media posts and business letters using real language, so you can be sure you are learning vocabulary and grammar that will be useful for you.

You can work through the workbook by itself or you can use it alongside our *Complete Russian* course or any other language course. This workbook has been written to reflect and expand upon the content of *Complete Russian* and is a good place to go if you would like to practise your reading and writing skills on the same topics.

Icons

- Discovery
- Vocabulary
- Writing
- Reading
- Personal tutor

Abbreviations

acc.	accusative	nom.	nominative
dat.	dative	perf.	perfective
fem.	feminine	pl.	plural
gen.	genitive	prep.	preposition
instr.	instrumental	sing.	singular
masc.	masculine		

It is important, but not always easy, to know where the stress should be placed when pronouncing a word in Russian. Therefore, in this book, you will find the stress in a word indicated by the use of **bold** text for the relevant vowel (syllables in Russian are always based around a vowel). If there is no **bold** text, this is because the placement of the stress is clear either because the word has only one vowel (and therefore is monosyllabic) or because the word contains the Russian letter ё, which always carries the stress.

Printed capital	Handwritten capital	Printed small	Handwritten small	Pronunciation
А	*А*	а	*а*	sounds slightly shorter than *a* in f*a*ther
Б	*Б*	б	*б*	sounds like *b* in *b*ox
В	*В*	в	*в*	sounds like *v* in *v*isit
Г	*Г*	г	*г*	sounds like *g* in *g*oat
Д	*Д*	д	*д*	sounds like *d* in *d*aughter
Е	*Е*	е	*е*	sounds like *ye* in *ye*t
Ё	*Ё*	ё	*ё*	sounds like *yo* in *yo*nder
Ж	*Ж*	ж	*ж*	sounds like *s* in plea*s*ure
З	*З*	з	*з*	sounds like *z* in *z*oo
И	*И*	и	*и*	sounds like *ee* in f*ee*t
Й	*Й*	й	*й*	sounds like *y* in bo*y*
К	*К*	к	*к*	sounds like *k* in *k*it
Л	*Л*	л	*л*	sounds like *l* in bott*l*e
М	*М*	м	*м*	sounds like *m* in *m*otor
Н	*Н*	н	*н*	sounds like *n* in *n*ovel
О	*О*	о	*о*	sounds like *aw* in l*aw*
П	*П*	п	*п*	sounds like *p* in *p*each
Р	*Р*	р	*р*	sounds like *r* in *r*at
С	*С*	с	*с*	sounds like *s* in *s*ip
Т	*Т*	т	*т,т*	sounds like *t* in *t*ired
У	*У*	у	*у*	sounds like *oo* in sh*oo*t
Ф	*Ф*	ф	*ф*	sounds like *f* in *f*ather
Х	*Х*	х	*х*	sounds like *ch* in lo*ch* (Scots)
Ц	*Ц*	ц	*ц*	sounds like *ts* in qui*ts*
Ч	*Ч*	ч	*ч*	sounds like *ch* in *ch*ick
Ш	*Ш*	ш	*ш*	sounds like *sh* in *sh*ift
Щ	*Щ*	щ	*щ*	sounds like *shch* in po*sh ch*ina
		ъ	*ъ*	hard sign – no separate sound
		ы	*ы*	sounds like *i* in *i*ll
		ь	*ь*	soft sign – no separate sound
Э	*Э*	э	*э*	sounds like *e* in l*e*t
Ю	*Ю*	ю	*ю*	sounds like *yu* in *yu*le
Я	*Я*	я	*я*	sounds like *ya* in *ya*k

THE DISCOVERY METHOD

There are lots of philosophies and approaches to language learning, some practical, some quite unconventional, and far too many to list here. Perhaps you know of a few, or even have some techniques of your own. In this book we have incorporated the Discovery Method of learning, a sort of awareness-raising approach to language learning. This means that you will be encouraged throughout to engage your mind and figure out the language for yourself, through identifying patterns, understanding grammar concepts, noticing words that are similar to English, and more. This method promotes language awareness, a critical skill in acquiring a new language. As a result of your own efforts, you will be able better to retain what you have learnt, use it with confidence, and, what's more, apply those same skills to continuing to learn the language (or, indeed, another one) on your own after you have finished this book.

Everyone can succeed in learning a language – the key is to know how to learn it. Learning is more than just reading or memorizing grammar and vocabulary. It is about being an active learner, learning in real contexts, and, most importantly, using what you have learnt in different situations. Simply put, if you figure something out for yourself, you are more likely to understand it. And when you use what you have learnt, you are more likely to remember it.

As many of the essential but (let's admit it!) challenging details, such as grammar rules, are introduced through the Discovery Method, you will have more fun while learning. Soon, the language will start to make sense and you will be relying on your own intuition to construct original sentences independently, not just reading and copying.

Enjoy yourself!

BECOME A SUCCESSFUL LANGUAGE LEARNER

1 **Make a habit out of learning**
   ▶ Study a little every day – between 20 and 30 minutes is ideal.
   ▶ Give yourself **short-term goals**, e.g. work out how long you will spend on a particular unit and work within this time limit, and **create a study habit**.
   ▶ Try to **create an environment conducive to learning** which is calm and quiet and free from distractions. As you study, do not worry about your mistakes or the things you cannot remember or understand. Languages settle gradually in the brain. Just **give yourself enough time** and you will succeed.

2 **Maximize your exposure to the language**
   ▶ As well as using this book, you can listen to radio, watch television or read online articles and blogs.
   ▶ Do you have a personal passion or hobby? Does a news story interest you? Try to access Russian information about them. It is entertaining and you will become used to a range of writing and speaking styles.

3 **Vocabulary**
   ▶ Group new words under **generic categories** (e.g. *food, furniture*) **situations** in which they occur (e.g. under *restaurant* you can write *waiter, table, menu, bill*) and **functions** (e.g. *greetings, parting, thanks, apologizing*).
   ▶ Write the words over and over again. Keep lists on your smartphone or tablet, but remember to switch the keyboard language so you can type Cyrillic.
   ▶ Cover up the English side of the vocabulary list and see if you remember the meaning of the word. Do the same for the Russian.
   ▶ Create flashcards, drawings and mind maps.
   ▶ Write Russian words on sticky notes and attach them to objects around your house.
   ▶ **Experiment with words.** Look for patterns in words – for example, Russian uses a lot of prepositions as prefixes: **в** (*in*) + ходи́ть (*to go*) = входи́ть (*to enter*)

4 **Grammar**
   ▶ **Experiment with grammar rules**. Sit back and reflect on how the rules of Russian compare with your own language or other languages you may already speak.
   ▶ Use known vocabulary to practise new grammar structures.
   ▶ When you learn a new verb form, write the conjugation of several different verbs you know that follow the same form.

5 **Reading**
The passages in this book include questions to help guide you in your understanding. But you can do more:

   ▶ **Imagine the situation**. Think about what is happening in the extract/passage and make educated guesses, e.g. a blog is likely to be about things someone has been doing.
   ▶ **Guess the meaning of key words before you look them up.** When there are key words you do not understand, try to guess what they mean from the context. If you are reading a Russian text and cannot get the gist of a whole passage because of one word or phrase, try to look at the words around that word and see if you can work out the meaning from context.

6 **Writing**
  ▶ Practice makes perfect. The most successful language learners know how to overcome their inhibitions and keep going.
  ▶ When you write an email to a friend or colleague, or you post something on social media, pretend that you have to do it in Russian.
  ▶ When completing writing exercises, see how many different ways you can write it, imagine yourself in different situations and try answering as if you were someone else.
  ▶ Try writing longer passages such as articles, reviews or essays in Russian, as this will help you to formulate arguments and convey your opinion, as well as helping you to think about how the language works.
  ▶ Try writing a diary in Russian every day, because this will give context to your learning and help you progress in areas which are relevant to you.

7 **Visual learning**
  ▶ Have a look at the infographics in this book. Do they help you to visualize a useful grammar point? You can keep to hand a copy of those you find particularly useful to help you in your studies, or put them on your wall until you remember them. You can also look up infographics on the Internet for topics you are finding particularly tricky to grasp, or even create your own.

8 **Learn from your errors**
  ▶ Making errors is part of any learning process, so do not be so worried about making mistakes that you will not write anything unless you are sure it is correct. This leads to a vicious circle: the less you write, the less practice you get and the more mistakes you make.
  ▶ Note the seriousness of errors. Many errors are not serious as they do not affect the meaning.

9 **Learn to cope with uncertainty**
  ▶ Do not overuse your dictionary. Resist the temptation to look up every word you do not know. Read the same passage several times, concentrating on trying to get the gist of it. If after the third time some words still prevent you from making sense of the passage, look them up in the dictionary.

Я ищу

I'm looking for . . .

In this unit you will learn how to:

- Use nominative, accusative and genitive cases
- Describe what you are buying
- Discuss food and clothes
- Discuss quantities

CEFR: Can use case endings for nouns and adjectives and handle numbers, quantities and cost (CEFR A1); Can understand an article about and write about food (CEFR B2)

Subject	Verb	Direct object
Иван	купил	пиджак и рубашку
Ivan	*bought*	*a jacket and a shirt*
Иван	встретил	Бориса и Анну
Ivan	*met*	*Boris and Anna*

Meaning and usage

Nominative, accusative and genitive cases

Russian has a case system, which applies special endings to nouns and adjectives according to their grammatical role in the sentence. As a result, word order is not fixed in Russian and words can be moved around for emphasis and effect. This means that understanding a sentence in Russian can be really helped by being able to recognize case endings.

There are six cases in Russian – the first three are:

1   Nominative case

This is used for the <u>subject</u> of a sentence. It is the 'dictionary form' of a noun – you can think of it as the 'default setting'.

<u>Иван</u> купил рубашку.   (<u>Ivan</u> bought a shirt.)
<u>Анна</u> купила блузку.   (<u>Anna</u> bought a blouse.)
<u>Пальто</u> стоит 500 рублей.   (<u>The coat</u> costs 500 roubles.)
<u>Студенты</u> купили футболку.   (<u>The students</u> bought a T-shirt.)

2   Accusative case

This is used for the underlined direct object of a sentence. It might be helpful to think of this in terms of 'accusing' someone or something:

e.g. *Anna* (**subject**) *accused* (**verb**) *Ivan* (**direct object**).

Because only feminine nouns have a separate accusative ending, a useful mnemonic for this is:

'A word you do something to, change a to y and я to ю.'

Иван купил рубашку.	*(Ivan bought a shirt.)*
Анна купила пиджак.	*(Anna bought a jacket.)*
Иван купил пальто.	*(Ivan bought a coat.)*
Студенты купили джинсы.	*(The students bought jeans.)*

There is also an animate accusative which is used for people and animals – masculine singular and both masculine and feminine plural. The animate accusative endings are, in fact, the same as the genitive.

Я увидела Ивана в магазине одежды.	*(I saw Ivan in the clothes shop.)*
Анна увидела студентов с покупками.	*(Anna saw the students with shopping.)*
Иван увидел учительниц недалеко от университета.	*(Ivan saw the (female) teachers not far from the university.)*

3   Genitive case

This is used for possession – this is the Russian equivalent of *'s, s'* and *of* in English. It is used after quantity words (a lot of, many of, a few of), and also always after numbers 5 and above (in Russian: 5 of jackets). One of the main uses of the genitive is to indicate absence – in Russian, this is expressed using нет + genitive.

Футболка Ивана стоит 50 рублей.	*(Ivan's T-shirt costs 50 roubles.)*
Пальто Анны – модно.	*(Anna's coat is fashionable.)*
Цвет платья красивый.	*(The colour of the dress is beautiful.)*
одежда студентов	*(the clothes of the students)*
У меня нет пиджака.	*(I do not have a jacket.)*

How to form the nominative and accusative cases

	Masculine inanimate	Masculine animate	Feminine	Neuter
Nominative	шарф	студент	шуба	место
Accusative	шарф	студента	шубу	место
Nominative	трамвай	герой	неделя/станция	здание
Accusative	трамвай	героя	неделю/станцию	здание
Nominative	автомобиль	учитель	дверь	платье
Accusative	автомобиль	учителя	дверь	платье

	Masculine plural inanimate	Masculine plural animate	Feminine plural inanimate	Feminine plural animate	Neuter plural
Nominative	шарфы	студенты	шубы	женщины	места
Accusative	шарфы	студентов	шубы	женщин_	места
Nominative	трамваи	герои	недели/станции	тёти	здания
Accusative	трамваи	героев	недели/станции	тёть	здания
Nominative	автомобили	учителя	двери	матери	платья
Accusative	автомобили	учителей	двери	матерей	платья

A Complete the sentences with the correct form of the missing noun.

1 Иван купил _____ в понедельник.

    a пиджаку   **b** пиджака   **c** пиджак

2 Иван купил _____ в среду.

    a рубашка   **b** рубашку   **c** рубашки

3 Анна увидела _____ , когда она была в центре города.

    a тётя   **b** тётю   **c** тёти

4 Иван увидел _____ на улице.

    a учителя   **b** учитель   **c** учители

5 Вечеринка – сегодня, и у меня новое платье и _____.

    a кофту   **b** кофта   **c** кофты

6 На вечеринке Анна видела _____.

    a Борис   **b** Борисы   **c** Бориса

B Complete the following sentences with the correct form of the noun in brackets, explaining in English your reasons for this choice.

Пример: Маша любит <u>Бориса</u>. (Борис) (masculine animate accusative)

1 Шёл дождь, а Иван забыл _____. (зонтик)

2 Анна долго искала_____. (дочь)

3 Профессор увидел _____. (студенты)

4 На день рождения Борис купил _____. (картина)

5 У меня в сумке _____. (платье)

6 Ты видел в магазине _____. (сувениры)?

How to form the genitive case

	Masculine	Feminine	Neuter
Nominative	шарф	шуба	место
Genitive	шарф<u>а</u>	шуб<u>ы</u>	мест<u>а</u>
Nominative	трамвай	неделя/станция	здание
Genitive	трамва<u>я</u>	недел<u>и</u>/станци<u>и</u>	здани<u>я</u>
Nominative	автомобиль	дверь	платье
Genitive	автомобил<u>я</u>	двер<u>и</u>	плать<u>я</u>

	Masculine plural	Feminine plural	Neuter plural
Nominative	шарф<u>ы</u>	шуб<u>ы</u>	мест<u>а</u>
Genitive	шарф<u>ов</u>	шуб	мест
Nominative	трамва<u>и</u>	недел<u>и</u>/станци<u>и</u>	здани<u>я</u>
Genitive	трамва<u>ев</u>	недель/станци<u>й</u>	здани<u>й</u>
Nominative	автомобил<u>и</u>	двер<u>и</u>	плать<u>я</u>
Genitive	автомобил<u>ей</u>	двер<u>ей</u>	плать<u>ев</u>

Meaning and usage

Translating *I have* etc. into Russian

1   Remember that the Russian for *I have* is у меня followed by the <u>nominative</u> case of the thing you have. You can add the word есть for emphasis – i.e. *I do have*. To say, for example, *Ivan has*, you simply use у + genitive case.

У меня (есть) новый пиджак.   (*I have a new jacket.*)

У Ивана (есть) новые брюки.   (*Ivan has new trousers.*)

У неё (есть) новая блузка.   (*She has a new blouse.*)

C   **Look at what Ivan and Anna have in their suitcases. Answer the following questions as if you were Ivan or Anna.**

Чемодан Ивана

шорты
джинсы
футболка
свитер
трусы
носки
кроссовки

Чемодан Анны

юбка
кофта
майка
вьетнамки
трусы
носки
купальник

1   Иван, у тебя есть шорты?   _____

2   Анна, у тебя есть купальник?   _____

3   Иван, ты забыл свитер?   _____

4   Анна, у тебя есть футболка?   _____

5   Иван, у тебя есть пиджак?   _____

6   Анна, у тебя есть платье?   _____

How to form quantity expressions requiring the genitive case

1   The genitive is used with the following expressions:

много	lots of, a lot of
мало	not much of
сколько?	how many?
несколько	a few
немного	few
большинство	the majority of, most of
достаточно	enough
бутылка	bottle
пачка	packet
банка	can, jar

Examples of the genitive case with quantity words:

много сахара   (lots of sugar)

достаточно молока   (enough milk)

банка рыбы   (a tin of fish)

Have you got enough of the required ingredients to make these pancakes?

Рецепт блинов

Блины с творогом	У меня есть …	Сколько у меня есть?
молоко – 500 мл	молоко – бутылка (500 мл)	достаточно молока
яйца – 3	яйца (коробка – 10)	
мука – 280 г	мука – 270 г	
сахар	–	
соль – 5 г	соль – пачка	
масло – 15 г	масло – пачка	
сметана – 100 г	сметана – банка (100 г)	
творог – 200 г	творог – полкило	

D   Complete the final column with an appropriate statement using as many different quantity expressions listed as possible.

# Reading

E **Read the beginning of this account of Ivan's shopping trip. Answer the question that follows in Russian.**

Суббота. В воскресенье Иван и Анна принимают друга, Бориса, на ужин. Анна должна работать в эту субботу, и Иван должен сделать покупки. В пятницу вечером Анна написала список продуктов на ужин и попросила Ивана купить всё пока она на работе. Иван встаёт поздно и хочет посмотреть футбол по телевизору. Поэтому он спешит в магазин и забывает список дома.

Какая проблема у Ивана? _____

F **Now read the rest of the account and answer the questions that follow in Russian.**

Суббота вечером. Анна приходит домой после тяжёлого дня на работе, пока Иван смотрит футбол по телевизору.

«Привет Иван! Ты всё купил?»

«Да, да – много продуктов купил.»

«Ты купил салат? Почему нет салата в холодильнике?»

«Салата не было. А я купил капусту.»

«Капусту? А я не хочу капусту! Почему ты купил капусту?»

«Я купил бутылку водки, 250 грамм ветчины, несколько помидоров и немного колбасы. Также шоколадный торт, банку икры и блины.»

«А почему у нас нет ни сахара, ни масла? У нас мало молока и недостаточно соли. А я написала в списке, что надо купить литр молока и пачку соли, не правда ли?»

«Да. Правда. Но, к сожалению, я забыл список дома. Я думаю, что я купил большинство продуктов. А сколько продуктов я забыл?»

« Ничего! Это не проблема …»

«Анна, ты такая добрая!»

«…супермаркет ещё открыт. Вот новый список:

    полкило сахара

    100 г масла

    литр молока

    пачка соли

    салат

    400 г колбасы

    буханка чёрного хлеба»

«Хорошо. Завтра утром, да?»

«Нет. Сейчас.»

«А футбол?»

«Нет футбола в списке! И я хочу смотреть танцевальное шоу.»

принимать	*to receive, accept*
должен/должна	*must*
список	*list*
спешить	*to hurry*
тяжёлый	*heavy*
к сожалению	*unfortunately*
буханка	*a loaf*

1 Почему Иван купил капусту?

_____

2 Что ещё он купил?

_____

3 У них дома есть достаточно масла?

_____

4 Сколько соли надо купить?

_____

Vocabulary

G Write a list of all the products that Anna and Ivan now have at home. Do not include the quantities, so make sure that the items are all listed in the nominative case.

1	
2	
3	
4	
5	
6	
7	
8	
9	
10	

H Choose a suitable quantity word from the box to complete the shopping list that follows.

плитка	банка	бутылка	кило	коробка	пачка

1 _____ вина   4 _____ чая

2 _____ шоколада   5 _____ икры

3 _____ конфет   6 _____ мяса

I **Identify the odd one out in each list.**

1 блузка, майка, футболка, джинсы

2 пальто, купальник, пиджак, шуба

3 икра, капуста, салат, картошка

4 сахар, шоколад, морковь, торт

5 вино, водка, лимонад, пиво

J **Choose the quantity expression that best describes each of the following sentences.**

1 В группе студентов есть восемь футболистов. Для команды это:

   a достаточно   **b** мало   **c** много

2 Я видел Ивана в понедельник, в среду и в субботу. На этой неделе это:

   a сколько раз   **b** пять раз   **c** несколько раз

3 Иван, Борис и Анна хотят играть в шахматы. Конечно это:

   a слишком много людей   **b** достаточно людей   **c** мало людей

4 Иван и Борис едят мясо, а Анна – вегетарианка. Кто в этой группе ест мясо?

   a все   **b** большинство   **c** немного

5 Я хочу купить юбку за 500 рублей и блузку за 250 рублей. У меня 750 рублей. Это:

   a мало   **b** много   **c** достаточно

Writing

K **While going shopping for groceries in Russia, keep your Russian friends up to date with a tweet™ from each shop that you visit. Write six tweets™, of up to 140 characters each.**

▶ Что вы покупаете?

▶ Сколько вы покупаете?

▶ В каких магазинах вы покупаете?

▶ Почему?

Now imagine some of the tweets™ that you might get in reply. Do they think you are buying too much?

Don't forget: make your tweets™ grammatically correct by using the accusative and the genitive when you need to.

Self-check

Tick the box which matches your level of confidence.

    1 = very confident   2 = need more practice   3 = not too confident

Как вы ду́маете? Вы хорошо́ понима́ете? Поста́вьте га́лочку:

    1 = хорошо́   2 = ну́жно бо́льше пра́ктики   3 = нехорошо́

	1	2	3
Recognize when to use the accusative, animate accusative and genitive cases			
Form the accusative, animate accusative and genitive cases			
Use a wide range of expressions of quantity followed by the genitive case			
Able to describe what and how much is being bought			

2 Приятного аппетита!

Enjoy your meal!

In this unit you will learn how to:

- ✔ Use dative, instrumental and prepositional cases
- ✔ Use a range of verbs that are followed by the instrumental case
- ✔ Describe a restaurant visit

CEFR: Can identify speaker viewpoints and attitudes as well as the information content (e.g. identify if a person likes or dislikes a restaurant, type of food, meal, etc.) (CEFR B2); Can state likes and dislikes (CEFR A2); Can give reasons and explanations for opinions (CEFR B1)

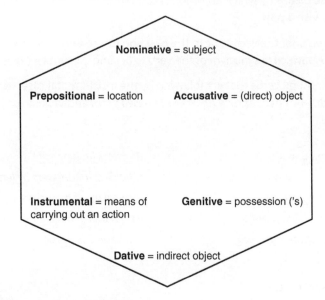

Nominative = subject

Prepositional = location   **Accusative** = (direct) object

Instrumental = means of carrying out an action   **Genitive** = possession ('s)

Dative = indirect object

Meaning and usage

Dative, instrumental and prepositional cases

The Russian case system applies particular endings to nouns and adjectives according to their grammatical role in the sentence. The first three cases are presented in Unit 1 – the nominative, accusative and genitive; the last three cases are the dative, instrumental and prepositional:

1 **Dative case**

This is used for the <u>indirect object</u> of a sentence. This is often indicated by *for* or *to* in English: a present <u>for Ivan</u>; I am writing <u>to him</u>.

It is also often used in modal constructions, e.g. мо́жно/на́до/нельзя́ *(can/should/must not)* and for expressing feelings or perceptions, e.g. хорошо́/пло́хо/гру́стно *(good/bad/sad)*.

Ив**а**н куп**и**л под**а**рок Бор**и**су.	*(Ivan bought a present for Boris.)*
Анна куп**и**ла бл**у**зку подр**у**ге.	*(Anna bought a blouse for a friend.)*
согл**а**сно письм**у**	*(according to the letter)*
Конц**е**рт понр**а**вился студ**е**нтам.	*(The students enjoyed the concert.)*
Офици**а**нту н**а**до раб**о**тать б**ы**стро.	*(The waiter has to work quickly.)*
Им хорош**о** в рестор**а**не.	*(They feel good in the restaurant.)*

2 Instrumental case

Used for the <u>means</u> by which an action is completed. This is often indicated by *with* in English, e.g. I write **with a pen**.

It is also used after the verb *to be* in the past and future tenses, and also many verbs used in its place, e.g. явл**я**ться (a synonym of the verb *to be*) and счит**а**ться (*to be considered*).

Three other useful verbs that are followed by the instrumental case are: заним**а**ться *(to occupy oneself* **with***)*, интересов**а**ться *(to interest oneself* **with***)* and увлек**а**ться *(to enjoy, be carried away* **with***)*.

Я пиш**у** карандаш**о**м.	*(I write with a pencil.)*
Дир**е**ктор отвеч**а**ет письм**о**м.	*(The director answers by letter.)*
бл**и**нчики с гриб**а**ми	*(pancakes with mushrooms)*
Он счит**а**ется чемпи**о**ном.	*(He is considered a champion.)*
Анна увлек**а**ется м**у**зыкой.	*(Anna enjoys music.)*

3 Prepositional case

Used to indicate position and only ever used with prepositions, the main ones of which are в (meaning *in*) and на (meaning *on*). It is also used with о, meaning 'about, concerning' (this becomes об when it is used before a word beginning with a vowel).

Бор**и**с в п**а**рке.	*(Boris is in the park.)*
Анна раб**о**тает на зав**о**де.	*(Anna works at the factory.)*
М**ы** пл**а**ваем в **о**зере.	*(We swim in the lake.)*
С**о**ня отдых**а**ет в гор**а**х.	*(Sonya is relaxing in the mountains.)*
кн**и**га об иск**у**сстве	*(a book about art)*

How to form the dative and prepositional cases

	Masculine	Feminine	Neuter
Nominative	шарф	шуба	мест_о_
Dative	шарф_у_	шуб_е_	мест_у_
Nominative	трамвай	неделя/станция	здание
Dative	трамва_ю_	недел_е_/станц_ии_	здани_ю_
Nominative	автомобиль	дверь	платье
Dative	автомобил_ю_	двер_и_	плать_ю_

	Masculine plural	Feminine plural	Neuter plural
Nominative	шарф_ы_	шуб_ы_	мест_а_
Dative	шарф_ам_	шуб_ам_	мест_ам_
Nominative	трамва_и_	недел_и_/станц_ии_	здани_я_
Dative	трамва_ям_	недел_ям_/станц_иям_	здани_ям_
Nominative	автомобил_и_	двер_и_	плать_я_
Dative	автомобил_ям_	двер_ям_	плать_ям_

Note that there are a group of masculine nouns that take an ending in -у in the prepositional singular when used with в *or* на. *Some common examples are:* в аэропорт_у_, на берег_у_, в год_у_, на льд_у_, в лес_у_, на мост_у_, в порт_у_, в сад_у_, в снег_у_ *and* в угл_у_.

	Masculine	Feminine	Neuter
Nominative	шарф	шуба	мест_о_
Prepositional	_о_ шарф_е_	_о_ шуб_е_	_о_ мест_е_
Nominative	трамвай	неделя/станция	здание
Prepositional	_о_ трамва_е_	_о_ недел_е_/ _о_ станц_ии_	_о_ здани_и_
Nominative	автомобиль	дверь	платье
Prepositional	_об_ автомобил_е_	_о_ двер_и_	_о_ плать_е_

	Masculine plural	Feminine plural	Neuter plural
Nominative	шарф**ы**	шуб**ы**	мест**а**
Prepositional	<u>о шарф**ах**</u>	<u>о шуб**ах**</u>	<u>о мест**ах**</u>
Nominative	трамва**и**	недел**и**/станци**и**	здани**я**
Prepositional	<u>о трамва**ях**</u>	<u>о недел**ях**</u>/<u>о станци**ях**</u>	<u>о здани**ях**</u>
Nominative	автомобил**и**	двер**и**	плать**я**
Prepositional	<u>об автомобил**ях**</u>	<u>о двер**ях**</u>	<u>о плать**ях**</u>

A Rewrite the following sentences, putting the underlined words into the singular. Then translate the rewritten sentences.

1 Тур**и**сты пр**о**бовали р**у**сскую ед**у** <u>в рестор**а**нах</u>.

_____

2 М**о**жно всегд**а** куп**и**ть вк**у**сные бутербр**о**ды <u>в аэропорт**а**х</u>.

_____

3 **А**нна и Бор**и**с заказ**а**ли <u>гост**я**м</u> р**у**сский борщ.

_____

4 <u>Муз**е**и</u> нах**о**дятся <u>в зд**а**ниях</u> в ц**е**нтре г**о**рода.

_____

5 <u>Официа**а**нтам</u> н**а**до раб**о**тать как м**о**жно быстр**е**е.

_____

6 Так**и**е дух**и** нр**а**вятся <u>ж**е**нщинам</u> в Росс**и**и.

_____

B Rewrite the following sentences, replacing the underlined phrases with their equivalents in brackets and changing the cases appropriately.

Прим**е**р: Я любл**ю** шокол**а**д (нр**а**виться). → Мн**е** нр**а**вится шокол**а**д.

1 <u>Студ**е**нт л**ю**бит</u> п**и**ццу. (нр**а**виться) _____

2 <u>Бор**и**су нр**а**вятся</u> пельм**е**ни. (люб**и**ть) _____

3 <u>**А**нна должн**а**</u> раб**о**тать сег**о**дня. (н**а**до) _____

4 <u>Г**о**сти гост**и**ницы м**о**гут у**у**жинать в рестор**а**не на п**е**рвом этаж**е**. (м**о**жно) _____

5 <u>Франц**у**зы л**ю**бят</u> круасс**а**ны на з**а**втрак. (нр**а**виться) _____

6 В рестор**а**не <u>мы н**е** м**о**жем кур**и**ть</u>. (нельз**я**) _____

How to form the instrumental case

	Masculine	Feminine	Neuter
Nominative	шарф	шуба	место
Instrumental	шарфом	шубой	местом
Nominative	трамвай	неделя/станция	здание
Instrumental	трамваем	неделей/станцией	зданием
Nominative	автомобиль	дверь	платье
Instrumental	автомобилем	дверью	платьем

	Masculine plural	Feminine plural	Neuter plural
Nominative	шарфы	шубы	места
Instrumental	шарфами	шубами	местами
Nominative	трамваи	недели/станции	здания
Instrumental	трамваями	неделями/станциями	зданиями
Nominative	автомобили	двери	платья
Instrumental	автомобилями	дверями	платьями

Меню

Бефстроганов

Котлеты по-киевски

Шницель

Курица

Рыба

Гарнир: картофель-фри, рис, овощи, картошка, вермишель

Блины

Начинка: мясо, грибы, сыр, капуста, икра, картошка

Пельмени

Начинка: картошка, фарш, говядина, свинина

C **Using the menu to help you with vocabulary, write the following dishes in Russian.**

Пример: Chicken with rice   Курица с рисом

1 Beef stroganoff with potatoes _____

2 Fish with vegetables _____

3 Schnitzel with pasta _____

4 Pancakes filled with mushrooms _____

5 Chicken Kiev with fries _____

6 Pelmeni (pastry parcel) filled with pork _____

Verbs followed by the instrumental

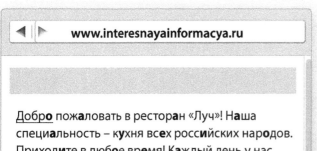

D Using the words in brackets, complete the following sentences.

1 Борис _____.
(интересоваться /музыка)

2 Анна _____.
(работать/врач)

3 Студенты _____. (стать/инженер)

4 Икра _____. (считаться/деликатес)

5 Это блюдо _____. (являться/шедевр)

6 Иван _____. (увлекаться/кулинария)

заниматься	*to occupy oneself (with)*
увлекаться	*to enjoy*
интересоваться	*to be interested in*
быть	*to be*
являться	*to be*
считаться	*to be considered*
становиться/стать	*to become*
работать	*to work (as)*

Reading

E Read this online description of a Russian restaurant then answer the question that follows in Russian.

www.interesnayainformacya.ru

Добро пожаловать в ресторан «Луч»! Наша специальность – кухня всех российских народов. Приходите в любое время! Каждый день у нас самые вкусные блюда с самыми первоклассными гарнирами. Мы находимся в прекрасном здании в живописном старом городе, где все официанты говорят на разных языках, и обслуживание является на высшем уровне. Мы работаем с полудня до полуночи – наши бизнес-ланчи считаются лучшими в городе, и цены всегда считаются доступными.

Добро пожаловать!	*Welcome!*
любой	*any*
кошмар	*nightmare*
обслуживание	*service*
принести	*to bring*

Где находится ресторан? _____

F Now read the online reviews and answer the questions that follow in Russian.

Мы с друзьями были в городе первый раз и захотели быстро пообедать в центре. Одному другу рекомендовали ресторан <<Луч>>, и мы быстро нашли его. Я заказала Борису бизнес-ланч – суп с грибами и пельмени со сметаной. Борису было очень хорошо – очень понравился ланч! Я заказала шницель с картофелем-фри. Я могу рекомендовать друзьям и туристам. Я понимаю, почему ресторан считается лучшим в городе!

(Анна, специалист по маркетингу)

Ресторан <<Луч>>? Я его считаю кошмаром! Обслуживание было медленным, официанты не интересовались клиентами, а занимались своими смартфонами. Еда оказалась холодной и невкусной. Жене я заказал курицу с овощами, дочери блины с картошкой и сыну Бефстроганов. Мне было жарко – значит, я заказал салат с грибами. Нельзя было есть ни жене, ни дочери, ни сыну, ни мне. Нельзя рекомендовать ни друзьям, ни туристам!

(Сергей, адвокат)

Я хотела сделать подарок другу на день рождения. Я слышала, что этот ресторан считается лучшим в городе. Другу было интересно попробовать вегетарианские блюда, и он заказал блины с картошкой и с капустой. К сожалению другу не понравилось, потому что блины были с капустой и с ветчиной. Было очевидно, что официанту было очень скучно. Он принёс другу омлет с сыром, но не с энтузиазмом. Я заказала лапшу с рыбой, потому что интересуюсь японской кухней, и надо сказать, что было очень вкусно.

(Соня, бизнесменка)

1 Почему **А**нна с друзь**я**ми в**ы**брали ресторан <<Луч>>?

_____

2 Как б**ы**ло Бор**и**су и почем**у**?

_____

3 Чт**о** д**у**мал Серг**е**й об официа**н**тах?

_____

4 Как**а**я пробл**е**ма был**а** у др**у**га С**о**ни?

_____

G Write a list in Russian of all the foods that are mentioned in the restaurant reviews. Explain in Russian which of them you would order and why.

_____

Vocabulary

H The following dishes come without side orders. Write how you would ask for them with the side orders mentioned.

> When changing case endings, always build in the extra stage of going back to the nominative first.

Прим**е**р: блин**ы** без ветчин**ы** → ветчин**а** → блин**ы** с ветчин**о**й

1 омл**е**т без с**ы**ра _____

2 суп без гриб**о**в _____

3 к**у**рица без кап**у**сты _____

4 пельм**е**ни без свин**и**ны _____

5 котл**е**ты без карт**о**феля-фри _____

6 чай без с**а**хара _____

I Find the words in the reading text that match the following definitions.

1 блю**до, кот**о**рое счит**а**ется **о**чень хор**о**шим, и гот**о**вится т**о**лько в **э**том одн**о**м м**е**сте. _____

2 то, что м**о**жно есть вм**е**сте с блю**до**м – наприм**е**р: карт**о**шка, смет**а**на _____

3 сов**е**товать друг**и**м _____

4 б**ы**стрый об**е**д для раб**о**чего челов**е**ка _____

5 уж**а**сная ситу**а**ция! _____

6 челов**е**к, кот**о**рый покуп**а**ет **и**ли зак**а**зывает _____

J Find the pairs of opposites in the box.

прекра́сный	совреме́нный	ти́хий	ме́дленный
бы́стрый	ужа́сный	традицио́нный	шу́мный

_____   _____   _____   _____

Writing

K Imagine that you have eaten at a Russian restaurant, maybe even at «Луч». Write an online review of about 100 words in Russian covering the following points.

▶ почему́ вы ходи́ли в рестора́н
▶ что вы заказа́ли
▶ что вы поду́мали об э́том
▶ рекоменду́ете ли вы э́тот рестора́н

_____

_____

_____

_____

_____

_____

_____

Self-check

Tick the box which matches your level of confidence.

1 = very confident   2 = need more practice   3 = not too confident

Как вы ду́маете? Вы хорошо́ понима́ете? Поста́вьте га́лочку:

1 = хорошо́   2 = ну́жно бо́льше пра́ктики   3 = нехорошо́

	1	2	3
Recognize when to use the dative, instrumental and prepositional cases			
Form the dative, instrumental and prepositional cases			
Use verbs that are followed by the instrumental case			
Able to describe eating out in Russia			

Кто на фотогра́фии?

Who is in the photograph?

In this unit you will learn how to:

✓ Use pronouns, including possessive pronouns

✓ Describe family relationships in detail

✓ Write a short autobiography

CEFR: Can understand texts that consist mainly of high-frequency everyday or job-related language (CEFR B1); Can write simple connected text on topics which are of personal interest (CEFR B1)

| Nominative | Accusative | Genitive | Dative | Instrumental | Prepositional |

Я знаю <u>его</u>, живу недалеко от <u>него</u>, звоню <u>ему</u> регуля́рно, встреча́юсь с <u>ним</u> ре́дко, а ду́маю о <u>нём</u> ка́ждый день.

(I know him, I live not far from him, phone him regularly, meet up with him rarely, but think about him every day.)

Meaning and usage

Personal pronouns

1   The Russian case system applies to personal pronouns (such as *I, you, me, them*) as well as nouns and adjectives. Therefore, personal pronouns in Russian have different forms according to their grammatical role in the sentence. However, sometimes the same spelling can be used for different cases, so it is a very good idea to try to memorize the following table:

Nominative	Accusative	Genitive	Dative	Instrumental	Prepositional
я	меня́	меня́	мне	мной	обо мне́
ты	тебя́	тебя́	тебе́	тобо́й	о тебе́
он	его́	его́	ему́	им	о нём
она́	её	её	ей	ей	о ней
оно́	его́	его́	ему́	им	о нём
мы	нас	нас	нам	на́ми	о нас
вы	вас	вас	вам	ва́ми	о вас
они́	их	их	им	и́ми	о них

Don't forget: the prepositional case is only ever used after a preposition – usually в (in) and на (on), but also о (about). Remember too that о is sometimes written as об- before a vowel and as обо before a double consonant – for example, обо мне.

A **Complete the paragraph with appropriate personal pronouns from the box. Be careful – you will not need all the personal pronouns in the box.**

ег**о**	её	ей	мен**я**
нам	ней	нём	он**а**

Вот мо**я** семь**я**: это мо**я** сестр**а**. **1** ____ зов**у**т Л**е**на. **2** ____ жив**ё**т в Москв**е**, недалек**о** от **3** ____. Я встреч**а**юсь с **4** ____ по субб**о**там. **5** ____ нр**а**вится хор**о**ший рестор**а**н в г**о**роде, и мы ч**а**сто об**е**даем в **6** ____.

 *If a personal pronoun beginning with a vowel is ever used after a preposition, the letter н is added – for example: not far from him = недалек**о** от нег**о**.*

B **Replace the underlined nouns with personal pronouns and explain your choice.**

Прим**е**р: Ты зн**а**ешь Ив**а**на?   Ты зн**а**ешь ег**о**?

– The original noun was in the accusative case and was animate.

1 Бор**и**с знак**о**м с **А**нной. _____

2 Что ты д**а**ришь Мар**и**и на день рожд**е**ния? _____

3 У Миха**и**ла есть сестр**а**? _____

4 Он**и** разгов**а**ривали о р**о**дственниках. _____

5 Никол**а**й сто**я**л п**е**ред Г**а**лей в **о**череди. _____

6 Мы в**и**дели друз**е**й в ц**е**нтре г**о**рода. _____

Meaning and usage

Possessive pronouns

1 Possessive pronouns are used in Russian to translate *my, your, his, her,* etc. They agree with the noun they describe in terms of gender, number and case.

The other possessive pronouns divide into two groups:

1 *my* and *your* (singular)

2 *our* and *your* (plural)

 Good news! The possessive pronouns for his, her and their have only one form:

*his = ег**о**, her = её, their = их*

*his brother = ег**о** брат*
*She knows his brother. = Он**а** зн**а**ет ег**о** бр**а**та.*

How to form the possessive pronoun

1 Here are all the forms of *my*:

	Masculine	Feminine	Neuter	Plural
Nominative	мой	моя	моё	мои
Accusative (inanimate/ animate)	мой/моего	мою	моё	мои/моих
Genitive	моего	моей	моего	моих
Dative	моему	моей	моему	моим
Instrumental	моим	моей	моим	моими
Prepositional	о моём	о моей	о моём	о моих

 C On the basis of the *my* table, complete the equivalent table for *your* (singular).

	Masculine	Feminine	Neuter	Plural
Nominative	твой			
Accusative (inanimate/ animate)		твою		
Genitive				твоих
Dative			твоему	
Instrumental				
Prepositional	о твоём			

2 Here are all the forms of *our*:

	Masculine	Feminine	Neuter	Plural
Nominative	наш	наша	наше	наши
Accusative (inanimate/ animate)	наш/нашего	нашу	наше	наши/наших
Genitive	нашего	нашей	нашего	наших
Dative	нашему	нашей	нашему	нашим
Instrumental	нашим	нашей	нашим	нашими
Prepositional	о нашем	о нашей	о нашем	о наших

D On the basis of the *our* table, complete the equivalent table for *your* (plural).

	Masculine	Feminine	Neuter	Plural
Nominative	ваш			
Accusative (inanimate/ animate)				
Genitive			вашего	
Dative				вашим
Instrumental	вашим			
Prepositional		о вашей		

E Fill in the gaps below with the missing possessive pronouns.

1 (я)   **Э**то _____ брат и _____ сест**ра**.

2 (ты)   **Э**то _____ друг и _____ под**ру**га?

3 (он)   Ты зн**а**ешь, где _____ **о**фис?

4 (мы)   Мы не заб**ы**ли ни_____ паспор**та** ни _____ бил**е**ты.

5 (она)   _____ дом нах**о**дится недалек**о** от _____ род**и**телей.

6 (он**и**)   Я ув**и**дел _____ маш**и**ну п**е**ред _____ д**о**мом.

7 (вы)   Вчер**а** я познак**о**мился с _____ б**а**бушкой.

дво**ю**родный брат	*cousin (male)*
дво**ю**родная сест**ра**	*cousin (female)*
св**о**дный брат	*half - /stepbrother*
св**о**дная сест**ра**	*half - /stepsister*
отчим	*stepfather*
ма**ч**еха	*stepmother*
плем**я**нник	*nephew*
плем**я**нница	*niece*
зять	*son-in-law*
нев**е**стка/снох**а**	*daughter-in-law*

 As you can see, talking about your relatives is quite complicated in Russian. The vocabulary you have been given should cover most situations, though do not be surprised if in conversation with Russians you hear some other words to describe blood ties (e.g. your brother's mother-in-law).

муж	*husband*	жен**а**	*wife*
свекр**о**вь	*husband's mother*	тёща	*wife's mother*
свёкор	*husband's father*	тесть	*wife's father*
деверь	*husband's brother*	**шу**рин	*wife's brother*
зол**о**вка	*husband's sister*	своя**ч**еница	*wife's sister*

F   Complete the following phrases.

Приме́р: Сын мое́й сестры́ – э́то мой племя́нник

1   Дочь моего́ бра́та – э́то ___ _____

2   Оте́ц мое́й жены́ – э́то ___ _____

3   Мать моего́ му́жа – э́то ___ _____

4   Жена́ моего́ отца́ – э́то ___ _____

5   Муж мое́й ма́тери – э́то ___ _____

G   Read Valentina's social media posts from her hen party and then imagine what the equivalent posts were for the stag party.

Приме́р: Ма́ма устро́ила мне деви́чник в ночно́м клу́бе.

– *Па́па устро́ил мне мальчи́шник в ночно́м клу́бе.*

1   Я давно́ не встреча́лась с мое́й двою́родной сестро́й. _____

2   К сожале́нию, не могла́ прийти́ моя́ люби́мая племя́нница. _____

3   Моя́ ма́чеха сове́товала мне мно́го не пить! _____

4   Я получи́ла ужа́сный пода́рок от сво́дной сестры́. _____

5   Моя́ бу́дущая золо́вка расска́зывала мно́го интере́сного о бра́те. _____

6   Да́же моя́ ба́бушка танцева́ла на столе́! _____

Meaning and usage

An additional possessive pronoun

1   Russian has an additional possessive which can be used with all persons – свой. Its endings are:

	Masculine	Feminine	Neuter	Plural
Nominative	свой	своя́	своё	свои́
Accusative (inanimate/ animate)	свой/своего́	свою́	своё	свои́/свои́х
Genitive	своего́	свое́й	своего́	свои́х
Dative	своему́	свое́й	своему́	свои́м
Instrumental	свои́м	свое́й	свои́м	свои́ми
Prepositional	о своём	о свое́й	о своём	о свои́х

2 A good way of thinking of this is to say that it means *one's own*; for example:

Я несу свою сумку.   *(I am carrying my <u>own</u> bag.)*

When you use свой to mean *my/your/our*, the meaning is essentially the same using мой/твой/наш/ваш. However, with *his/her/their*, the meaning is different. Look at these two sentences:

Иван знает Бориса и позвонил его сестре. Потом он позвонил своей сестре.

(Ivan knows Boris and phoned his (Boris's) sister. Then he phoned his <u>own</u> (Ivan's) sister.)

3 Note that свой is never used with the subject of a sentence:

Его сестра позвонила ему.   *(His sister rang him.)*

H **Choose the correct word to complete the sentences.**

1 Анна встретилась со _____ бабушкой.

   a своя   **b** своим   **c** своей

2 Борис встретился со _____ бабушкой.

   a свой   **b** своим   **c** своей

3 Марина и Николай подарили цветы _____ родителям.

   a свои   **b** своим   **c** своих

4 Они жили у _____ друзей в Томске.

   a свои   **b** своих   **c** своей

5 Мы позвонили _____ коллегам в понедельник.

   a своим   **b** свои   **c** своей

6 _____ брат увидел Галю на вокзале.

   a свой   **b** Её   **c** своего

Reading

I Read this fictional online encyclopaedia entry, then answer the question that follows in Russian.

---

www.interesnayainformacya.ru

Серов Николай Михайлович (р. 1 апреля 1969, Ларигуб) – предприниматель, промышленник, фабрикант, председатель городского комитета предпринимателей и бизнесменов, с января 2008 года – спонсор Ларигубского театра оперы и балета. Основатель и совладелец интернет-компании «Матрёшкин мир». Живёт в Москве и Тянджине с семьёй.

Какая профессия у Николая Серова? _____

J Now read Nikolai's biography and answer the questions that follow in Russian.

Биография

Ранние годы

Николай родился в Ларигубе, в семье инженера Михаила и врача Елизаветы. Семья переехала в Москву, и он учился в московской школе № 192, математической спецшколе. Особенно понравилось ему изучать экономику. В 1987 году поступил на экономический факультет МГУ. Окончил МГУ с красным дипломом, и распределили его работать на завод уральских сувениров в Перми.

Профессиональная карьера

Началась профессиональная деятельность Серова после распада СССР. Скоро после окончания второго года работы в Перми он решил вернуться к своей семье в Москву и основать свой бизнес по производству сувениров и художественных изделий. Его настоящий успех начался с 2002 года, когда он стал совладельцем фабрики на севере Китая. В финансировании этого дела помогли Серову его тесть и тёща, и его заместительницей стала его свояченица.

Личная жизнь

Встретился со своей будущей супругой Ириной в 1994 году во время работы в комитете молодых московских предпринимателей. Поженились в 1998 году. Родился сын (2001), дочь (2004), сын (2007). Шурин Алексей Родионов – известный художник – заинтересовался компанией Серова, и вместе они разработали новый набор матрёшек для производства на китайской фабрике, которой Родионов стал совладельцем с Серовым. Зимой семья Серовых живёт в Тянджине, весной и осенью в Москве, а летом на юге Испании.

To say 'in' a season, you use the instrumental case in Russian (with no preposition): весной *(in spring),* летом *(in summer),* осенью *(in autumn),* зимой *(in winter).*

предприниматель	*entrepreneur*	производство	*production*
промышленник	*industrialist*	изделие	*product*
фабрикант	*manufacturer*	настоящий	*real, genuine*
основатель	*founder*	заместитель(ница)	*deputy*
совладелец	*co-owner*	супруга	*spouse*
распределить	*to assign, to send*	разработать	*to develop*
деятельность	*activity*		

1 Какая была профессия у отца и матери Николая?

_____

2 Где начал Николай свою профессиональную карьеру?

_____

3 Когда и почему он стал по-настоящему успешным бизнесменом?

_____

4 Где живут члены его семьи в течение года?

_____

K For extra practice, imagine you were Nikolai Serov and retell your life story in the я form.

Vocabulary

L For each group of words, identify the odd one out.

1 бабушка, дедушка, мама, сестра

2 тёща, тесть, шурин, деверь

3 муж, свекровь, свёкор, свояченица

4 отец, мать, племянница, тесть

5 сводный брат, сводная сестра, мачеха, племянник

M Change the following words to their plural forms. Be careful – many of these words are irregular, so you will need to use a dictionary to help you.

1 мать _____

2 сестра _____

3 брат _____

4 отец _____

5 бабушка _____

6 дочь _____

7 сын _____

8 дядя _____

N Choose the appropriate word from the box to complete the following paragraph. Be careful – you will not need to use all the words in the box.

его	сестра	своя	мать	её	матери	мужа	жена

Говорить о своей семье по-русски? Какой кошмар! Сначала надо знать, кто говорит – муж о родственниках жены, или **1** _____ о родственниках мужа. Если он говорит о её **2** _____ – это его тёща. Его **3** _____ – это её свекровь. Её отец – это **4** _____ тесть, а её свёкор – это его отец. Брат **5** _____ – это её деверь. Шурин – это брат жены. Самое трудное, по-моему, это свояченица (**6** _____ жены) и золовка (сестра мужа). Кто не согласится? Настоящий кошмар!

Writing

O Write an entry for yourself for an online encyclopaedia. It does not have to be true but should be interesting. Write about 100 words in Russian.

> Don't forget: an encyclopaedia entry needs to be in the third person (он/она) so be particularly careful with your use of свой.

▶ Как вы проводили ранние годы?

▶ Какая была ваша карьера?

▶ Опишите личную жизнь

_____

_____

_____

_____

_____

_____

_____

_____

_____

Self-check

Tick the box which matches your level of confidence.

    1 = very confident   2 = need more practice   3 = not too confident

Как вы думаете? Вы хорошо понимаете? Поставьте галочку:

    1 = хорошо   2 = нужно больше практики   3 = нехорошо

	1	2	3
Recognize when to use personal pronouns			
Recognize when to use possessive pronouns			
Use personal and possessive pronouns with appropriate case endings			
Able to describe extended family in detail			

Это тебе очень идёт!

It really suits you!

In this unit you will learn how to:

- ✓ Use long and short form adjectives
- ✓ Describe clothes
- ✓ Give opinions on clothes
- ✓ Describe fashion

CEFR: Can write about everyday aspects of their environment (people, places, job) (CEFR A2); Can scan longer text in order to locate desired information and understand relevant information in everyday material, such as letters, brochures and short official documents (CEFR B1)

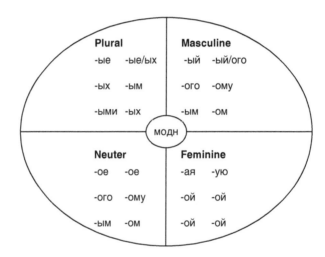

Meaning and usage

Adjectives: long form

1 Look at these phrases. Which words are adjectives and what do you notice about their endings?

На витрине модная, красная блузка.

(In the window is a fashionable, red blouse.)

Это хорошо идёт с чёрным пиджаком.

(This goes well with the black jacket.)

Она отказалась от зелёного платья.

(She rejected the green dress.)

Он был в серых брюках.

(He was in grey trousers.)

2 You will have noticed that adjectives in Russian agree with the noun that they are describing in number, gender and case. Although word order in Russian is quite flexible, adjectives are usually found in the same place as you would expect them to be in English.

How to form adjectives

1 Most adjectives follow a standard pattern of endings:

	Masculine	Feminine	Neuter	Plural
Nominative	новый	новая	новое	новые
Accusative (inanimate/ animate)	новый/ нового	новую	новое	новые/ новых
Genitive	нового	новой	нового	новых
Dative	новому	новой	новому	новым
Instrumental	новым	новой	новым	новыми
Prepositional	о новом	о новой	о новом	о новых

2 There is a spelling rule which affects many words in Russian:

After к, г, х, ж, ч, ш and щ: you cannot write ы but have to write и instead.

Many adjectives in Russian are affected by this spelling rule, as -кий is a common ending.

 A **Applying the spelling rule, fill in the endings for the adjective маленький (small).**

	Masculine	Feminine	Neuter	Plural
Nominative	маленький	маленькая	маленькое	маленькие
Accusative (inanimate/ animate)	маленьк__/__	маленьк__	маленьк__	маленьк__/__
Genitive	маленьк__	маленьк__	маленьк__	маленьк__
Dative	маленьк__	маленьк__	маленьк__	маленьк__
Instrumental	маленьк__	маленьк__	маленьк__	маленьк__
Prepositional	о маленьком	о маленьк__	о маленьк__	о маленьк__

3 There is also a very small group of adjectives that are known as 'soft' adjectives, as they have the soft endings of и (instead of ы), я (instead of a) and e (instead of o). One of the most common soft adjectives is си́ний (*royal blue*).

 There are two words in Russian for blue – си́ний (*dark blue*) *and* голубо́й (*light blue*).

B Complete the following table.

	Masculine	Feminine	Neuter	Plural
Nominative	синий	синяя	синее	синие
Accusative (inanimate/ animate)	син__/__	син__	син__	син__/__
Genitive	син__	син__	синего	син__
Dative	син__	синей	син__	син__
Instrumental	син__	син__	син__	синими
Prepositional	о синем	о син__	о син__	о син__

4 The good news is that Russian adjectives always follow one of these three patterns and so are therefore much more regular than nouns. The only exception to this is a small number of adjectives which have the stress on the final adjective ending. In this case, the only change is that the masculine singular nominative and inanimate accusative end in -**о**й rather than -ый, such as in the adjectives больш**о**й *(big)* and молод**о**й *(young)*.

C Choose the correct adjective endings in the following phrases.

1 У мен**я** _____ г**а**лстук.

 a кр**а**сная **b** кр**а**сную **c** кр**а**сный

2 Я куп**и**л _____ дж**и**нсы.

 a с**и**ний **b** с**и**нее **c** с**и**ние

3 **Э**то – п**у**говица от _____ руб**а**шки.

 a б**е**лая **b** б**е**лой **c** б**е**лые

4 Он**а** нос**и**ла плащ с_____ пл**а**тьем.

 a дл**и**нным **b** дл**и**нной **c** дл**и**нном

5 В ки**о**ске н**е** было _____ колг**о**ток.

 a чёрный **b** чёрной **c** чёрных

6 Он**и** подошл**и** к _____ кост**ю**му.

 a кор**и**чневому **b** кор**и**чневую **c** кор**и**чневая

D Complete the following phrases with the appropriate form of the adjective in brackets.

1 У нег**о** _____ т**у**фли. (м**о**дный)

2 Он**а** был**а** в _____ бр**ю**ках. (жёлтый)

3 Мой брат отказ**а**лся от _____ ш**а**рф**а**. (шерстян**о**й)

4 Ей понр**а**вился _____ пидж**а**к. (к**о**жаный)

5 Он нос**и**л футб**о**лку под _____ к**о**фтой. (с**и**ний)

6 Я ненав**и**жу **э**ту _____ м**а**йку. (ор**а**нжевый)

E Complete the following phrases by translating the words in brackets into Russian.

1 В го́роде есть _____. *(expensive shops)*

2 Им понра́вились _____. *(the cheap prices)*

3 Он чу́вствовал холо́дный ве́тер
  че́рез _____. *(the light coat)*

4 Её но́вые кроссо́вки бы́ли похо́жи
  на_____. *(fashionable shoes)*

5 Мы иска́ли везде́ в
  це́нтре_____. *(silk socks)*

6 Когда́ я был в Пари́же, я ви́дел
  мно́го _____. *(luxurious scarves)*

> Although in English the same form of a word can be both a noun and an adjective (silk, a silk scarf), *in Russian an adjective must always have adjectival endings (*шёлк, шёлковый шарф*). The good news is that this makes adjectives very easy to spot in Russian and avoids confusion in translation.*

Meaning and usage

Adjectives – short form

1 On most occasions when we meet adjectives in Russian, they will be in the long form. However, occasionally a short form is used for emphasis. The clue is, once again, the word order in English:

   these new shoes – э́ти но́вые ту́фли (long form)

   these shoes are new – э́ти ту́фли – но́вы (short form)

2 The short form is never used before a noun, only exists in the nominative and, as the name suggests, is shorter than the long form.

How to form short adjectives

Short adjectives are regular in their formation:

Masculine	нов
Feminine	нова́
Neuter	но́во
Plural	но́вы

Usually, the long form can be used as an alternative to the short form, but there are four occasions on which the short form **must** be used:

1 when an adjective is followed by a preposition. For example, *look like:* он похо́ж на отца́ *(he looks like his father)*

2 when an adjective is followed by a verb. For example, *ready to*: она́ гото́ва купи́ть *(she is ready to buy)*

3 when an adjective indicates a temporary state. For example, *they are (not permanently) ill*: он**и** больн**ы**

4 when an adjective is followed by a case. For example, *we are happy with our shopping*: мы дов**о**льны пок**у**пками

1 *Adjectives of colour **never** have a short form.*

2 *Adverbs are, in fact, short form neuter adjectives.*

3 *Note the following specific short forms used to indicate too big (*вел**и**к, велик**а**, велик**о**, велик**и***) and too small (*мал, мал**а**, мал**о**, мал**ы***):* эти т**у**фли велик**и** *(these shoes are too big),* эта руб**а**шка мал**а** *(this shirt is too small).*

F **Translate the following phrases into Russian.**

1 My shoes are too small. _____

2 My favourite skirt is lilac. _____

3 We are pleased with the new clothes. _____

4 The jacket is beautiful! _____

5 They were ready to buy an expensive fur coat. _____

6 The trousers were too small.

_____

G **You have lost one of your two suitcases. Describe what you can see and what is missing, using the examples and vocabulary box to help you.**

Прим**е**р: Я в**и**жу жёлт**ы**е вьетн**а**мки, но у мен**я** нет кр**а**сных шорт.

вьетн**а**мки	*flip-flops*
купа**а**льник	*swimsuit*
плат**о**к	*headscarf*
к**у**ртка	*short coat*
п**о**яс	*belt*

Что б**ы**ло в чемод**а**нах:	*What I still have in my remaining suitcase:*
кр**а**сные ш**о**рты	*yellow flip-flops*
н**о**вый купа**а**льник	*summer jacket*
уд**о**бная футб**о**лка	*sunglasses*
л**е**тний пиджа**а**к	*comfortable T-shirt*
лёгкая к**у**ртка	*fashionable hat*
жёлтые вьетн**а**мки	
шёлковый плат**о**к	
с**о**лнечные очк**и**	
б**е**лая ма**а**йка	
м**о**дная шл**я**па	

Reading

H Read the first part of this fashion show blog, then answer the question that follows in Russian.

---

www.interesnayainformacya.ru

Что нового в мире моды

Добро пожаловать на наш весенний показ моды. Мы рады находиться в столице недалеко от Кремля в красивом и элегантном здании, которое достойно отражает всю красоту нашей блестящей новой коллекции.

Где проходит этот показ моды?_____

I Now read the rest of the fashion show flyer and blog entries and answer the questions that follow in Russian.

Для мужчин тема весны – элегантность. Всем нужен традиционный костюм либо чёрного, либо синего цвета. Ткань может быть в полоску, но не советуется в клетку. Полоска должна хорошо смотреться, и она придаёт дополнительную элегантность костюму. На наш взгляд, лучшая комбинация – рубашка проста, а галстук интересен, может быть контрастного цвета. Брюки и пиджак, конечно, лучше выглядят, если они ни длинны, ни коротки, чтобы можно было восхищаться блестящими кожаными туфлями.

модный мужик Куда мне костюм? Я не в офисе работаю, и ваш совет для меня глуп!
У меня в шифоньере одни джинсы да футболки. Такая элегантность – вечна и универсальна.

фэшионистка модный мужик? По-моему, просто мужик! Костюм никогда не выходит из моды. Он – прекрасен, надёжен, солиден.

Для женщин, тема весны – свежесть и уверенность в себе. Брюки, платья, юбки – на ваш выбор в этом году. Многие модельеры рекомендуют контрастные цвета, особенно светлую одежду с тёмной обувью. Стоит носить на талии контрастный пояс. Все аксессуары должны быть пропорциональны росту. В нашей коллекции сумки – оригинальны, пояса – незабываемы, и шарфы – разноцветны. Рукава в этом сезоне – узки и длинны, а туфли на высоких каблуках. Цвета сезона – бордовый, песочный, пурпурный и серый.

фэшионистка Откуда ваши цвета сезона? Пурпурный и серый? Даже моя бабушка не так старомодна!

мода123 Спасибо за ваши советы. Они понятны, деликатны и конструктивны. Особенно понравилась идея о поясе. Всегда забываю про пояс, но зря!

1 Какой галстук нужен для «лучшей комбинации»?

_____

2 Почему «модныймужик» не согласен с советами этого показа моды?

_____

3 Что важно, когда выбираешь аксессуары?

_____

4 Что думает «фэшионистка» о рекомендованных цветах для женщин?

_____

Vocabulary

J For each group of words, identify the odd one out.

1 майка, футболка, юбка, рубашка

2 белый, синий, чёрный, коричневый

3 шарф, платок, пояс, джинсы

4 кроссовки, шорты, туфли, вьетнамки

5 блестящий, великолепный, элегантный, старомодный

K Give the noun that can be formed from the following adjectives.

Пример: свежий → свежесть

1 новый _____   4 весенний _____

2 модный _____   5 элегантный _____

3 традиционный _____   6 кожаный _____

 # Writing

L **You have seen an online survey. Write about 100 words in Russian, describing the following in your answers.**

▶ что вы носите каждый день и почему

▶ в чём вы были, когда вы выходили вечером в прошлый раз и почему

▶ кошмарную одежду, по-вашему

▶ идеальную одежду, по-вашему

_____

_____

_____

_____

_____

_____

_____

_____

_____

_____

Self-check

Tick the box which matches your level of confidence.

1 = very confident   2 = need more practice   3 = not too confident

Как вы думаете? Вы хорошо понимаете? Поставьте галочку:

1 = хорошо   2 = нужно больше практики   3 = нехорошо

	1	2	3
Use long form adjectives in all cases			
Use short form adjectives/adverbs			
Understand a complex text about fashion			
Able to describe clothes in detail			

5 Вам понравилось?

Did you like it?

In this unit you will learn how to:

- ✔ Use comparative and superlative adjectives and adverbs
- ✔ Give opinions about media
- ✔ Compare and contrast
- ✔ Understand the history of Russian media

CEFR: Can give opinions on familiar matters such as media and culture (CEFR B1); Can write accounts of experiences, describing feelings and reactions in simple connected text (CEFR B1)

Positive	Comparative	Superlative
Это интер**е**сный фильм	Это б**о**лее интер**е**сный фильм. / **Э**тот фильм – интер**е**снее	Это с**а**мый интер**е**сный интер**е**сный фильм.
*This is an **interesting** film*	*This is a more **interesting** film. / This film is more **interesting**.*	*This Is the most **interesting** film.*

Meaning and usage

Comparative and superlative adjectives and adverbs

 A **Look at these phrases. Explain what с**а**мый means and how it works.**

Это интер**е**сный фильм. *(This is an interesting film.)*

Это с**а**мый интер**е**сный фильм. *(This is the … interesting film.)*

Я смотр**ю** увлек**а**тельную перед**а**чу по ср**е**дам. *(I watch an entertaining programme on Wednesdays.)*

Я смотр**ю** с**а**мую увлек**а**тельную перед**а**чу по ср**е**дам. *(I watch the … programme on Wednesdays.)*

How to form superlative adjectives

1 The word с**а**мый can be used in Russian to make an adjective a *superlative*. In English, there are two ways of forming a superlative: adding the word *most* (this is a direct translation of the Russian с**а**мый) or adding the suffix *-est*. С**а**мый in Russian is an adjective and therefore follows the standard adjectival pattern of endings:

There are just two common adjectives which have a special form of the superlative:

хор**о**ший *(good)* → л**у**чший *(best)*

плох**о**й *(bad)* → х**у**дший *(worst)*

	Masculine	Feminine	Neuter	Plural
Nominative	самый	самая	самое	самые
Accusative	самый/ого	самую	самое	самые/ых
Genitive	самого	самой	самого	самых
Dative	самому	самой	самому	самым
Instrumental	самым	самой	самым	самыми
Prepositional	о самом	о самой	о самом	о самых

Самый can be added to any long form adjective to create a superlative.

B **Using the words in brackets, form superlative sentences.**

Пример: (интересный, книга) → На столе лежит <u>самая интересная книга</u>.

1 (популярный, фильм) → В кинотеатре идёт _____

2 (полезный, передача по кулинарии) → Мы ужинали после _____

3 (знаменитый, телеведущий) → У журналиста была встреча с _____

4 (оригинальный, боевики) → От этого режиссёра, мы привыкли к _____

5 (надёжный, вебсайт) → Мы читали об этом на _____

6 (хороший, газета) → Я купил _____

C **Look at these phrases. Explain what более means and how it works.**

Это интересный фильм.	(This is an interesting film.)
Это более интересный фильм.	(This is a … interesting film.)
Я смотрю увлекательную передачу по средам.	(I watch an entertaining programme on Wednesdays.)
Я смотрю более увлекательную передачу по средам.	(I watch a … programme on Wednesdays.)

How to form comparative adjectives

1   The word более can be used in Russian to make an adjective a *comparative*. In English, there are two ways of forming a comparative: adding the word *more* (this is a direct translation of the Russian более) or adding the suffix *-er* (as in the second example in the infographic). Using более is the long form of the comparative adjective in Russian and so can only be used when the adjective comes **in front of** the noun. Note in the examples that the word более never changes, although the adjectives used with it continue to agree with the nouns that they describe in the usual way. The word for *less* (менее) works in exactly the same way as более:

Это менее интересный фильм.   (*This is a less interesting film.*)

2 Note that there are three common pairs of adjectives that **do not** use более to form the comparative:

хороший *good*	лучший *better*	плохой *bad*	худший *worse*
большой *big*	больший *bigger*	маленький *small*	меньший *smaller*
старый *old*	старший *older*	молодой *young*	младший *younger*

D **Complete the sentences below using the words in brackets to help you.**

1 По-моему, _____ (more interesting) фильмы снимаются сейчас, чем в прошлом.

2 Я никогда не читала _____ (better) статью.

3 У него были _____ (more original) идеи в начале карьеры.

4 Я хочу стать _____ (more successful) режиссёром, чем Спилберг.

5 Я получил _____ (worse) впечатление от продолжения этого сериала.

6 Молодёжь скачивает _____ (more modern) музыку.

3 If the adjective comes **after** the noun, Russian usually uses an alternative form of the comparative called the short form. This is constructed by replacing the adjective ending (-ый/-ая/-ое/-ые, etc.) with -ee, which never changes, and is often followed by чем, meaning *than*.

этот фильм интереснее, чем книга.   *(This film is more interesting than the book.)*

Unfortunately, there are quite a few irregular short form comparative adjectives. Among the most common are:

хороший *good*	лучше *better*	лёгкий *light*	легче *lighter/easier*
плохой *bad*	хуже *worse*	дорогой *expensive*	дороже *more expensive*
большой *big*	больше *bigger*	дешёвый *cheap*	дешевле *cheaper*
маленький *small*	меньше *smaller*	простой *simple*	проще *simpler*
старый *old*	старше *older*	близкий *close*	ближе *closer*
молодой *young*	моложе *younger*	далёкий *distant*	дальше *further*

E Using the words in brackets, form comparative sentences.

Приме́р: Я чита́л бо́лее интере́сный блог. → Э́тот блог интере́снее.

1 Сего́дня была́ бо́лее дли́нная диску́ссия в э́том ток-шо́у. → Э́та диску́ссия

_____

2 На Но́вый год переда́чу вела́ бо́лее краси́вая кинозвезда́. → Э́та кинозвезда́
была́_____

3 Бо́лее информати́вный журна́л продава́лся онла́йн. → Э́тот журна́л _____

4 Я предпочита́ю сериа́лы с бо́лее просто́й исто́рией. → Я предпочита́ю сериа́лы, где
исто́рия _____

5 Есть бо́лее бы́стрый до́ступ к интерне́ту в го́роде. → В го́роде, до́ступ к
интерне́ту _____

6 В интерне́т-магази́не есть хоро́ший вы́бор бо́лее дешёвых това́ров. → В интерне́т-
магази́не, това́ры _____

F You are trying to decide which of the three films from the table you are going to buy. Write a short paragraph comparing them.

Приме́р: Фильм А длинне́е, чем фильм В, но са́мый дли́нный фильм – Б.

		Фильм А	Фильм Б	Фильм В
дли́нный?	длина́	140 мину́т	172 мину́ты	93 мину́ты
дешёвый?	сто́имость ДВД	350 рубле́й	300 рубле́й	200 рубле́й
но́вый?	год	2014	2003	1983
хоро́ший?	рейтинг	★★★	★★★★★	★★★★
дорого́й?	сто́имость произво́дства	12.3 млн рубле́й	10.3 млн рубле́й	2 млн рубле́й
успе́шный?	при́быль	15 млн рубле́й	45 млн рубле́й	23 млн рубле́й

4 Adverbs in Russian are short form neuter adjectives. Comparative adverbs, therefore, usually end in -ee (apart from irregular comparatives which end in -e). Superlative adverbs are usually formed by following the comparative adverbs with either всего or всех (in English, literally: *of all*).

Гла́вный актёр игра́л лу́чше всех.   (*The main actor played best of all.*)

Поле́знее всего́ купи́ть смартфо́н   (*It is most useful (of all) to buy a smartphone*
с интерне́том.   *with internet connection.*)

G   Read the following definitions and match them with the correct word in the box.

знамен**и**тость	*(celebrity)*
ск**а**чивать/скач**а**ть	*(to download)*
СМИ	*(media)*
соци**а**льные с**е**ти	*(social networks)*
стать**я**	*(article)*
телевед**у**щий	*(television presenter)*

1   пр**е**сса, интерн**е**т, телев**и**дение _____

2   получ**а**ть/получ**и**ть (наприм**е**р, м**у**зыку) по интерн**е**ту _____

3   то, что п**и**шет репортёр для газ**е**ты _____

4   **о**чень изв**е**стный и усп**е**шный челов**е**к _____

5   челов**е**к, кот**о**рый ведёт ш**о**у по телев**и**дению _____

6   комп**ь**ютерные прогр**а**ммы, при п**о**мощи кот**о**рых м**о**жно общ**а**ться с друзь**я**ми

_____

📖 Reading

H   Read the first part of this article about Russian media, then answer the question that follows in Russian.

М**о**жно счит**а**ть, что своб**о**дной пр**е**ссы никогд**а** н**е** было в Росс**и**и. При цар**и**зме все публик**а**ции подверг**а**лись с**а**мой жест**о**кой ценз**у**ре – наприм**е**р, л**и**чным ц**е**нзором у вел**и**кого р**у**сского по**э**та, Алекс**а**ндра П**у**шкина, был сам царь, Никол**а**й I.

Существов**а**ла ли своб**о**дная пр**е**сса в Росс**и**и при цар**и**зме?

_____

I   Now read the rest of the article and answer the questions that follow in Russian.

Ситу**а**ция не измен**и**лась п**о**сле Окт**я**брьской Револ**ю**ции в 1917-ом год**у**. Б**ы**ло с**о**здано Гл**а**вное управл**е**ние по дел**а**м литерат**у**ры и изд**а**тельств (Главл**и**т), кот**о**рое отвеч**а**ло за пол**и**тику госуд**а**рства в отнош**е**нии ценз**у**ры. Пр**е**жде всег**о** Главл**и**т составл**я**л сп**и**ски произвед**е**ний, запрещённых к опубликов**а**нию, как, наприм**е**р «Д**о**ктор Жив**а**го». Главл**и**т т**а**кже тр**е**бовал маркс**и**стские предисл**о**вия, не т**о**лько для кл**а**ссиков Росс**и**и, но ос**о**бенно для б**о**лее совр**е**менной литерат**у**ры.

Госуд**а**рство управл**я**ло постан**о**вкой всех драмат**и**ческих, музык**а**льных и кинематограф**и**ческих произвед**е**ний. С теч**е**нием вр**е**мени сов**е**тские вл**а**сти ст**а**ли контрол**и**ровать люб**ы**е публ**и**чные зр**е**лища и выступл**е**ния, от с**а**мых скр**о**мных л**е**кций и докл**а**дов до эстр**а**дных и д**а**же музык**а**льно-танцев**а**льных веч**е**ров. Ценз**у**рный реж**и**м знач**и**тельно не мен**я**лся до пери**о**да «перестр**о**йки» в конц**е** '80-х год**о**в. Перестр**о**йка внесл**а** б**о**лее существ**е**нные коррект**и**вы в де**я**тельность Главл**и**та. П**о**сле расп**а**да СССР в декабре 1993 года Конституция Российской Федерации запретила цензуру, и по мнению многих экспертов, российские средства массовой информации (СМИ) стали свободнее, чем когда-либо.

Со временем в России государство более косвенным путём заново получило контроль над основными общенациональными телеканалами, и «оппозиционные» журналисты считают, что добывать информацию становится всё труднее и труднее. По недавнему опросу относительное большинство россиян считают, что отечественное телевидение всё же достаточно полно освещает события дня. Те, кто не доверяет телевидению, обычно лучшим и самым надёжным источником информации выбирают для себя интернет-ресурсы, блоги и соцсети.

V		
в отношении	*with regard to*
запрещать/ запретить	*to ban*
зрелище	*spectacle*
отечественный	*Russian ('of the Fatherland')*
доверять + *dat.*	*to trust*

1 Почему был создан Главлит?

_____

2 Кто давал разрешение на публичные зрелища в СССР?

_____

3 Когда запретили цензуру в России?

_____

4 Легко ли работать журналистом в России сейчас?

_____

5 Кроме телевидения и традиционной прессы, откуда можно получать информацию в России?

_____

Vocabulary

J Highlight all the instances of comparatives and superlatives in the reading text. Note what cases are they in and how you would translate them into English.

K Write the opposite of the following words.

1 лучше _____

2 дороже _____

3 интереснее _____

4 легче _____

5 старше _____

6 дальше _____

L Using comparatives or superlatives, write a Russian sentence giving your preferences for the following options. Use phrases from the box to express your opinion.

я думаю, что	*(I think that)*	по моему мнению	*(in my opinion)*
я считаю, что	*(I consider that)*	на мой взгляд	*(in my view)*
по-моему	*(in my opinion)*	мне кажется, что	*(it seems to me that)*

Пример: грамматика/информатика → Я думаю, что грамматика интереснее, чем информатика.

1 телевизор/радио _____

2 ходить в кино/смотреть на ДВД _____

3 смотреть крикет по телевизору/общаться с друзьями по интернету _____

4 посылать СМС/звонить по телефону/встречаться _____

5 компьютер/смартфон/планшет _____

6 газета/вебсайт/новости по телевизору _____

M Give an opinion on the questions below and justify it with at least one reason.

1 Что интереснее – смотреть фильм или читать книгу? _____

2 Что полезнее для здоровья – сидеть перед экраном компьютера или заниматься спортом?
_____

3 Что удобнее – смартфон или планшет? _____

4 Что лучше – детектив или мыльная опера? _____

5 Что быстрее – покупать в магазине или онлайн? _____

6 Что ленивее – смотреть телевизор весь день или играть в компьютерные игры весь день?_____

Writing

N You want to subscribe to a video-streaming service to be able to watch films and TV serials. Answer these registration questions, writing about 100 words of Russian.

▶ Опишите себя (возраст, пол, и т.д.)

▶ Какой жанр передач вы предпочитаете и почему?

▶ Какой жанр передач вам не нравится и почему?

▶ Что важнее для вас – история? персонажи? исторический период? режиссёр? спецэффекты?

▶ Что важнее всего – цена или доступ к самым последним выпускам?

_____

_____

_____

_____

_____

_____

_____

_____

_____

 When you are giving your preferences, aim to make as many comparisons as you can and give reasons for your favourite options.

Self-check

Tick the box which matches your level of confidence.

1 = very confident   2 = need more practice   3 = not too confident

Как вы думаете? Вы хорошо понимаете? Поставьте галочку:

1 = хорошо   2 = нужно больше практики   3 = нехорошо

	1	2	3
Use superlative adjectives and adverbs			
Use comparative adjectives and adverbs			
Understand a complex text about media			
Able to express preferences and opinions using comparatives and superlatives			

6 Что ты делаешь в свободное время?

What do you do in your free time?

In this unit you will learn how to:

✔ Use verbs in the present tense

✔ Describe hobbies

✔ Offer opinions about hobbies

CEFR: Can express themselves on everyday topics using more complex constructions and vocabulary (CEFR B1); Can write accounts of experiences, describing feelings and reactions in simple connected text (CEFR B1)

I play		-аю	I speak		-ю
you play		-аешь	you speak		-ишь
he/she plays	игр-	-ает	he/she speaks	говор-	-ит
we play		-аем	we speak		-им
you play		-аете	you speak		-ите
they play		-ают	they speak		-ят

Meaning and usage

The present tense

1   There is only one form of the present tense in Russian, which is used to translate the various forms of the present tense in English:

	I relax
я отдыхаю	I am relaxing
	I do relax

How to form the present tense

1   Present tense verbs in Russian usually follow a logical pattern. The regular verbs can be split into two main groups – as in the infographic:

▶ those whose infinitive ends in -ать/-ять – these are referred to as Conjugation I

▶ those whose infinitive ends in -ить/-еть – these are referred to as Conjugation II

 Don't forget the spelling rule that can affect Conjugation II verbs in the я and они forms: you can never write ы, ю or я after г, к, х, ж, ч, ш, щ; instead write и, у and а.

2 When forming the present tense, you first need to identify the verb stem (this is usually formed by removing ать/ять/ить/еть) and then just add the appropriate ending to match the subject of the verb:

Don't forget that if you are using two verbs together (as in, for example, I prefer to swim) you leave the second verb in the infinitive: я предпочит**аю** пл**а**вать.

Я пл**а**в**аю**   (*I swim*)

Я звон**ю**   (*I ring/phone*)

3 Even though the ending of a present tense verb makes it clear who the subject is, it is still usual in Russian to use a pronoun.

A   Put the verb in brackets in the correct form and then translate the sentence into English.

1 Мы всегд**а** (игр**а**ть) _____ в к**а**рты по п**я**тницам.

2 М**и**ша не (л**ю**бить) _____ ход**и**ть на конц**е**рты.

3 Как**и**е перед**а**чи вы (смотр**е**ть) _____ со сво**и**ми детьм**и**?

4 Р**у**сские ч**а**сто (чит**а**ть) _____ зараб**е**жную литерат**у**ру.

5 Я ненав**и**жу (получ**а**ть) _____ и-м**е**йлы от друз**е**й; я (предпочит**а**ть) _____ говор**и**ть с друзь**я**ми по интерн**е**ту.

6 Ты ч**а**сто (навещ**а**ть) _____ семь**ю**?

How to form the present tense of irregular verbs

The good news is that even irregular verbs in Russian are usually recognizably regular once you know the stem because the endings will always broadly follow one of the two basic conjugations. It is possible to group these irregular verbs together.

1 verbs in -авать, -овать, -евать (these verbs often originate from other languages). Look at the table below and try to spot the pattern:

фотографировать (to photograph)			танцевать (to dance)		
I photograph		-ую	*I dance*		-ую
you photograph		-уешь	*you dance*		-уешь
he/she photographs	фотографир	-ует	*he/she dances*	танц	-ует
we photograph		-уем	*we dance*		-уем
you photograph		-уете	*you dance*		-уете
they photograph		-уют	*they dance*		-уют

You will have noticed that the stem has been formed by replacing the syllable -ов-/-ев- in the infinitive with -у- in the endings.

2 Second conjugation verbs whose stem changes in the first person singular only:

б		бл	любить (to love)	я люблю (ты любишь …)
в		вл	ловить (to catch)	я ловлю (ты ловишь …)
м		мл	кормить (to feed)	я кормлю (ты кормишь …)
п	→	пл	купить (to buy)	я куплю (ты купишь …)
д/з		ж	видеть (to see)	я вижу (ты видишь …)
с		ш	просить (to ask)	я прошу (ты просишь …)
т		ч	лететь (to fly)	я лечу (ты летишь …)

3 Single syllable first conjugation verbs.

The three most common examples of this are:

петь	(to sing)	пить	(to drink)	мыть	(to wash)
я	пою	я	пью	я	мою
ты	поёшь	ты	пьёшь	ты	моешь
он/она	поёт	он/она	пьёт	он/она	моет
мы	поём	мы	пьём	мы	моем
вы	поёте	вы	пьёте	вы	моете
они	поют	они	пьют	они	моют

B **Complete the sentences with an appropriate verb from the box, putting the verb in the correct form.**

танцевать	рисовать	любить	пробовать	просить
пить	видеть	петь	лететь	мыть

1 На день рождения я всегда _____ шампанское.

2 По вечерам Иван часто _____ картины.

3 На выходные я _____ в Париж из аэропорта моего города.

4 Они _____ много на дискотеке.

5 На вечеринках мы с друзьями _____ весёлые песни.

6 Мороженое? Я не _____, а обожаю!

7 Когда погода хорошая, она _____ машину.

8 Когда я уезжаю на целый день я _____ соседа смотреть за моей собакой.

9 **Е**сли ты _____ красивую футболку, купи!

10 Вы _____ новые блюда, когда вы находите новый ресторан?

We can identify some other verbs which seem to be even more irregular, although again once we know the stem, the endings normally continue to follow the basic patterns:

4 First conjugation verbs with stems ending in a consonant. The two most common are:

ждать *(to wait)*		идти *(to go)*	
я	жд**у**	я	ид**у**
ты	жд**ёшь**	ты	ид**ёшь**
он/он**а**	жд**ёт**	он/он**а**	ид**ёт**
мы	жд**ём**	мы	ид**ём**
вы	жд**ёте**	вы	ид**ёте**
он**и**	жд**ут**	он**и**	ид**ут**

5 Common verbs with unusual changes from their infinitive to their stem:

брать *(to take)*		звать *(to call)*		жить *(to live)*	
я	бер**у**	я	зов**у**	я	жив**у**
ты	бер**ёшь**	ты	зов**ёшь**	ты	жив**ёшь**
он/он**а**	бер**ёт**	он/он**а**	зов**ёт**	он/он**а**	жив**ёт**
мы	бер**ём**	мы	зов**ём**	мы	жив**ём**
вы	бер**ёте**	вы	зов**ёте**	вы	жив**ёте**
он**и**	бер**ут**	он**и**	зов**ут**	он**и**	жив**ут**
ехать *(to go (by transport))*		писать *(to write)*		мочь *(to be able to)*	
я	**е**ду	я	пиш**у**	я	мог**у**
ты	**е**дешь	ты	пиш**ешь**	ты	м**о**жешь
он/он**а**	**е**дет	он/он**а**	пиш**ет**	он/он**а**	м**о**жет
мы	**е**дем	мы	пиш**ем**	мы	м**о**жем
вы	**е**дете	вы	пиш**ете**	вы	м**о**жете
он**и**	**е**дут	он**и**	пиш**ут**	он**и**	м**о**гут

6 Verbs that combine elements of both conjugations. Fortunately, there are only two common examples:

есть *(to eat)*		хотеть *(to want)*	
я	ем	я	хоч**у**
ты	ешь	ты	хо**ч**ешь
он/он**а**	ест	он/он**а**	хо**ч**ет
мы	едим	мы	хот**им**
вы	едите	вы	хот**ите**
он**и**	едят	он**и**	хот**ят**

C **Change the following sentences from singular to plural and vice versa.**

Пример: Ка́ждый день я беру́ раке́тку. → Ка́ждый день мы берём раке́тку.

1 Ка́ждый день я пишу́ дневни́к. _____

2 Мы е́дем в теа́тр сего́дня ве́чером. _____

3 Мои́ друзья́ не едя́т мя́со. _____

4 Ты хо́чешь де́лать поку́пки? _____

5 В кинотеа́тре идёт интере́сный фильм. _____

6 Вы мо́жете игра́ть в ка́рты в сре́ду? _____

D **Using your knowledge of all types of irregular present tense verbs in Russian, put the verb in brackets into the correct form in the following sentences.**

1 Я всегда́ (брать) _____ зо́нтик, е́сли плоха́я пого́да.

Note that there is a small group of verbs ending in -ать (such as лежа́ть and слы́шать – to hear) that are Conjugation II verbs.

2 Они́ (мочь) _____ прийти́ к нам по́сле обе́да.

3 Твоя́ подру́га Све́та (ждать) _____ у вхо́да в метро́.

4 По воскресе́ньям, де́душка ча́сто (спать) _____ в кре́сле по́сле обе́да.

5 Моя́ тётя ча́сто (организова́ть) _____ прогу́лки в лесу́ для всей семьи́.

6 Та́ня никогда́ не (сиде́ть) _____ до́ма пе́ред экра́ном – она́ о́чень акти́вная же́нщина.

E **Fill in the table below with the correct forms of the verbs.**

	to listen	*to go for a walk*	*to watch*	*to go (on foot)*	*to have lunch*
(infinitive)					
я					
ты					
он/она́					
мы					
вы					
они́					

 # Reading

F   Read the first part of this online post and answer the question that follows in Russian.

---

www.interesnayainformacya.ru

Уважаемые читатели! Просим вас ответить на наши вопросы в этом небольшом опросе о свободном времени. На основе этих данных мы сможем рекомендовать местным властям какие возможности для отдыха нужно развивать в вашем городе.

Почему надо принимать участие в этом опросе?

G   Now read these replies to the survey and answer the questions that follow in Russian.

Таня   15–30 лет   31–55 лет   56–80 лет

Как вы проводите вечера дома во время недели?

Я работаю в офисе, а по вечерам в свободное время я люблю отдыхать. В основном мне помогает отдыхать мой любимый планшет. Конечно посещаю соцсети, чтобы поддерживать контакты с подругами. Брожу по интернету час или два каждый вечер.

Выходите ли вы по выходным?

По выходным мы с мужем выходим в кино или в ресторан. Это не совсем просто потому, что надо ехать в центр города. Жаль, что нет ни кинотеатра, ни хороших ресторанов в нашем районе.

Какое ваше любимое хобби?

Смотрю телевизор нечасто и раз в неделю хожу в спортзал на кружок йоги. Но моё любимое хобби не фитнес, а экзотическая кулинария. Люблю искать по интернету новые рецепты и готовить оригинальные блюда для семьи и гостей.

Как вы проводите вечера дома во время недели?

Я пенсионерка и провожу вечера дома перед телевизором. Также люблю готовить, и ужинаю в гостиной пока смотрю любимые телесериалы. Предпочитаю мексиканские передачи – я знаю, что это чепуха, но это так красиво!

Выходите ли вы по выходным?

Да, по крайней мере раз в неделю. Мы с бывшими коллегами ужинаем друг у друга по очереди каждую субботу. Обсуждаем детей и внуков, и, конечно, самые последние приключения мексиканских героев.

Какое ваше любимое хобби?

Страшно люблю триктрак. Играем с бывшими коллегами и также участвую в областных соревнованиях. В этом году – я чемпионка, и регулярно играю, чтобы ещё раз победить всех конкурентов.

область	region
чепуха	nonsense
триктрак	backgammon
соревнование	competition

1   Почему Таня любит свой планшет?

_____

2   Почему Таня ездит в центр города по выходным?

_____

3   Где Таня находит новые рецепты?

_____

4   Почему Люда любит телесериалы?

_____

5   Как мы знаем, что Люда хорошо играет в триктрак?

_____

H   Have you noticed anything about the verbs in this reading passage? This is a feature of the informal style of writing that an internet survey would encourage.

I   For extra practice, review the responses to the survey and write a brief report with recommendations for new facilities that would benefit residents.

J Rewrite the following sentences using present tense verbs.

Пример: Я люблю чтение. → Я читаю.

1 Я люблю плавание. → _____

2 Любимое хобби Ивана – песни. → _____

3 Маша и Даша любят книги. → _____

4 Я предпочитаю игру в шахматы. → _____

5 Для тебя, самое важное – это бег. → _____

6 Мы обожаем рисование. → _____

K Rephrase the following sentences in the same way as the example.

Пример: Иван танцует на дискотеке. → Иван любит танцевать на дискотеке.

1 Мои друзья едят пирожные. → _____

2 Мы берём бутерброды на пикник. → _____

3 Вы ждёте друзей после школы? → _____

4 Его сестра поёт фольклорные песни. → _____

5 Я пишу открытки на день рождения. → _____

6 Почему ты не моешь собаку после прогулки? → _____

Vocabulary

L Find a word or words in the reading text that matches the following definitions.

1 вебсайты, где можно разговаривать с друзьями _____

2 инструкции, чтобы готовить блюда _____

3 едим вечером _____

Writing

M You are relaxing with your family. Record your impressions on the микроблог site – don't forget you have only 140 characters for each of the following four entries in Russian:

▶ Что вы делаете, и как это?

▶ Что делают другие в семье и почему?

▶ Какая погода?

▶ Вы рекомендуете место, которое вы посещаете?

Once you have responded as yourself, imagine the replies that other members of your family would message back to you.

_____

_____

_____

_____

_____

_____

_____

_____

_____

_____

Self-check

Tick the box which matches your level of confidence.

1 = very confident   2 = need more practice   3 = not too confident

Как вы думаете? Вы хорошо понимаете? Поставьте галочку:

1 = хорошо   2 = нужно больше практики   3 = нехорошо

	1	2	3
Form present tense of regular verbs			
Form present tense of irregular verbs			
Describe a wide range of free-time activities			
Express opinions about people's free-time activities			

7 Мой день

My day

In this unit you will learn how to:

● Use reflexive verbs

● Use the passive voice

● Compare your daily routine with that of others

CEFR: Can describe daily routine (CEFR A2); Can scan longer text in order to locate desired information and understand relevant information in everyday material, such as questionnaires, brochures and short official documents (CEFR B1)

я одеваю (*I dress*)	я одеваюсь (*I dress myself*)

Meaning and usage

Reflexive verbs

A Look at the following sentences. What do you notice about the verbs?

Я одева**ю**сь в спа**ль**не.	(*I get dressed in the bedroom.*)
Когд**а** ты занима**е**шься м**у**зыкой?	(*When do you do (occupy yourself with) music?*)
Он**и** куп**а**ются в м**о**ре.	(*They bathe in the sea.*)

1 The verbs in the examples in **A** are reflexive verbs and you will have noticed that this means they have an additional ending. This is usually -ся, but becomes -сь if the letter in front of it is a vowel.

The basic use of a reflexive verb is to describe an action where the subject of the verb is doing the action to themselves, such as *to dress oneself*. Reflexive verbs are very common in Russian because there are various other uses of reflexives:

a reciprocal verbs – which normally involve two people:

Степ**а**н и Ир**и**на встреч**а**ются по субб**о**там.	(*Stepan and Irina meet (each other) on Saturdays.*)

b verbs in the reflexive form used as a way of expressing the passive:

Зубн**а**я п**а**ста продаётся в   *(Toothpaste is sold in supermarkets.)*
     супермаркетах.

c many of the verbs in Russian to express feelings or attitudes:

Мы волн**у**емся немн**о**го, потом**у** что   *(We are a little anxious because we*
     у нас н**о**вый котёнок.   *have a new kitten.)*

B **Put the verbs in the following sentences into the correct form and translate them into English.**

1   Мой день (начин**а**ться) _____ р**а**но.

2   Я (умыв**а**ться) _____ в семь час**о**в.

3   Я (причёсываться) _____ п**е**ред з**е**ркалом.

4   Он (просып**а**ться) _____ п**о**здно по воскрес**е**ньям.

5   Он**и** (встреч**а**ться) _____ в рестор**а**не на об**е**д.

6   Вы (возвращ**а**ться) _____ дом**о**й на трамв**а**е.

C **Choose the most appropriate option for the following sentences.**

1   У мен**я** в**а**жная встр**е**ча с дир**е**ктором. Я сиж**у** в ег**о** о**ф**исе и …

    a заним**а**юсь   **b** волн**у**юсь   **c** умыв**а**юсь

2   Он**и** предлаг**а**ют пойт**и** на н**а**шу люб**и**мую **о**перу, и мы …

    a соглаш**а**емся   **b** б**о**ремся   **c** просып**а**емся

3   П**о**сле дл**и**нного дня на раб**о**те, он**а** р**а**но …

    a встреч**а**ется   **b** лож**и**тся   **c** удивл**я**ется

4   При встр**е**че ст**а**рые друзь**я** …

    a прощ**а**ются   **b** успок**а**иваются   **c** цел**у**ются

5   На **у**лице сто**и**т зл**а**я соб**а**ка. Пётр …

    a бо**и**тся   **b** улыб**а**ется   **c** куп**а**ется

6   Бал**е**т … в в**о**семь час**о**в

    a начин**а**ется   **b** руг**а**ется   **c** одев**а**ется

D **Look at these two sentences and decide which one is active and which one is passive.**

a   Зубн**а**я п**а**ста продаётся в супермаркете.
b   Супермаркет продаёт зубн**у**ю п**а**сту.

E **Complete the following blog post with appropriate verbs from the box. Be careful – you will not need all of the verbs.**

| готовится | просыпаюсь | одеваюсь | умываюсь |
| готовлю | чищу | возвращаюсь | принимаю |

Я 1 _____ в шесть час**о**в и 2 _____ з**а**втрак на к**у**хне. Пок**а** з**а**втрак
3 _____, я 4 _____ душ и 5 _____. Пот**о**м я 6 _____
на к**у**хню.

2 As previously mentioned, a reflexive verb can often be used to express the passive voice in Russian, i.e. 'toothpaste **is sold**'. Although there is a proper form of the passive in Russian this is used a lot less frequently than in English. There are also two other ways of expressing the passive in **Russian**:

a use the он**и** form of a verb in Russian without the pronoun:

Зубн**у**ю п**а**сту прода**ю**т в супермаркете.

(Toothpaste they sell in the supermarket. → Toothpaste is sold in the supermarket.)

b reverse the word order of an active sentence:

М**а**ша покуп**а**ет зубн**у**ю п**а**сту. (active) → Зубн**у**ю п**а**сту покуп**а**ет М**а**ша. (passive)

(Masha buys toothpaste. → Toothpaste buys Masha. → Toothpaste is bought by Masha.)

F **Using one of the last two explained methods, make the following active sentences passive.**

1 Он**и** гот**о**вят **у**жин. _____

2 Все молод**ы**е л**ю**ди сл**у**шают м**у**зыку по утр**а**м. _____

3 Мо**и** род**и**тели всегд**а** см**о**трят ф**и**льмы по вечер**а**м. _____

4 Мо**я** б**а**бушка обож**а**ет кроссв**о**рды. _____

5 Он**и** м**о**ют пос**у**ду к**а**ждый день. _____

6 В н**а**шей семь**е** т**о**лько я покуп**а**ю вегетари**а**нскую ед**у**. _____

G **Read the account of Misha's strange day and change it where needed to make it more plausible.**

Прим**е**р: Я з<u>асып**а**ю</u> в 6 час**о**в и б**ы**стро вста**ю**. → Я <u>просып**а**юсь</u> в 6 час**о**в и б**ы**стро вста**ю**.

Я ид**у** в гар**а**ж и приним**а**ю душ. Пот**о**м я раздев**а**юсь и конч**а**ю гот**о**вить **у**жин. В 06:45 я смотр**ю** веч**е**рние н**о**вости по р**а**дио, и пот**о**м я сним**а**ю пальт**о** и отправл**я**юсь на раб**о**ту. Я лож**у**сь в трамв**а**й и **е**ду в центр г**о**рода. Я зак**а**нчиваю раб**о**тать в 8 час**о**в утр**а** и начин**а**ю раб**о**тать в 6 час**о**в в**е**чера. **У**тром я возвращ**а**юсь домой и ем з**а**втрак. Об**ы**чно я просып**а**юсь дов**о**льно р**а**но, в два час**а** н**о**чи. Я засып**а**ю в сад**у** и кр**е**пко раб**о**таю до утр**а**.

засып**а**ть/засн**у**ть	*to fall asleep*	отправл**я**ться/отпр**а**виться	*to set off*
лож**и**ться/лечь	*to lie down*	просып**а**ться/просн**у**ться	*to wake up*
начин**а**ться/нач**а**ться	*to start, be started*	сад**и**ться/сесть	*to sit down*
одев**а**ться/од**е**ться	*to get dressed*		

# Reading

H Your Russian friend is on secondment abroad and has written an email to you. Read the first paragraph and answer the question that follows in Russian.

От:	Новиков, С.А.
Кому:	Фергасан, Р.
Тема:	Командировка

Привет!
Как ты знаешь, я не в России, потому что работаю за границей. Много очень похоже на жизнь и работу дома, но кое-что отличается. Я пишу, чтобы рассказать об этом. Надеюсь, что это тебе интересно.

Почему Слава пишет вам? _____

I Now read the rest of the email and answer the questions that follow in Russian.

Я удивляюсь тому, как рано начинают работать здесь! Надо быть на работе к восьми часам, тогда как в России я начинаю около десяти. Когда я прихожу на работу я проверяю свои и-мейлы, но также часто есть заседания с клиентами на завтрак. Едим круассаны и пьём кофе пока обсуждаем важные контракты и все возможные аспекты деятельности фирмы и это для меня непривычно.

В России иногда мы с коллегами едим второй завтрак – это как настоящий обед. А здесь нет времени на это – часто нет времени даже на обед. Иногда организуется бизнес-ланч с клиентами, но чаще всего я работаю перед компьютером целый день без перерыва. Трудно поверить, но иногда я даже скучаю по нашей столовой на работе в России. Рабочий день здесь кончается около шести, и это неудобно если надо сходить на почту, потому что почта закрывается намного раньше, чем в России. Вообще многие заведения закрываются позже в России, чем здесь. Обычно по пути домой в России я захожу на рынок и покупаю всё, что нужно на вечер, хотя иногда трудно ехать с покупками на трамвае. Друг, у которого я живу здесь, редко ходит по магазинам. Обычно вечером он достаёт уже готовое блюдо из морозильника и разогревает в микроволновке. Это конечно хорошо, но всё-таки я скучаю немного по свежей русской кухне.

Пока,

Слава

кое-что	*something*	непривычный	*unaccustomed*
отличаться	*to differ*	скучать	*to miss*
заседание	*meeting*	заведение	*establishment*

1 Почему Слава удивляется началу рабочего дня за рубежом?

_____

2 Что он думает о заседаниях на завтрак?

_____

3 Почему он считает конец рабочего дня неудобным?

_____

4 Когда он в России, что он обычно делает по пути домой?

_____

5 Предпочитает ли Слава типичный ужин за рубежом?

_____

 J For extra practice, compare the details given above with your own daily routine and note similarities and differences.

Vocabulary

K Give the reflexive verbs for the following definitions.

1 кончаю спать _____

2 надеваешь одежду _____

3 чищу лицо и руки _____

4 выходят из дома _____

5 делаете хорошую причёску _____

6 едем обратно _____

7 снимаю одежду _____

8 иду спать _____

L Match the activities with the people.

1 Павел встаёт рано

2 Ирина поздно работает

3 Наташа всегда моет посуду

4 Петя чистит зубы три раза в день

5 Настя купается каждое утро

6 Володя долго читает перед сном

a ... хочет купить посудомоечную машину

b ... начинает работать в семь часов утра

c ... у него красивая улыбка

d ... страдает от бессонницы

e ... возвращается домой после восьми часов вечера

f ... живёт в доме, где находится бассейн

M Give the opposite for the following verbs.

1 просып**а**ться _____ 4 закрыв**а**ть _____

2 раздев**а**ться _____ 5 встав**а**ть _____

3 начин**а**ть _____ 6 возвращ**а**ться _____

▶ Writing

N Your annual health check is due and your doctor asks you to complete a report about your typical working day. In about 100 words of Russian, cover the following points.

- ▶ когд**а** вы раб**о**таете
- ▶ на выходн**ы**е
- ▶ в **о**тпуске л**е**том
- ▶ в **о**тпуске зим**о**й

> *Try to include comparatives and superlatives in the paragraphs when describing your routine at different times.*

_____

_____

_____

_____

_____

_____

_____

_____

_____

_____

Self-check

Tick the box which matches your level of confidence.

1 = very confident   2 = need more practice   3 = not too confident

Как вы д**у**маете? Вы хорош**о** понима**е**те? Пост**а**вьте г**а**лочку:

1 = хорош**о**   2 = н**у**жно б**о**льше пр**а**ктики   3 = нехорош**о**

	1	2	3
Form reflexive verbs			
Use a variety of constructions to convey passive meaning			
Understand a description of daily routine			
Able to describe your daily routine and compare it to others			

Какие у тебя планы?

What are your plans?

In this unit you will learn how to:

- ✔ Describe events in the past
- ✔ Describe events in the future
- ✔ Understand aspect in Russian

CEFR: Can use the past and future tenses in Russian (CEFR B1) and write a narrative about a family holiday (CEFR B2)

Past	Present	Future
он **делал** *he did, was doing* он**а делала** *she did, was doing* он**и делали** *they did, were doing*	он **делает** *he does, is doing* он**а делает** *she does, is doing* он**и делают** *they do, are doing*	он **будет делать** *he will do, will be doing* он**а будет делать** *she will do, will be doing* он**и будут делать** *they will do, will be doing*
он **сделал** *he did, has done, had done* он**а сделала** *she did, has done, had done* он**и сделали** *they did, have done, had done*		он **сделает** *he will do, will have done* он**а сделает** *she will do, will have done* он**и сделают** *they will do, will have done*

Meaning and usage

Tenses in Russian

There are only three tenses in Russian and they are easy to form. Nearly all Russian verbs exist as a pair: one is known as the *imperfective aspect* and the other is known as the *perfective aspect*. Let's look at the imperfective first:

How to form the past tense

 A Look at the following table – how is the past tense formed?

делать	(to do)
я де**л**ал / я де**л**ала	мы де**л**али
ты де**л**ал / ты де**л**ала	вы де**л**али
он де**л**ал	он**и** де**л**али
он**а** де**л**ала	
он**о** де**л**ало	

 *Remember that in the present tense, there is usually no verb to be in Russian (он – в кинотеа**т**ре – he is in the cinema). In the past tense, the infinitive* быть *follows the usual pattern:*

быть

он**о** б**ы**ло

он был

он**и** б**ы**ли

он**а** был**а**

1 As you will have noticed, there is a limited number of endings for the past tense. To form the past tense, you remove the -ть from the infinitive and add the following:

masculine singular -л	
feminine singular -ла	all plurals -ли
neuter singular -ло	

There are *very* few exceptions to this pattern. The most common are:

идти *(to walk)*	шёл	шла	шло	шли
мочь *(to be able to)*	мог	могла	могло	могли
есть *(to eat)*	ел	ела	ело	ели
класть *(to place, lay)*	клал	клала	клало	клали

2 Reflexive verbs follow the same pattern for the past tense. To form them, remove the reflexive ending from the infinitive, form the past tense in the usual way and then add on the appropriate reflexive ending. Remember, if a reflexive ending follows a consonant, it is spelt -ся but if it follows a vowel, it is spelt -сь. For example: занима**т**ься *(to do, occupy oneself with)* becomes:

он занима**л**ся   он**а** занима**л**ась   он**о** занима**л**ось   он**и** занима**л**ись

B Put the following present tense sentences into the past tense.

1   Я игра**ю** в кр**и**кет по субб**о**там. _____

2   Он**и** см**о**трят телев**и**зор к**а**ждый день. _____

3   Ты п**и**шешь регул**я**рно, М**а**ша? _____

4   Вы занима**е**тесь м**у**зыкой? _____

5   Мы танц**у**ем по ср**е**дам. _____

6   Ив**а**н идёт в киноте**а**тр в субб**о**ту. _____

How to form the future tense

C   Look at the following table – how is the future tense formed?

делать		to do	
я б**у**ду д**е**лать		мы б**у**дем д**е**лать	
ты б**у**дешь д**е**лать		вы б**у**дете д**е**лать	
он/он**а**/он**о** б**у**дет д**е**лать		он**и** б**у**дут д**е**лать	

You will have noticed that this form of the future tense is formed with the help of an additional verb – быть – followed by the infinitive. There is only one exception to this pattern.

The future tense of the verb to be *is, in fact, slightly exceptional: simply use the appropriate form of* быть *– you do not need to follow it with an infinitive:*

Я б**у**ду в п**а**рке.   *I will be in the park.*

D   Put the following present tense sentences into the future tense.

1   Я игра**ю** в кр**и**кет по субб**о**там. _____

2   Он**и** см**о**трят телев**и**зор к**а**ждый день. _____

3   Ты п**и**шешь регул**я**рно, М**а**ша? _____

4   Вы занима**е**тесь м**у**зыкой? _____

5   Мы танц**у**ем по ср**е**дам. _____

6   Ив**а**н идёт в киноте**а**тр в субб**о**ту. _____

Meaning and usage

Aspect

1   Although Russian verbs have only three tenses – past, present and future – the majority of them exist as a pair of **aspects**: one **imperfective** and one **perfective**.

Most of the verbs that you will use will be **imperfective** – this aspect is the only one that you can use in the present tense and, if it is used in the past and the future, it conveys an action that is either repeated, continuing or incomplete:

Present tense	он чит**а**ет	*he reads / he is reading / he does read*
Past tense – imperfective	он чит**а**л	*he used to read / he was reading / he read*
Future tense – imperfective	он б**у**дет чит**а**ть	*he will read / he will be reading*

The **perfective** aspect is never used for the present tense because it conveys an action that is either single or complete. Note that what appears to be the present tense of a perfective verb is, in fact, the future (you could think of it as being a 'future in disguise'!):

Present tense	–	–
Past tense – perfective	он прочит**а**л	*he has read / he did read / he had read*
Future tense – perfective	он прочит**а**ет	*he will read / he will have read*

 Remember: he read *in English could be translated either by an imperfective or a perfective verb in Russian. Using the imperfective stresses the* <u>process</u> *of reading* (Он чит**а**л, пок**а** он**а** раб**о**тала. He was reading while she was working.) *whereas the perfective stresses the* <u>result</u> (Он прочит**а**л до конц**а**. He read through to the end.)

How to form aspectual pairs

1   There are three main ways of forming **pairs of aspects**:

	Imperfective	Perfective
Adding a prefix to form the perfective	чит**а**ть *to read*	<u>про</u>чит**а**ть *to read*
Adding an infix to form the imperfective	расск**а**зыв**а**ть *to tell*	расск**а**з**а**ть *to tell*
Imperfective as a first conjugation verb and perfective as a second conjugation verb	приглаш**а**ть *to invite*	пригла<u>с**и**ть</u> *to invite*

 It is usual to list an imperfective verb before a perfective verb in reference material. In a dictionary, you will always be directed to the aspectual pair of any verb that you look up. Occasionally, pairs of aspects are very different verbs. A few common examples are: говор**и**ть/сказ**а**ть (to say), брать/взять (to take), сад**и**ться/сесть (to sit down), лож**и**ться/лечь (to lie down).

E   Look at the following sentences, decide if they are in the present or future tense and then translate them.

1   Я куплю билет завтра. _____

2   Маша всегда пишет открытки на каникулах. _____

3   Тебе так понравится Москва! _____

4   Я не знаю, что он скажет. _____

5   Гид рассказывает историю памятника. _____

6   Ты сможешь купить мне матрёшку. _____

F   Choose the correct verb, based on aspect, to complete these sentences and justify your choice.

1   Обычно в отпуске я (провожу/проведу) время в саду каждый день.

2   В среду я (поеду/буду ездить) в аэропорт, у меня самолёт рано утром.

3   После следующей поездки я окончательно (буду говорить/скажу), когда поеду снова.

4   Завтра я быстро (буду смотреть/посмотрю) информацию о поездах и закажу билет.

G   Three of the verbs in the following list do not have a perfective form. Suggest a reason for this for each of the three verbs.

договариваться/договориться	to agree (on)
загорать (no perfective)	to sunbathe
заказывать/заказать	to order
запрещать/запретить	to ban
искать (no perfective)	to look for
нанимать/нанять	to hire
находить/найти	to find
осматривать/осмотреть	to look round
подписывать/подписать	to sign
регистрироваться/ зарегистрироваться	to register
терять/потерять	to lose
торговаться (no perfective)	to haggle

 **Reading**

H Read the first part of this advert online for an apartment swap and answer the question that follows in Russian.

---

 www.interesnayainformacya.ru

Моя современная квартира находится в самом центре города в живописном старом районе. Я регулярно обедаю в кафе и ресторанах этой части города, где я пробую экзотические блюда. Рядом находится большой парк, с театром на открытом воздухе.

Вас интересует эта квартира и почему? _____

I Now read the visitor comments on the advert and answer the questions that follow in Russian.

26-02-16

Эта квартира была недалеко от центра, но район нам с мужем не показался живописным, хотя может быть это было из-за погоды. Было ужасно холодно, дул северный ветер, и бесконечно шёл дождь. Некоторые рестораны были закрыты – может быть на зиму? – но мы нашли один («Сказка»), где сервис был на высшем уровне, и блюда были очень вкусные. Всё стоило недорого, но в основном мы нашли только местную кулинарию. Конечно, из-за погоды парк был нам не нужен, и мы проводили много времени в квартире.

Рейчел (Оттава)

08-06-17

Спасибо большое! Мы с женой жили две недели в вашей прекрасной квартире, и нам очень понравилось. Мы два раза ходили на спектакль в парке и проводили много времени в торговом центре в пригороде. Городской транспорт работал без проблем и стоил недорого. В квартире было всё, что мы хотели, и мы там готовили завтрак и ужин почти каждый день. Мебель была не самая современная, и один раз моя жена села на стул, и он сломался. Мы конечно оставили деньги, но потом эти деньги нам вернули, потому что не была наша вина.

Мат (Мельбурн)

19-07-17

Мы с друзьями решили, что в этом году в отпуске мы познакомимся со старой архитектурой и традициями восточной Европы. Можно сделать это у вас? Для нас будет идеально, если мы …

… увидим исторические памятники

… посмотрим по крайней мере один спектакль

… будем загорать в зелёном месте

Пьер (Манчестер)

1 Почему Рейчел думает, что этот район не показался ей с мужем живописным?

_____

2 Какое впечатление получили Рейчел с мужем о ресторане «Сказка»?

_____

3 Какое впечатление получили они о городском транспорте?

_____

4 Были ли у них какие-нибудь проблемы в квартире?

_____

5 Думаете ли вы, что для Пьера с друзьями будет идеально провести отпуск в этой квартире?

_____

Vocabulary

J Complete the postcard with the appropriate verbs from the box.

Будем	веселились	хотим	загорали	пишем		
отдыхала	купили	была	обещают	было	идёт	разговаривали
навестим	плавали					

Привет друзья из Владивостока!

Мы **1** _____ вам из гостиницы, потому что, к сожалению, сегодня

2 _____ дождь. Вчера **3** _____ намного лучше –

4 _____ хорошая погода и Маша **5** _____

весь день на пляже. Несколько раз мы **6**_____

в море и один раз **7** _____ мороженое. Мы

8 _____ на солнце, **9** _____ друг с

другом и **10** _____. Завтра, **11** _____

хорошую погоду и мы **12** _____ торговый

центр города. **13** _____ долго гулять по

магазинам, потому что мы

14 _____ купить хорошие сувениры.

Жалко, что вас с нами нет!

КОМУ: Павлову, Н.И и
         Семёновой, Э.М.

КУДА: ул.Мира д.45, кв. 2,

г. Екатеринбург Свердловский

обл. 620075 - РОССИЯ

живописный	*picturesque*
проводить/провести	*to spend (time)*
готовить/приготовить	*to cook*
ломаться/сломаться	*to break*
оставлять/оставить	*to leave (behind)*

K State which tense(s) you would use after the following expressions.

1 завтра _____
2 позавчера _____
3 в следующую субботу _____
4 в прошлом году _____

5 на позапрошлой неделе _____
6 каждый месяц _____
7 послезавтра _____
8 прошлым летом _____

✍ Writing

L   Write a holiday blog entry for your Russian friends. In about 100 words of Russian make sure that you tell them the following.

- ▶ что вы обычно делаете в отпуске
- ▶ что вы делали во время последней поездки
- ▶ как вы собираетесь провести следующий отпуск
- ▶ вы предпочитаете отпуск летом или зимой

_____

_____

_____

_____

_____

_____

_____

_____

_____

Self-check

Tick the box which matches your level of confidence.

1 = very confident   2 = need more practice   3 = not too confident

Как вы думаете? Вы хорошо понимаете? Поставьте галочку:

1 = хорошо   2 = нужно больше практики   3 = нехорошо

	1	2	3
Use different tenses			
Use different aspects			
Understand a complex text about holidays			
Able to describe holiday activities in detail			

Какой у тебя режим?

What is your fitness regime?

In this unit, you will learn how to:

✓ Tell the time

✓ Discuss healthy living

✓ Describe how you keep healthy

CEFR: Can tell the time (CEFR A1) and can write in detail about sport and fitness (CEFR B2); Can read articles and reports concerned with contemporary problems in which the writers adopt particular attitudes or viewpoints (CEFR B2)

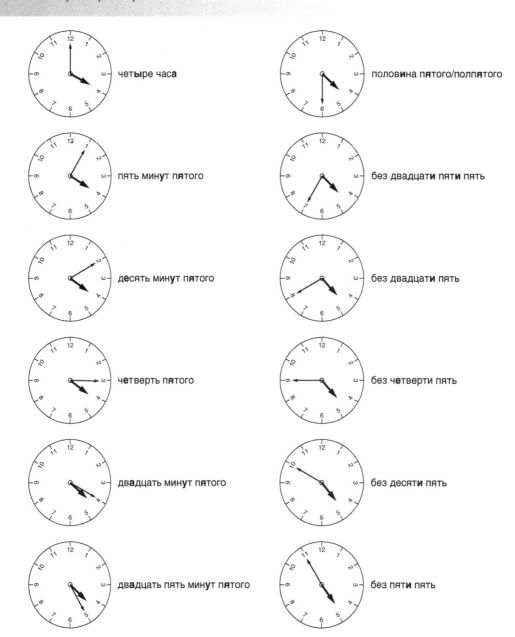

четыре часа

пять минут пятого

десять минут пятого

четверть пятого

двадцать минут пятого

двадцать пять минут пятого

половина пятого/полпятого

без двадцати пяти пять

без двадцати пять

без четверти пять

без десяти пять

без пяти пять

Meaning and usage

Telling the time

1 Just as in English, there are two different ways of telling the time in Russian: the digital method used with the 24-hour clock (e.g. four fifteen, twenty-three fifty-nine) and the analogue method used with the 12-hour clock (e.g. a quarter past four).

A Look at the clock faces at the start of the unit. Which method is this and what do you notice about the numbers used?

2 Telling the time in Russian involves using both **cardinal** and **ordinal** numbers. You should be familiar with cardinal numbers because they are used for counting and quantities: один, два, три, etc. Ordinal numbers translate *first, second, third,* etc., and we need to know up to 12th in order to be able to tell the time in Russian.

B Complete the following grid to give you all the ordinal numbers you need for analogue time-telling. Use the words in the box for help with the answers.

восемь	двенадцать	шестой	пять	два	одиннадцатый	четвёртый
десятый	третий	одиннадцать	седьмой	десять	девятый	
три	пятый	шесть	второй	четыре	восьмой	двенадцатый
семь	девять					

1	Час	Первый
2	_____ часа	
3	_____ часа	
4	_____ часа	
5	_____ часов	
6	_____ часов	
7	_____ часов	
8	_____ часов	
9	_____ часов	
10	_____ часов	
11	_____ часов	
12	_____ часов	

3 Ordinal numbers are needed to tell the time from the hour to the following half-hour.

C Look again at the clock diagrams: give the direct translation into English of пять минут пятого. Explain the grammar used here.

As you will have noticed, when telling the analogue time in Russian from the hour to the following half-hour, you are in fact saying that it is a number of minutes <u>of</u> the following hour.

D Complete the following table by translating the times in the same way as the given example.

пять мин**у**т п**я**того	4:05	*5 minutes of the fifth (hour)*
д**е**сять мин**у**т п**я**того	4:10	
ч**е**тверть п**я**того	4:15	
дв**а**дцать мин**у**т п**я**того	4:20	
дв**а**дцать пять мин**у**т п**я**того	4:25	
полов**и**на п**я**того/полп**я**того	4:30	

*Note that in spoken Russian, полов**и**на (п**я**того) can be replaced by пол(п**я**того). If the number starts with a vowel, there is a hyphen after the пол: пол-од**и**ннадцатого (half past ten).*

When telling the analogue time in Russian to the hour, you are in fact saying that it is *without* a number of minutes + the following hour.

E Complete the following table by translating the times in the same way as the given example.

без двадцат**и** пят**и** пять	4:35	*without 25 five*
без двадцат**и** пять	4:40	
без ч**е**тверти пять	4:45	
без дес**я**ти пять	4:50	
без пят**и** пять	4:55	

F Match the times with the clocks.

шесть час**о**в	без двадцат**и** двен**а**дцать
ч**е**тверть дев**я**того	без пят**и** час
полдес**я**того	дв**а**дцать пять мин**у**т тр тьего

Saying 'at' a time in Russian is quite straightforward: you use в unless the time begins with без or пол-

*at 4:25 = в дв**а**дцать пять мин**у**т п**я**того*

*at 4:30 = полп**я**того*

*at 4:35 = без двадцат**и** пят**и** пять*

G Choose the correct time.

1 без ч**е**тверти чет**ы**ре

   a 3:45   **b** 4:15   **c** 4:45

2 полвтор**о**го

   a 12:30   **b** 1:30   **c** 2:30

3 в ч**е**тверть седьм**о**го

   a at 4:30   **b** at 6:15   **c** at 6:45

4 без двадцат**и** в**о**семь

   a 7:20   **b** 7:40   **c** 8:40

5 в дв**а**дцать мин**у**т четвёртого

   a at 12:15   **b** at 3:20   **c** at 3:40

6 п**о**лдень

   a 00:00   **b** 11:30   **c** 12:00

H Write out these times in full using the analogue method in Russian.

8:05	11:20	8:45	10:30
1 _____	2 _____	3 _____	4 _____

2:25	6:40	12:10	1:15
5 _____	6 _____	7 _____	8 _____

I Reorder the frequency expressions in each group from the earliest to latest, or least to most frequent. Refer to the vocabulary box for help.

1 в м**о**лодости   в д**е**тстве   в ст**а**рости

_____

2 н**о**чью   **у**тром   днём   в**е**чером

_____

3 ч**а**сто   р**е**дко   об**ы**чно   иногд**а**

_____

4 давн**о**   сейч**а**с   нед**а**вно

_____

в детстве	*in childhood*	недавно	*recently*
в молодости	*in younger years*	ночью	*during the night*
в старости	*in old age*	обычно	*usually*
вечером	*in the evening*	редко	*rarely*
давно	*a long time ago*	сейчас	*(right) now*
днём	*during the afternoon*	утром	*in the morning*
иногда	*sometimes*	часто	*often*

Reading

J Read the beginning of this article and answer the question that follows in Russian.

> Вы часто устаёте на работе? Вы редко просыпаетесь с радостью? Вы обычно хотите есть скоро после обеда? Вы иногда едете на лифте, потому что нет сил подниматься по лестнице? Если вы отвечаете «Да!» хотя бы на один из этих вопросов, мы советуем вам серьёзно подумать о своём здоровье и о своём повседневном режиме. Диета и фитнес могут сильно влиять на самочувствие и работоспособность каждого человека.

О чём пишет автор этого текста? _____ _____

K Now read the rest of the article and answer the questions that follow in Russian.

> Что предлагают эксперты по отношению к хорошей диете? Конечно надо питаться регулярно и в меру. Свежие овощи являются хорошим источником витаминов, но важно помнить, что надо разнообразить питание, чтобы получать все нужные витамины и минералы. Если на прошлой неделе вы ели много мяса, то на этой неделе, не забывайте о рыбе. Во время рабочего дня естественно захотеть сладкого: свежие фрукты и ягоды очень полезны и могут удовлетворить потребность в сладком.
>
> По выходным важно заниматься спортом. Вот наш идеальный режим выходного дня:
>
> С семи до восьми часов: бег по улицам или желательно по лесу. После завтрака забывайте про фитнес на пару часов. Хорошо встречаться с друзьями на обед,

но если хотите потом поплавать в бассейне, это разрешается только через час после еды. Если вы давно не плавали, не плавайте долго – лучше постепенно привыкать в течение месяца. По вечерам долго не сидите перед экраном. Здоровый человек всегда ложится спать до полуночи.

Конечно, все знают, что здоровый человек редко пьёт алкоголь и никогда не курит. Также, если хочешь быть здоровым, избегаешь фаст-фуд, жирные продукты и чрезмерно сладкие напитки. Всё хорошо, если в меру – только наркотики запрещаются безоговорочно! Если вы делаете усилия, чтобы следовать нашим советам, то за месяц вы почувствуете себя намного здоровее.

хотя бы	*at least*	питаться (impf. only)	*to eat*
повседневный	*daily*	источник	*source*
предлагать/предложить	*to suggest*	постепенно	*gradually*
по отношению к (+ dat.)	*in relation to*	в течение	*during*

1 Почему эксперты рекомендуют свежие овощи?

_____

2 Где и когда лучше бегать?

_____

3 Можно ли плавать после обеда?

_____

4 В котором часу рекомендуется ложиться спать?

_____

Note the use of various prepositions in time phrases in this text:

после (+ gen.)	*(after)*
на неделе	*(in the week)*
по (+ dat. pl.)	*(on … days)*
с (+ gen.) … до (+ gen.) …	*(from … until …)*
на (+ acc.)	*(for (followed by an amount of time in the future))*
через (+ acc.)	*(in/after a period of time)*
до (+ gen.)	*(before)*
за (+ acc.)	*(within)*

Vocabulary

L **Find verbs in the text that have the same root as the following nouns.**

Приме́р: письм**о**   пи́шет (пис**а́**ть)

1 отв**е́**т   _____

2 сов**е́**т   _____

3 вли**я́**ние   _____

4 зан**я́**тие   _____

5 бег   _____

6 встр**е́**ча   _____

7 пл**а́**вание   _____

M **Find the opposite for the following words in the text.**

1 р**е́**дко   _____

2 задаёте вопр**о́**с   _____

3 сл**а́**бо   _____

4 забыв**а́**ть   _____

5 б**у́**дущей   _____

6 г**о́**рькое   _____

7 запрещ**а́**ется   _____

8 больн**о́**й   _____

N **Match the questions with the answers.**

1 По как**и́**м дням вы игр**а́**ете в бадминт**о́**н?   **a** до раб**о́**ты

2 Когд**а́** вы з**а́**втракаете?   **b** за два дня

3 Мы по**е́**дем ч**е́**рез три дня **и́**ли семь дн**е́**й?   **c** по пя́тницам

4 За ск**о́**лько дней вы см**о́**жете зак**о́**нчить **э́**тот про**е́**кт?   **d** с нач**а́**ла нед**е́**ли

5 Когд**а́** ты начин**а́**ешь свой н**о́**вый реж**и́**м?   **e** с шест**и́** до девят**и́** час**о́**в в**е́**чера

6 Когд**а́** ты нах**о́**дишься на веч**е́**рних к**у́**рсах?   **f** ч**е́**рез нед**е́**лю

Writing

O **Answer a Russian online fitness survey. Cover the following points in about 100 words of Russian.**

▶ что вы об**ы**чно ед**и**те и как**о**й заряд**к**ой вы занима**е**тесь

▶ что вы **е**ли и что вы д**е**лали в пр**о**шлые выходн**ы**е

▶ что вы собира**е**тесь д**е**лать в б**у**дущем, что**о**бы ул**у**чшить **у**ровень ф**и**тнеса

▶ что вы не б**у**дете д**е**лать в б**у**дущем, потом**у** что вы зн**а**ете, что **э**то пл**о**хо для ф**и**тнеса

_____

_____

_____

_____

_____

_____

_____

_____

_____

Self-check

Tick the box which matches your level of confidence.

1 = very confident   2 = need more practice   3 = not too confident

Как вы д**у**маете? Вы хорош**о** понима**е**те? Пост**а**вьте г**а**лочку:

1 = хорош**о**   2 = н**у**жно б**о**льше пр**а**ктики   3 = нехорош**о**

	1	2	3
Recognize and tell the time			
Able to use a wide variety of time and frequency expressions and prepositions			
Understand a complex text about healthy living			
Describe how you keep fit and healthy			

 # В зав**и**симости от пог**о**ды

It depends on the weather

In this unit you will learn how to:

✔ Discuss the weather

✔ Negate verbs

✔ Use a range of negative constructions

CEFR: Can talk about the weather in the past, present and future tenses (CEFR B1) and form a range of negative constructions (CEFR A1)

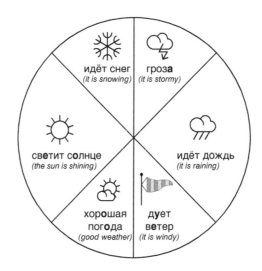

Meaning and usage

Using the negative

1 Look at these sentences about the weather.

 A Identify which expressions involve a verb and how these verbs are made negative.

Не св**е**тит с**о**лнце. *(The sun isn't shining.)*

Не идёт дождь. *(It isn't raining.)*

Не д**у**ет в**е**тер. *(The wind isn't blowing.)*

Нет с**о**лнца. *(There is no sun.)*

Нет дожд**я**. *(There is no rain.)*

Нет в**е**тра. *(There is no wind.)*

When you want to make a verb negative in Russian (e.g. the sun *isn't* shining), you simply add не as a separate word in front of the verb, no matter which tense the verb is in.

2 When there is no separate verb and you want to say *there is/are no …*, Russian uses the word нет followed by the genitive case. In the past tense, нет becomes н**е** было (pronounced as one word) and in the future tense it becomes не б**у**дет:

Вчера не было солнца, сегодня нет
солнца и завтра не будет солнца.

*(Yesterday there was no sun, today there is
no sun, tomorrow there will be no sun.)*

B **The weather is a disappointment! Change the
following expressions to describe bad weather.**

Note that the English word no
is translated by нет *whereas*
not *is translated by* не.

1 светит солнце _____

2 тепло _____

3 нет тумана _____

4 было жарко _____

5 завтра будет хорошая погода _____

6 не идёт дождь _____

3 Negative adverbs in Russian require a double negative:

Я никогда не загораю, когда
идёт дождь.

*(literally: I never not sunbathe
when it is raining.)*

C **Match the English and Russian negative adverbs.**

1	никогда	**a**	from nowhere
2	нигде	**b**	never
3	никуда	**c**	in no way
4	никак	**d**	to nowhere
5	ниоткуда	**e**	nowhere

D **Complete the sentences using a negative adverb and the verb given in brackets.**

1 Когда гроза, я _____ (плавать) в море.

2 Был туман везде и Иван _____ (видеть) машину.

3 Если будет очень жарко, мы _____ (ходить), а будем загорать в саду.

4 Полина искала паспорт, но _____ (найти).

5 Если ты устанешь на работе, ты _____ (захотеть) пойти вечером.

6 _____ (идти) снег в августе.

4 Negative pronouns in Russian also require a **double negative**:

Никто не любит плохую погоду.

(No one *likes bad weather.)*

Они ничего не делали, пока было
так холодно.

(They didn't do anything while it was so cold.)

Forms of the negative pronouns

1   These two negative pronouns have different endings if they are used in different cases:

Nominative	никто	ничто
Accusative	никого	ничего
Genitive	никого	ничего
Dative	никому	ничему
Instrumental	никем	ничем
Prepositional	ни о ком	ни о чём

As shown by the prepositional, if you need to use a preposition with the negative pronouns, you simply write them as three words with the preposition in the middle:

Из-за дождя я ни с кем не встречался.   *(Due to the rain, I did not meet up with anyone.)*

E   **Fill in the gaps in the sentences using a word from the box.**

никуда   никто   нигде   никому   ничего   ни о чём

1   Миша _____ не говорит, кроме погоды.

2   _____ не знает, будет ли ураган на следующей неделе.

3   Мы _____ не ездили на каникулы, потому что занимались ремонтом дома.

4   Было так жарко, что туристы _____ не делали.

5   Из-за плохой погоды, _____ не продаётся клубника.

6   _____ не нравится слишком жаркая погода.

F   **Look at the following sentences. Explain the difference between verbs used with никуда and verbs used with некуда.**

Они никуда не ходят, когда   *(**They don't go anywhere** when it is*
   идёт снег.   *snowing.)*

В деревне некуда ходить, когда   *(In the countryside **there is nowhere to***
   идёт снег.   ***go** when it is snowing.)*

2 There is an additional type of negative pronoun and adverb in Russian (column B in the table), which is followed by an infinitive:

A		B	
никто	*no one*	некого	*there is no one*
ничто	*nothing*	нечего	*there is nothing*
никогда	*never*	некогда	*there is never*
нигде	*nowhere*	негде	*there is nowhere*
никуда	*to nowhere*	некуда	*there is to nowhere*

G Choose the correct negative to complete the following sentences.

1 _____ делать, когда погода плохая.

2 Я _____ не забываю зонтик, если обещают дождь.

3 Туристы _____ не могли смотреть достопримечательности, потому что было пасмурно.

4 Так много людей загорали на солнце, что _____ было лежать на пляже.

5 _____ не предсказал сильный ветер.

6 Хорошо будет погулять в парке, но _____ будет, если будет гроза.

H Give the weather word that best matches the definition.

1 очень сильный ветер _____

2 не очень светло, но не идёт дождь _____

3 длинная струя замёрзшей воды _____

4 облако, которое обещает дождь _____

5 покрыть лёгким дождём _____

6 дожди с громом и молнией на море _____

V

моросить	*to drizzle*
пасмурно	*overcast*
сосулька	*icicle*
туча	*raincloud*
ураган	*hurricane*
шторм	*gale (at sea)*

📖 Reading

I Read the beginning of this article and answer the question that follows in Russian.

Никто не мог не заметить, что климат меняется во всём мире. Бабушки рассказывают о прекрасных, тёплых летах и лютых зимних морозах прошлого, когда можно было предсказывать с уверенностью, какая погода будет в каком сезоне.

О чём говорит автор этой статьи? _____

Теперь совсем не так: экстремальные погодные явления — штормовой ветер и мощные осадки — повторяются так регулярно, что никто не знает, что будет дальше, и мы всё больше и больше интересуемся метеорологией и прогнозами погоды на завтра!

В течение последних 20-и лет всё чаще наблюдаются мощные ураганы, со снегопадами или проливными дождями, с нарушением авиационного и дорожного движения. Скорость ветра постоянно увеличивается, температура ключевых элементов климата, как Гольфстрим, аномально высокая и превышает норму на несколько градусов, циклоны и антициклоны оказываются сильнее, что и вызывает опасные явления в любой стране, хотя иногда в ослабленном виде.

Эксперты предполагают, что около 40% так называемых «природных катастроф» приходится на наводнения и тесно связанные с ними оползни. Причиной наводнений и оползней могут быть неожиданные проливные дожди или необычно быстрое таяние снежного покрова и ледников. Оползни приносят крайне значительный ущерб населённым пунктам, находящимся на высоких берегах рек, а от наводнений больше всего страдают города и деревни, расположенные в долинах рек.

Экстремальная погода, конечно, не всегда враг человека. Не надо забывать, что сельское хозяйство многих тропических стран зависит во многом от наводнений, вызываемых муссонными дождями. Не в этом проблема, а в более опасных быстроразвивающихся, или внезапных наводнениях и паводках на реках, возникающих при прохождении атмосферных фронтов и циклонов, вызывающих сильные дожди на значительной территории. Усугубляющими факторами может быть деятельность человека, хотя даже сегодня не все согласны, что мы играем значительную роль в глобальном изменении климата.

явление	occurrence, phenomenon	оползень	landslip
		таяние	melting
осадки	precipitation	снежный покров	blanket of snow
проливной	torrential	ледник	iceberg
наводнение	flood	паводок	flooding

1 Что нарушается во время мощных ураганов?

_____

2 Какая «природная катастрофа» повторяется чаще всего?

_____

3 Что вызывают проливные дожди и таяние снежного покрова и ледников?

_____

4 Почему можно сказать, что экстремальная погода – друг человека?

_____

5 При каких условиях сильные дожди становятся проблемой?

_____

Vocabulary

K Put these weather expressions in ascending order of severity.

1 тепло, жара, холод, солнечный удар, прохлада _____

2 снежинки, снег, вьюга, мокрый снег, дождь _____

3 ветерок, ураган, шторм, ветер _____

4 тучи, чистое небо, смерч, гроза, облака _____

5 метель, проливные дожди, кратковременные дожди, град _____

6 наводнение, сильные дожди, оползень, засуха, моросить _____

L Using this screen shot of your weather app, describe yesterday's weather in Russian.

_____

_____

_____

M Use each set of words to make a sentence.

Пример: никто, холодно, лежать на пляже → Никто не лежал на пляже, потому что было холодно.

1 никуда, очень жарко, ходить

_____

2 негде, сидеть, ресторан, гроза

_____

3 никто, хотеться, плавать, шторм

_____

4 некуда, ездить, туристы, ураган

_____

5 никогда, скучно, хорошая погода, отпуск

_____

6 некогда, кататься на велосипеде, метель, лютый мороз

_____

Writing

N The holiday brochure claimed you can ski in the morning yet sunbathe in the afternoon. Keep your friends and family up to date with regular Russian tweets™ from your holiday, covering the following points:

▶ какая погода?
▶ чем занимаетесь?
▶ всё как в брошюре?
▶ где будете отдыхать в следующем году и почему?

_____

_____

_____

_____

_____

_____

_____

_____

_____

_____

Self-check

Tick the box which matches your level of confidence.

1 = very confident   2 = need more practice   3 = not too confident

Как вы думаете? Вы хорошо понимаете? Поставьте галочку:

1 = хорошо   2 = нужно больше практики   3 = нехорошо

	1	2	3
Describe weather in the past, present and future			
Use negative adverbs and pronouns with conjugated verbs and infinitives			
Understand a complex text about weather			
Able to use a range of specialized vocabulary to describe the weather			

11 Куда?
Where are you going?

In this unit you will learn how to:

- ✓ Use the many verbs of motion
- ✓ Describe in detail how you move around
- ✓ Give and understand instructions with imperatives
- ✓ Give and understand travel advice

CEFR: Can give detailed instructions (CEFR A2); Can summarize, report and give opinion about accumulated factual information on familiar matters with some confidence (CEFR B1); Can recognize significant points in straightforward newspaper articles on familiar subjects (e.g. article about health) (CEFR B1)

ходить *(to go often, by foot)*	идти *(to go once, by foot)*	пойти *(to go, by foot)*	ездить *(to go often, by transport)*	ехать *(to go once, by transport)*	поехать *(to go, by transport)*
я хожу	я иду	я пойду	я езжу	я еду	я поеду
ты ходишь	ты идёшь	ты пойдёшь	ты ездишь	ты едешь	ты поедешь
он/она ходит	он/она идёт	он/она пойдёт	он/она ездит	он едет	он поедет
мы ходим	мы идём	мы пойдём	мы ездим	мы едем	мы поедем
вы ходите	вы идёте	вы пойдёте	вы ездите	вы едете	вы поедете
они ходят	они идут	они пойдут	они ездят	они едут	они поедут

Meaning and usage

Verbs of motion

1   Russian is very precise when it talks about **going** to places. For this it uses **verbs of motion** and there are several decisions to make in identifying the correct verb to use. The first choice is between using a means of transport (e.g. **е**здить/**е**хать) *or* going 'under your own steam' (e.g. ход**и**ть/идт**и**).

2   The second choice is the usual choice of which **aspect** to use:

  ▶   if it is a **single, completed** action then you use the **perfective**, as usual:
  ▶   Бор**и**с по**е**хал в **о**фис и н**а**чал раб**о**тать в 9 час**о**в.
  ▶   *(Boris <u>travelled</u> to the office and started to work at 9 o'clock.)*
  ▶   if the action is not **single and completed**, then you use one of two possible **imperfectives**:
  ▶   На пр**о**шлой нед**е**ле Бор**и**с **е**здил в **о**фис на трамв**а**е к**а**ждый день.
  ▶   *(Last week Boris <u>travelled</u> to the office on the tram every day.)*
  ▶   Бор**и**с **е**хал в **о**фис, когд**а** он зам**е**тил колл**е**гу в авт**о**бусе.
  ▶   *(Boris <u>was travelling</u> to the office when he noticed a colleague on the bus.)*

3   The third choice is the choice of which one of the two possible **imperfective** verbs of motion to use:

  ▶   If you are describing an action done on many occasions and/or in many directions, you use the **multidirectional** imperfective – ход**и**ть/**е**здить:
  ▶   На пр**о**шлой нед**е**ле Бор**и**с **е**здил в **о**фис на трамв**а**е к**а**ждый день.
  ▶   (Last week Boris <u>travelled to</u> the office on the tram every day.)
  ▶   If you are describing an action done on one occasion and in one direction, you use the **unidirectional** imperfective – идт**и**/**е**хать:
  ▶   Бор**и**с **е**хал в **о**фис, когд**а** он зам**е**тил колл**е**гу в авт**о**бусе.
  ▶   *(Boris <u>was travelling</u> to the office when he noticed a colleague on the bus.)*

4   The past tense of the **unidirectional imperfective** verb идт**и** and the **perfective** verb пойт**и** is irregular:

идт**и**	шёл, шла, шло, шли	пойт**и**	пошёл, пошл**а**, пошл**о**, пошл**и**

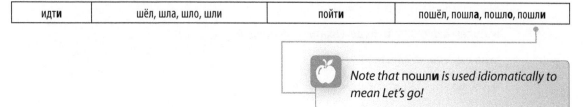

Note that пошл**и** *is used idiomatically to mean Let's go!*

A Match the following clauses to make sentences.

1 Были свободные места, и я мог читать газету,

2 Я слушаю музыку каждый день,

3 Мой рабочий день завтра начнётся рано,

4 Есть остановка троллейбуса около дома,

5 Сегодня мой день рождения,

6 В прошлом году я отдыхал в Сочи

a когда я хожу в магазины.

b итак я езжу регулярно в центр города.

c когда я ехал на поезде.

d и вечером я иду в ресторан.

e и я ездил туда на поезде.

f итак я пойду сразу после быстрого завтрака.

B Choose the correct verb to complete the following sentences.

1 Было бы интересно купить билет на Транссибирскую магистраль, но ...

a ездить   b ехать   c поехать

восемь дней на поезде было бы трудно.

2 В будущем я куплю дом около вокзала и буду ...

a ходить   b идти   c пойти

на вокзал каждый день.

3 В августе Максим ...

a ездил   b ехал   c поехал

в Париж, был три дня дома, а сейчас он в Берлине.

4 Сегодня Марина опоздала на работу, а завтра она ...

a будет ездить   b будет ехать   c поедет

намного раньше.

5 Мы купили дачу за городом и ...

a будем ездить   b будем ехать   c поедем

туда как можно чаще.

6 Я люблю возвращаться домой пешком, так как я ...

a хожу   b иду   c пойду

и смотрю на витрины.

Prefixed verbs of motion

1   In the same way that English uses **phrasal verbs**, Russian can add various prefixes to verbs of motion to give even more information about the type of movement being described. The most common **prefixed verbs of motion** describing motion 'under your own steam':

Маша перешла через улицу.   (Masha crossed the road.)

Мой дедушка заходит к нам каждую   (My grandfather pops in to see us every
неделю.   week.)

C   Using the terms in the box, complete the table for some common <u>prefixed verbs of motion</u> describing motion 'under your own steam'.

к + dat.	из + gen.	вокруг + gen.	через + acc.	мимо + gen.
с + gen.	в + acc.	по + dat.	за + acc.	на + acc.

Prefix	Prefixed verbs	Meaning	Following preposition(s) if required
в (во-)	входить/войти	to enter	в + acc., на + acc.
вы-	выходить/выйти	to exit	
при-	приходить/прийти	to arrive	
у-	уходить/уйти	to leave	
пере-	переходить/перейти	to cross	
про-	проходить/пройти	to go through	
за-	заходить/зайти	to call in/pop in	
об-/обо-	обходить/обойти	to go round	

2   As soon as a verb of motion is prefixed, it reverts to the usual pattern of having one imperfective and one perfective.

Маша переехала через реку на   (Masha crossed the river in her car.)
машине.

Мой дедушка заезжает к нам   (My grandfather pops in to see us every
каждую неделю на автобусе.   week on the bus.)

D Using the terms in the box, complete the table for the most common <u>prefixed verbs of motion</u> describing motion using transport.

к + dat.	из + gen.	вокруг + gen.	через + асс.	мимо + gen.
с + gen.	в + асс.	по + dat.	за + асс.	на + асс.

Prefix	Prefixed verbs	Meaning	Following preposition(s) if required
в (во-)	въезжать/_____	*to enter*	
вы-		*to exit*	
при-		*to arrive*	
у-	уезжать/уехать	*to leave*	
пере-		*to cross*	
про-		*to go through*	
за-		*to call in/pop in*	
об-/обо-	объезжать/	*to go round*	

E Complete the following sentences with an appropriate <u>prefixed verb of motion</u>.

1 Они ехали 40 часов и наконец _____ в Москву.

2 Мы очень рады были _____ через мост, потому что таким образом мы сэкономили много времени.

3 В котором часу ты _____ из дома, потому что я хочу пойти с тобой?

4 После сильных дождей надо было _____ затопленную дорогу.

5 Сейчас Ольга _____ к бабушке в центре города каждую субботу.

6 После длинной поездки он с удовольствием _____ в гараж.

Other verbs of motion

Verb of motion	Meaning
бегать/бежать/побежать	*to run*
плавать/плыть/поплыть	*to swim*
летать/лететь/полететь	*to fly*
носить/нести/понести	*to carry (on foot)*
возить/везти/повезти	*to carry (by transport)*
водить/вести/повести	*to lead*
ползать/ползти/поползти	*to crawl*
лазить/лезть/полезть	*to climb*

All of these other verbs of motion have prefixed forms as well. The past tense of some of these verbs is slightly irregular:

нести	везти	вести	ползти	лезть
нёс, несл**а**, несл**о**, несл**и**	вёз, везл**а**, везл**о**, везл**и**	вёл, вел**а**, вел**о**, вел**и**	полз, ползл**а**, ползл**о**, ползл**и**	лез, л**е**зла, л**е**зло, л**е**зли

F Give the <u>prefixed verbs of motion</u> for the following. State the imperfective followed by the perfective for each one.

1 to run out _____

2 to carry in _____

3 to export (to transport away) _____

4 to fly in _____

5 to swim through _____

6 to introduce (to lead in) _____

Meaning and usage

Imperatives

Look at the following four sentences. What do you notice about the form of the verbs?

Конч**и**та! Покуп**а**й р**у**сскую в**о**дку, потом**у** что **э**то с**а**мая л**у**чшая в**о**дка в м**и**ре!

(Conchita! Buy Russian vodka, because it is the best vodka in the world!)

Уваж**а**емые гр**а**ждане! Покуп**а**йте в**о**дку, потом**у** что **э**то с**а**мый л**у**чший нап**и**ток в м**и**ре!

(Ladies and gentlemen! Buy vodka, because it is the best drink in the world!)

Конч**и**та! Идёшь в магаз**и**н? Куп**и** мне бут**ы**лку р**у**сской в**о**дки на вечер**и**нку сег**о**дня!

(Conchita! Are you going to the shop? Buy me a bottle of Russian vodka for the party tonight!)

Уваж**а**емые покуп**а**тели! Сег**о**дня в распрод**а**же – в**о**дка. Куп**и**те!

(Dear customers, today vodka is on special offer. Buy it!)

1 You can see from the four example sentences that, if you wish to tell someone to do something, you have a choice both of **aspect** and **number**. In other words, you need to decide first whether or not this is a single, completed action, how many people you are addressing and how well you know them.

	Yes	No
Single, completed action?	perfective	imperfective
More than one person?	use a plural imperative	use a singular or plural imperative
Do you know them well?	consider using a singular imperative	use a plural imperative

Forms of the imperative

1   How to form the singular imperative:

Final letter of the stem	Stress in the я form	Imperative
a vowel	(does not apply)	+й
покупа-ют		покупай
a consonant	stress on the last syllable	+и
куп-ят	куплю	купи
a consonant	stress not on the last syllable	+ь
остав-ят	оставлю	оставь
two consonants	(does not apply)	+и
молч-ат		молчи

2   The choice of the **aspect** in a **negative imperative** changes the meaning slightly.

не + imperfective imperative	**не** + perfective imperative
advises against or forbids an action	gives an urgent warning
Не бросай мусор!	Осторожно, не урони молоко!
Don't drop litter!	*Careful, don't drop the milk!*

3   How to form the **plural imperative**:

 G   Look at this table and work out how to form the plural imperative. Explain the rule.

Final letter of the stem	Stress in the я form	Imperative
a vowel	(does not apply)	sing.+й покупай
покупа-ют		pl. покупайте
a consonant	stress on the last syllable	sing. +и купи
куп-ят	куплю	pl. купите
a consonant	stress not on the last syllable	sing. +ь оставь
остав-ят	оставлю	pl. оставьте
two consonants	(does not apply)	sing. +и молчи
молч-ат		pl. молчите

4   It is very easy to form a **reflexive imperative**:

add -ся after a consonant	возвращайся! *(come back!)*
add -сь after a vowel	вернитесь! *(go back!)*

H **Give the appropriate imperative for the following situations.**

Пример: Я купил газету. <u>Купи</u> <u>газету</u>!

1 Я прочитал эту статью. _____

2 Мы посмотрим выставку. _____

3 Маша не забыла заседание. _____

4 Иван не уходит рано. _____

5 Мария Фёдоровна приходит в семь часов. _____

6 Привет! Я зашёл к вам, как вы мне сказали. _____

📖 Reading

I **Read the beginning of this memo and answer the question that follows in Russian.**

От: Акулова, С.Н.

Кому: Топоровой, В.И.

Привет Вика.

Я пишу, потому что я услышал, что ты едешь в Лондон на следующей неделе. Я езжу туда довольно часто и думаю, что тебе будет интересно услышать мои советы о поездке туда.

Почему Вика получила этот меморандум?

_____

_____

J **Now read the rest of the memo and answer the questions that follow in Russian.**

Я обычно летаю в Лондон авиакомпанией «Бритиш». Я вылетаю рано утром и прилетаю в Лондон около полудня по местному времени. В аэропорту я сажусь в метро и еду в центр. Когда я приезжаю в центр, я иду пешком в гостиницу. Когда я уезжаю, я заказываю такси в аэропорт – по-моему, это удобнее.

Ездить по Лондону на метро – очень легко, хотя не очень дёшево по сравнению с Москвой. Если по ошибке проезжаешь нужную станцию, это редко проблема, так как станции находятся недалеко друг от друга. Если вы заблудились, то легко подойти к любому местному жителю и спрос**и**ть, как найт**и** дор**о**гу. Когд**а** переезж**а**ешь из одног**о** м**е**ста в друг**о**е, м**о**жно сл**у**шать пле**е**р, **и**ли чит**а**ть газ**е**ты – их разда**ю**т беспл**а**тно.

Когд**а** прилет**и**шь в Л**о**ндон в п**е**рвый раз, сад**и**сь в такс**и** и поезж**а**й пр**я**мо в гост**и**ницу. Из гост**и**ницы выход**и** как м**о**жно ч**а**ще, чт**о**бы смотр**е**ть достопримеч**а**тельности. Сход**и** в Брит**а**нский муз**е**й, наприм**е**р. Нельз**я** обойт**и** всё ср**а**зу, кон**е**чно, но попр**о**буй зайт**и** в гл**а**вные з**а**лы. Когд**а** вх**о**дишь в муз**е**й, ост**а**вь пальт**о** в гардер**о**бе, как в Росс**и**и. Постар**а**йся про**е**хать ч**е**рез все больш**и**е мост**ы** на авт**о**бусе, чт**о**бы посмотр**е**ть на г**о**род. Ешь р**ы**бу с карт**о**шкой и пей п**и**во! Не уезж**а**й из Л**о**ндона без хор**о**ших сувен**и**ров, но не забыв**а**й, что тр**у**дно нест**и** тяжёлый чемод**а**н.

Жел**а**ю теб**е** сч**а**стл**и**вого пут**и**! Когд**а** прилет**и**шь обр**а**тно, приход**и** в г**о**сти и расскаж**и**, как съ**е**здила. М**о**жно до**е**хать до нас на трамв**а**е **и**ли на тролл**е**йбусе – не б**о**йся, что **э**то сл**и**шком далек**о**! Сообщ**и** из Л**о**ндона, чем занима**е**шься – будь хор**о**шей тур**и**сткой!

сад**и**ться/сесть	*to take a seat; to get on (transport)*
заблуд**и**ться (*perf.*)	*to lose one's way*
как м**о**жно ч**а**ще	*as often as possible*
сход**и**ть (*perf.*)	*to make a trip to (on foot)*
сч**а**стл**и**вого пут**и**!	*bon voyage!*
съ**е**здить (*perf.*)	*to make a trip to (by transport)*

Ешь р**ы**бу с карт**о**шкой и пей п**и**во!

*Note two slightly irregular, but important, imperatives in the memo: ешь/**е**шьте (eat!), пей/н**е**йте (drink!).*

1   На как**о**м в**и**де тр**а**нспорта **е**дет Ак**у**лов из аэроп**о**рта и в аэроп**о**рт?

_____

_____

2   Что Ак**у**лов сов**е**тует д**е**лать, **е**сли вы заблуд**и**лись в Л**о**ндоне?

_____

_____

3 Советует ли Акулов всё время оставаться в гостинице в Лондоне?

_____

_____

4 Что говорит Акулов о мостах в Лондоне?

_____

_____

5 Что предлагает Акулов сделать после поездки?

_____

_____

Vocabulary

K Using your knowledge of prefixes, match the following nouns with their meanings.

1	в**ы**ход	**a**	approach
2	подх**о**д	**b**	entrance
3	обх**о**д	**c**	departure; retirement; resignation
4	вход	**d**	round (of doctor or postman); bypass
5	ух**о**д	**e**	crossing; transition
6	перех**о**д	**f**	exit

L Complete the following sentences with the most appropriate verb of motion from the box.

въ**е**хал	в**ы**шла	заход**и**ла	обош**ё**л	при**е**хал	у**е**хала

1 Чтобы пойти на п**о**чту, я _____ из магаз**и**на и пошл**а** нал**е**во.

2 Крист**о**фф _____ весь г**о**род, но не нашёл ресторан « Бр**и**столь».

3 Нат**а**ша _____ ко мне **у**тром, когд**а** мен**я** н**е** было.

4 Артём _____ в г**о**род в 18:00.

5 Мо**я** б**а**бушка _____ из Москв**ы** в 1948 год**у**.

6 Мой от**е**ц _____ на зав**о**д, чт**о**бы отд**а**ть мне мо**и** ключ**и**.

M Write a command for the following situations.

Приме́р: **А**не на́до купи́ть откры́тку.   **А**ня! Купи́ откры́тку! _____

1   Ча́ду на́до учи́ть но́вые ру́сские слова́ ка́ждый день. _____

2   Са́ша бу́дет просма́тривать брошю́ры. _____

3   Сла́ва хо́чет верну́ться домо́й на такси́. _____

4   На́дя не должна́ забы́ть день рожде́ния де́душки. _____

5   Всем на́до есть пять по́рций фру́ктов и́ли овоще́й в день. _____

6   Ива́н Ива́нович до́лжен написа́ть мемора́ндум дире́ктору. _____

Writing

N Write a memo to a business associate about taking a trip to Moscow. Cover the following points in your advice, in about 100 words of Russian.

▶   Как и отку́да лу́чше всего́ пое́хать?
▶   Где жить?
▶   Как проводи́ть свобо́дное вре́мя?
▶   Каки́е сувени́ры купи́ть?

_____

_____

_____

_____

_____

_____

_____

_____

_____

_____

_____

Self-check

Tick the box which matches your level of confidence.

    1 = very confident   2 = need more practice   3 = not too confident

Как вы ду́маете? Вы хорош**о** понима́ете? Пост**а**вьте г**а**лочку:

    1 = хорош**о**   2 = н**у**жно б**о**льше пр**а**ктики   3 = нехорош**о**

	1	2	3
Form and use 'simple' verbs of motion			
Translate English phrasal verbs using Russian prefixed verbs of motion			
Give commands			
Understand and give detailed advice to travellers			

12 С праздником!

Let's celebrate!

In this unit, you will learn how to:

- ✅ Use a wide variety of verbs
- ✅ Use *which, that, **who*** and *whom*
- ✅ Give information about festivals and celebrations
- ✅ Form more complex sentences by using a relative pronoun

CEFR: Can recognize significant points in straightforward newspaper articles on familiar subjects (CEFR B1); Can write a description of an event (CEFR B1)

Город называется Смоленск. Я жив**у** в Смол**е**нске.

(The city is called Smolensk. I live in Smolensk.)

г**о**род ← gender/number = masculine singular

→ case = в + prepositional

Г**о**род, в кот**о**ром я жив**у**, называ**е**тся Смол**е**нск.

(The city in which I live is called Smolensk.)

Meaning and usage

The relative pronoun кот**о**рый *(who, which, what, that)*

Г**о**род, в кот**о**ром я жив**у**, называ**е**тся Смол**е**нск.   *(The city in which I live is called Smolensk.)*

1 The way that Russian links together shorter sentences to make longer sentences is to use the relative pronoun кот**о**рый. Although called a pronoun, this word actually has the same endings as an adjective. There are two stages to choosing the correct ending for кот**о**рый in a longer sentence:

   a Look backwards to the gender of the noun to which кот**о**рый refers. In the sentence about Smolensk, this would be masculine, as the noun г**о**род is masculine.

   b Look forwards to decide the case ending for кот**о**рый. In the sentence about Smolensk this would be the prepositional singular, as you are saying *in which* I live.

2 There are many ways to translate кот**о**рый into English, depending on how the longer sentence is constructed and also on how formal a translation you make. A good starting point to translate кот**о**рый is usually *which* or *that*; however it can also be translated by *who, whom* or simply left out in English. Look at the following examples:

Книга, которую я читаю, очень интересная.

*(The book **that** I am reading is very interesting. / The book **which** I am reading is very interesting. / The book I am reading is very interesting.)*

Мой друг, который работает в университете, любит крикет.

*(My friend, **who** works at the university, loves cricket. / My friend **that** works at the university loves cricket.)*

Студент, которого я знаю, живёт в Москве.

*(The student **whom** I know lives in Moscow. / The student **that** I know lives in Moscow. / The student I know lives in Moscow.)*

*If you ever want to say who in Russian as a question word, you do not use **который** but кто.*

Кто живёт в Томске?   *(Who lives in Tomsk?)*

How to form the relative pronoun

A **Bearing in mind, as mentioned above, that the relative pronoun has the same endings as an adjective, complete the table:**

	Masculine	**Feminine**	**Neuter**	**Plural**
Nominative	который	которая	которое	которые
Accusative (inanimate/animate)	котор__/__	котор__	котор__	котор__/__
Genitive	котор__	котор__	котор__	котор__
Dative	котор__	котор__	котор__	котор__
Instrumental	котор__	котор__	котор__	котор__
Prepositional	о котор__	о котор__	о котор__	о котор__

B **Complete the sentences with the correct form of который.**

1 Мы жили в городе, _____ находится на юго-западе России.

    a которые   **b** который   **c** котором

2 Мы хотим гостиницу, _____ стоит недорого.

    a которая   **b** которую   **c** которые

3 Мои друзья знают озеро, в _____ можно плавать летом.

    a котором   **b** которое   **c** которая

4 Подруга, _____ нравится мода, покупает одежду в Париже.

    a которая   **b** которую   **c** которой

5 Машина, на _____ они приехали, стоит около дома.

    a котором   **b** которая   **c** которой

6 Картины, _____ они смотрели в музее, очень известные.

    a которые   **b** котором   **c** которых

C Complete the sentences with the correct form of который.

1 Гид, с _____ мы говорили, очень умный человек.

2 Мы посетили музей, _____ находится недалеко от парка.

3 Мы подарим друзьям подарки, _____ мы купили в универмаге.

4 Памятник, у _____ мы встретимся в 7 часов, очень знаменитый.

5 Мост, _____ нам очень нравится, построили 200 лет назад.

6 Школьникам, _____ посещают музей, надо оставить рюкзак в гардеробе.

D Make each of the following pairs of short sentences into one longer sentence with the correct form of который.

1 Я часто хожу в парк. Парк находится на севере города. _____

2 Мы говорили о фильме. Мы смотрели фильм вчера в кинотеатре недалеко от центра города. _____

3 Озеро очень чистое. Максим плавал в озере. _____

4 Библиотека огромная. Мы живём за библиотекой. _____

5 Гид много знает о картинах. Гид работает в галерее. _____

6 Мы увлекались катанием на коньках с нашими новыми друзьями. Наши новые друзья живут в пригороде Томска. _____

Meaning and usage

Verbs and the cases that follow them

встречаться/встретиться	to meet	+ с (prep.) and instrumental
договариваться/договориться	to agree with	+ с (prep.) and instrumental
заказывать/заказать	to order	+ accusative
звонить/позвонить	to phone	+ dative
знакомиться/познакомиться	to get to know	+ с (prep.) and instrumental
отдавать/отдать	to give sth. to sb.	+ accusative + dative
отмечать/отметить	to mark, celebrate	+ accusative
показывать/показать	to show sth. to sb.	+ accusative + dative
прикладывать/приложить	to attach sth. to sth.	+ accusative + к (prep.) and dative
радовать/обрадовать	to please	+ accusative
рекомендовать	to recommend sth. to sb.	+ accusative + dative
участвовать	to take part in sth.	+ в (prep.) and prepositional

E   **Using the verbs from the table and the words in brackets, complete the sentences below.**

Пример: До праздника, мы <u>показали подарки друзьям</u>. (показать/подарки/друзья)

1   На празднике я _____. (познакомиться/русский студент)

2   На празднике мы _____. (встретиться/родители)

3   На празднике мы _____. (отдать/подарки/дети)

4   На празднике все_____. (участвовать/парад)

5   На праздник они _____. (рекомендовать/мы/еда)

6   После праздника _____. (она/радовать/фотографии)

📖 Reading

F   **Read the beginning of this blog describing recent celebrations in Russia, then answer the question that follows in Russian.**

> Это мой блог на этой неделе, который я пишу как всегда в воскресенье. Посмотрите на фотографию, которая показывает, как нам с друзьями было весело! Было много интересных событий, о которых я хочу написать на этой неделе, потому что мы отмечали праздник Первое мая, который отмечают как праздник весны.

Что показывала фотография? _____

До праздника надо было поговорить с друзьями, с которыми мы хотели отметить Первое мая. Многие работают со мной и не было трудно договориться с ними. Мы обсудили ресторан, в котором мы хотели встретиться, и еду, которую мы предпочитали. Шампанское, которое рекомендовали в ресторане, мы заказали без комментариев. Друзья, которые не работают с нами и которым надо было позвонить до праздника, все были довольны нашими решениями.

Первого мая погода, которая всегда играет важную роль в успехе любого праздника, обрадовала нас, потому что было солнечно и тепло. Друзья с работы познакомились с друзьями, которые не работают с нами, на демонстрации, которая была как всегда в центре города. До обеда был парад, в котором мы не участвовали, но который мы смотрели с интересом. Потом мы пошли в ресторан, который находится недалеко от центра, и заняли места, которые мы заказали.

Еда в ресторане была очень вкусная, хотя мне не очень понравилось шампанское, которое рекомендовал ресторан. Зато моя подруга, которую я не видел почти месяц, отдала мне подарок, который она купила мне на день рождения, который был в середине апреля. Как можно видеть на фотографии, которую я прикладываю, в конце концов был очень весёлый день, который мы все будем долго помнить!

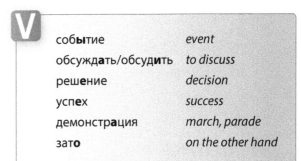

событие	*event*
обсуждать/обсудить	*to discuss*
решение	*decision*
успех	*success*
демонстрация	*march, parade*
зато	*on the other hand*

1 Почему надо было поговорить с друзьями до праздника?

_____

2 Понравились ли рекомендации ресторана?

_____

3 Опишите погоду, которая была на праздник.

_____

4 Куда они ходили до обеда?

_____

5 Понравились ли еда и шампанское?

_____

6 Что можно видеть на фотографии?

_____

Vocabulary

H **Complete the sentences with an appropriate verb taken from the text.**

Пример: На день рождения мы <u>подарили</u> ему хороший подарок.

1 Мы все _____ о фильме, который мы хотели смотреть.

2 Мы с друзьями _____ вкусный обед в ресторане.

3 Посмотри на фотографию, которую я _____ к этому письму.

4 Мои друзья _____ по телефону вчера.

5 Я решила _____ Новый год в Австралии.

6 Мы были очень довольны после хорошей новости, которая _____ нас.

I **Match the phrase in the question with the sentence with the same meaning.**

1 мы обсудили ресторан

   a мы говорили о том, где делать покупки   **b** мы говорили о том, где смотреть спектакль   **c** мы говорили о том, где есть

2 рекомендовали в ресторане

   a говорили, что плохо   **b** говорили, что хорошо   **c** говорили, что дорого

3 было солнечно

   a светило солнце   **b** светит солнце   **c** будет солнце

4 мы смотрели с интересом

   a не было скучно   **b** не было полезно   **c** не было вкусно

5 мне не очень понравилось

   a я ненавидел   **b** я не любил   **c** я обожал

6 в середине апреля

   a первое апреля   **b** пятнадцатое апреля   **c** тридцатое апреля

J   Match the definitions with a word in the text.

1   день п**о**сле субб**о**ты и до понед**е**льника _____

2   с людьм**и**, кот**о**рые мне нр**а**вятся _____

3   вин**о**, кот**о**рое всегд**а** пьют на пр**а**здниках _____

4   не ж**а**рко, но не х**о**лодно _____

5   м**е**сто, в кот**о**ром об**ы**чно раб**о**тают официа**а**нты _____

6   что д**а**рят, наприм**е**р, на день рожд**е**ния _____

Writing

K   You have been to a party. Write a blog entry for this, describing an imaginary photograph from the event. Write around 100 words in Russian, covering the following points.

▶   Где вы отмеч**а**ли пр**а**здник?

▶   С кем вы б**ы**ли?

▶   Что вы д**е**лали?

▶   Что вам понр**а**вилось б**о**льше всег**о**?

_____

_____

_____

_____

_____

_____

_____

_____

_____

_____

_____

_____

When you are writing or speaking in English using longer sentences, consider which word you are using that would be the equivalent of кот**о**рый _in Russian. Which do you tend to use most in English:_ which, that, who, whom _or, in fact, do you not use any separate word at all?_

Self-check

Tick the box which matches your level of confidence.

1 = very confident   2 = need more practice   3 = not too confident

Как вы думаете? Вы хорошо понимаете? Поставьте галочку:

1 = хорошо   2 = нужно больше практики   3 = нехорошо

	1	2	3
Recognize when to use который in longer sentences			
Form longer sentences using который			
Use verbs in Russian that are followed by a variety of different cases			
Describe a festival or similar event			

13 Если бы!

If only!

In this unit you will learn how to:

✓ Discuss illnesses

✓ Recognize and use the conditional and subjunctive moods

CEFR: Can understand a detailed health report (CEFR B2); Can write accounts of experiences, describing feelings and reactions in simple connected text (CEFR B1)

Если я **е**ла мн**о**го, у мен**я** бол**е**л жив**о**т.
(If I ate a lot, my stomach hurt.)
Если я ем мн**о**го, у мен**я** бол**и**т жив**о**т.
(If I eat a lot, my stomach hurts.)
Если я б**у**ду есть мн**о**го, у мен**я** б**у**дет бол**е**ть жив**о**т.
(If I am going to eat a lot, my stomach is going to hurt.)
Если я съем мн**о**го, у мен**я** забол**и**т жив**о**т.
(If I eat a lot, my stomach will start to hurt.)
}
real conditions

Если бы я **е**ла мн**о**го, у мен**я** бол**е**л бы жив**о**т.
(If I had eaten a lot, my stomach would have hurt.)
(If I were to have eaten a lot, my stomach would have hurt.)
(If I were to eat a lot, my stomach would hurt.)
(If I were going to eat a lot, my stomach would be going to hurt.)
Если бы я съ**е**ла мн**о**го, у мен**я** забол**е**л бы жив**о**т.
(If I had eaten a lot, my stomach would have started hurting.)
}
hypothetical conditions

The Russian for I have a stomach ache *is* У мен**я** бол**и**т жив**о**т, *which literally means 'I have hurting the stomach'. You use this construction for all parts of the body.*

Meaning and usage

Possible and impossible conditions

1   The Russian word **е**сли *(if)* can be used in two different ways to introduce **conditions**. Russian makes a difference between **real** (possible) conditions and **hypothetical** (unlikely) conditions.

2   In the first set of sentences, the condition is **real** because it can occur. To convey this, the tenses used are what you would expect.

3 In the second set of sentences, the condition is **hypothetical** because the implication is that it won't happen. To convey this, Russian uses **е**сли at the start of the condition clause with a past tense verb and бы, and a past tense verb and бы in the main clause. Note that in Russian no other tense can be used in **hypothetical** conditions.

4 As the examples show, **е**сли sentences can be translated into English in a variety of ways depending on the context.

5 If **е**сли comes at the start of the first part of a condition sentence, then то may be used at the start of the second part of the sentence as a stylistic variation, especially in longer sentences.

Если я б**у**ду приним**а**ть витам**и**ны регул**я**рно и заним**а**ться сп**о**ртом к**а**ждый день, то я б**у**ду ч**у**вствовать себ**я** намн**о**го л**у**чше.

(If I take vitamins regularly and do sport every day, then I will feel a lot better.)

Если бы я приним**а**ла витам**и**ны регул**я**рно и заним**а**лась сп**о**ртом к**а**ждый день, то я ч**у**вствовала бы себ**я** намн**о**го л**у**чше.

(If I were to take vitamins regularly and do sport every day, then I would feel a lot better.)

(If I were to have taken vitamins regularly and done sport every day, then I would have felt a lot better.)

(If I had taken vitamins regularly and done sport every day, then I would have felt a lot better.)

> Note that the English verb would *is not always translated into Russian by the conditional. It is sometimes simply* **reported speech**, *such as*
> Он сказ**а**л, что он к**у**пит аспир**и**н. *(He said he* **would** buy some aspirin.)

A **Use е**сли to form <u>real conditions</u> with the prompts below.

Прим**е**р: пить в**о**дку; бол**е**ть голов**а**; я → **Е**сли я пью в**о**дку, у мен**я** бол**и**т голов**а**.

1 чит**а**ть мн**о**го; бол**е**ть глаз**а**; я _____

2 ход**и**ть без ш**а**пки; бол**е**ть г**о**рло; р**у**сские _____

3 раб**о**тать в сад**у**; бол**е**ть спин**а**; б**а**бушка _____

4 ход**и**ть к врач**у**; иногд**а** получ**а**ть рец**е**пт; паци**е**нты _____

5 запис**а**ться на прив**и**вку; не забол**е**ть гр**и**ппом; раб**о**тники здравоохран**е**ния

_____

6 не заним**а**ться сп**о**ртом (в б**у**дущем); не быть в ф**о**рме (в б**у**дущем); студ**е**нты

_____

B Use **если** to form <u>hypothetical conditions</u> with the prompts below.

1 не есть сладкое; не болит зуб; Зигмунд _____

2 не забыть деньги; купить аспирин; Зинаида _____

3 жить на юге; нет простуды; я _____

4 нет аллергии; принимать антибиотики; ребёнок _____

5 не кататься на коньках; не сломать ногу; ты _____

6 перестать курить; чувствовать себя лучше; любой человек _____

C Translate the following sentences. Where more than one translation is possible, give every valid variant.

1 Если туристы ходят в России без шарфа зимой, то они будут кашлять.

_____

_____

2 Если бы ты встала очень быстро, ты упала бы в обморок.

_____

_____

3 Если бы мальчик ел очень холодное мороженое, наверно, у него была бы ангина.

_____

_____

4 Если пробовать слишком экзотические блюда, вполне возможно, что будет понос.

_____

_____

5 Если тебя очень сильно тошнит и у тебя температура, то тебя может вырвать.

_____

_____

6 Если мужчины пьют много пива и не упражняются физически, то у них повышенный риск инсульта.

_____

_____

The conditional mood

1 The past tense of a verb + бы can be used without a **е**сли clause and is the **conditional** mood in Russian. It sometimes can also be used to make requests more politely, although this is used far less frequently than in English:

Я хоч**у** отдохн**у**ть.   (*I want to relax.*)

Я хот**е**л бы отдохн**у**ть.   (*I would like to relax.*)

Look at these sentences:

Я зн**а**ю, что у вас бол**и**т гол**о**ва от р**у**сской грамм**а**тики.

(*I know that your head hurts because of Russian grammar.*)

Я хоч**у**, чт**о**бы у вас не бол**е**ла голов**а** от р**у**сской грамм**а**тики.

(*I want your head not to hurt because of Russian grammar.*)

2 Russian uses что (+ usual tense) to introduce an actual fact, but чт**о**бы (+ past tense ONLY) to express that you want something to happen. Чт**о**бы followed by the past tense is the **subjunctive** mood in Russian.

D **These common verbs are followed either by что or чтобы. Put them in the correct column. Make your decision based on whether the verb relates to a fact or a desired event.**

д**у**мать	жел**а**ть	знать	каз**а**ться	предлаг**а**ть	прос**и**ть
сл**ы**шать	сов**е**товать	сообщ**а**ть	счит**а**ть	тр**е**бовать	хот**е**ть

что	чтобы

There are some verbs that can be followed by either что or чт**о**бы, depending on the meaning. The most common ones are: говор**и**ть/сказ**а**ть (*to speak/say*) and пис**а**ть/написать (*to write*), for example:

Ир**и**на сказ**а**ла, что Бор**и**с приним**а**ет табл**е**тки.

(*Irina said that Boris takes tablets.*)

Ир**и**на сказ**а**ла, чт**о**бы Бор**и**с приним**а**л табл**е**тки.

(*Irina said that Boris should take tablets. / Irina told Boris to take tablets.*)

E **Choose the correct sentence in English to match the Russian.**

1 Врачи говорят, чтобы все ели пять порций свежих продуктов в день.

   a Doctors say that everyone eats five portions of fresh produce per day.

   b Doctors say that everyone should eat five portions of fresh produce per day.

2 Студенты говорят, что это недорого выпивать часто.

   a Students say that it is not expensive to drink alcohol often.

   b Students say that it should not be expensive to drink alcohol often.

3 Мой тренер никогда не скажет, что я редко плаваю.

   a My trainer will never say that I swim rarely.

   b My trainer will never say that I should swim rarely.

4 Эксперты пишут в статьях, чтобы никто не курил в машине.

   a Experts write in articles that no one smokes in a car.

   b Experts write in articles that no one should smoke in a car.

5 Медсестра сказала, чтобы я лежал в постели два дня.

   a The nurse said that I was lying in bed for two days.

   b The nurse said that I should lie in bed for two days.

6 Почему Марина написала, что её семья здоровая?

   a Why has Marina written that her family is healthy?

   b Why has Marina written that her family should be healthy?

F **Complete these sentences with the most appropriate word from the box.**

ангина	*(tonsillitis)*	понос	*(diarrhoea)*
диабет	*(diabetes)*	прививка	*(inoculation)*
инфаркт	*(heart attack)*	рецепт	*(prescription)*
лекарство	*(medicine)*		

1 У него довольно часто болит сердце, и он боится, что у него будет _____.

2 После того, как у дедушки установили, что у него _____, он должен избегать сахара.

3 Некоторые считают, что если у тебя _____, то полезно кушать мороженое.

4 Слава не любит, чтобы ему делали _____, потому что он ненавидит иглы.

5 Они считают, что у них хороший врач, так как он всегда даёт _____ на _____.

6 Он уверен, что у него _____ после того, как он съел креветки.

 # Reading

G Read the beginning of this online news article and answer the question that follows in Russian.

◀ | ▶   www.interesnayainformacya.ru

Чем мы болеем?

В двадцать первом веке, чем мы болеем чаще всего? Какие самые распространённые заболевания, с которыми встречается современный человек? Прежде всего, нам надо прислушиваться к своему телу. Если бы мы только нашли время для себя, мы могли бы избегать многих проблем.

О чём говорит автор этой статьи?

_____

_____

H Now read the rest of the article and answer the questions that follow in Russian.

Эксперты считают, что для возникновения болезни есть как минимум четыре основные причины. Первая причина заболеваний – это наше неправильное питание. Кроме того, что мы неправильно питаемся, мы ещё и неправильно пьём. Третья причина заболеваний—экологическая нагрузка на организм человека. Врачи мира пришли к единому выводу: больше половины заболеваний можно считать экологически обусловленными. Четвёртая причина наших заболеваний – это агрессия бактерий, вирусов, грибков, и других паразитов.

Существуют так называемые «детские» болезни, например, коклюш, ветрянка, корь и свинка. Сегодня такие болезни всё реже встречаются из-за почти универсальных прививок. Если ребёнку ввели вакцину, вряд ли будет он болеть этими заболеваниями, которые в прошлом были очень опасные. Первое место в списке самых распространённых заболеваний у взрослых занимают головные боли и мигрени, и на втором месте – простуды и грипп. Учёные считают, что именно ухудшение экологической ситуации в мире, стресс на работе и дома значительно влияют негативно на иммунитет и на развитие этих заболеваний. Также организму человека не хватает витаминов и жизненно важных элементов. Всё это приводит к ослаблению организма, который не способен противостоять вирусным инфекциям.

Для того, чтобы повысить наш иммунитет и сопротивляемость к болезням, необходимо заниматься спортом, принимать витамины и правильно питаться. Если у нас будет более сознательный подход у нас будет намного больше шансов наслаждаться длинной и здоровой жизнью!

вводить/ввести вакцину	*to administer a vaccine*
грибок	*fungus*
обусловленный	*conditional upon, dependent on*
распространённый	*widespread*
сопротивляемость	*resistance*

1 Какая первая причина заболеваний?

_____

2 Какая четвёртая причина заболеваний?

_____

3 Почему «детские» болезни не так часто встречаются сегодня?

_____

4 Чем болеют взрослые чаще всего?

_____

5 Что нужно, чтобы повысить иммунитет и сопротивляемость к болезням?

_____

I **Considering their meaning, decide whether these words are likely to be followed by что or чтобы.**

1 нужно   _____

2 рад   _____

3 понятно   _____

4 необходимо   _____

5 можно   _____

6 уверен   _____

Vocabulary

J **Identify which word is the odd one out. Give a reason for your choice.**

1 тошнить, понос, вырвать, кашель

2 корь, свинка, ветрянка, инфаркт

3 ухо, кишки, живот, печень

4 микроб, лекарство, вирус, грибок

5 витамины, аспирин, никотин, парацетамол

6 засыпать, упражняться, бегать, плавать

K **Find a word in this unit with the same stem as the following.**

1 рвота   _____

2 лечить   _____

3 распространяться   _____

4 иммунизировать   _____

5 простудиться   _____

6 слабый   _____

Writing

L **You are due to fly to Russia but you miss the plane due to illness. Write a diary entry about the experience, covering the following points in about 100 words of Russian.**

▶ Какая болезнь?

▶ Чем бы вы занимались, если бы вы не опоздали на самолёт?

▶ С кем бы вы встречались?

▶ Если вы хотите избежать таких проблем в будущем, что надо делать?

_____

_____

_____

_____

_____

_____

_____

_____

_____

Self-check

Tick the box which matches your level of confidence.

1 = very confident   2 = need more practice   3 = not too confident

Как вы думаете? Вы хорошо понимаете? Поставьте галочку:

1 = хорошо   2 = нужно больше практики   3 = нехорошо

	1	2	3
Able to recognize whether a condition is real or hypothetical			
Use the conditional mood			
Use the subjunctive mood			
Able to use a range of specialized vocabulary to discuss health and illness			

14 Что случилось?

What happened?

In this unit you will learn how to:

- Form indirect statements and indirect questions
- Talk about problems
- Describe an accident
- Report what someone has said or asked

CEFR: Can understand and give reactions to problems and accidents (CEFR B1); Can write accounts of experiences, describing feelings and reactions in simple connected text (CEFR B1)

> Я знал, что дешёвый смартфон иногда ломается.

> Я знаю, что дешёвый смартфон иногда ломается.

> Продавец скажет, что дешёвый смартфон иногда ломается.

> *I knew that a cheap smartphone sometimes broke.*

> *I know that a cheap smartphone sometimes breaks.*

> *A shop assistant will say that a cheap smartphone sometimes breaks.*

> Я знал, что смартфон сломается.

> Я знаю, что смартфон сломается.

> Продавец скажет, что смартфон сломается.

> *I knew that a smartphone would break.*

> *I know that a smartphone will break.*

> *A shop assistant will say that a smartphone will break.*

> Я знал, что смартфон сломался.

> Я знаю, что смартфон сломался.

> Продавец скажет, что смартфон сломался.

> *I knew that the smartphone had broken.*

> *I know that the smartphone broke.*

> *A shop assistant will say that the smartphone broke.*

Meaning and usage

Indirect speech

1 All of the sentences in the infographic contain **indirect statements** – where you are reporting what someone has said or an event. You will have noticed from the infographic that Russian is much more consistent and logical in its choice of tenses than English.

2 The tense rule for indirect statements is very straightforward: the tense in an indirect statement in Russian is the tense in which the original statement is made.

3 Be careful! There is a far greater range and choice of possible tenses in indirect statements in English than in Russian. In particular, English can use *would* (implying a conditional) in an indirect statement, whereas Russian uses the conditional only for **hypothetical conditions**.

A **Give the original statement for the reported speech.**

Пример: **А**ня усл**ы**шала, что Макс**и**м потер**я**л баг**а**ж. → «Макс**и**м потер**я**л баг**а**ж.»

1 Тур**и**ст п**о**нял, что он потер**я**л бум**а**жник. _____

2 Б**а**бушка бо**и**тся, что упадёт на льду. _____

3 Продавц**ы** с**е**рдятся, когд**а** покуп**а**тели рвут од**е**жду в магаз**и**не.

_____

4 Г**о**сти зам**е**тят, когд**а** официа**н**т разольёт кр**а**сное вин**о**. _____

5 Уч**и**тель ув**и**дел, что студ**е**нт урон**и**л п**а**пку. _____

6 Никт**о** не рад, когд**а** разбив**а**ют з**е**ркало. _____

4 One of the main uses of indirect statements is to report speech:

«Ты опозд**а**ешь, Мар**и**я!» сказ**а**л д**е**душка. (*'You will be late, Maria!' said her grandfather.*) → Д**е**душка сказ**а**л, что Мар**и**я опозд**а**ет. (*Her grandfather said that Maria would be late.*)

B **Turn these statements into reported speech.**

1 Полиц**е**йский сказ**а**л: «Маш**и**на столкн**у**лась со столб**о**м.» _____

2 М**а**ма всегд**а** предупрежд**а**ет: «Ив**а**н! Ты упадёшь!» _____

3 Ст**у**дентка был**а** ув**е**рена: «Я урон**ю** уч**е**бники.» _____

4 Врач сообщ**и**ла: «Ты слом**а**л себ**е** р**у**ку, м**а**льчик!» _____

5 Уб**о**рщица спрос**и**ла: «Кто разл**и**л к**о**фе?» _____

6 Экскурсов**о**ды ч**а**сто говор**я**т: «Тур**и**сты забыв**а**ют п**а**спорт.» _____

Meaning and usage

Indirect questions

1 The rule that applies to tenses in **indirect statements** also applies to **indirect questions**. Again, a little care is needed because in English **indirect questions** often use *if* when we really mean *whether*, whereas Russian is much more precise:

whether = ли

«Вы потеряли паспорт, Николай?», спросил экскурсовод → Экскурсовод спросил, потерял <u>ли</u> Николай паспорт.

2 You will have noticed that the word order in an **indirect question** is different to a **direct question**. The rule is: identify the most important word in the direct question (which is very often the verb) and then start the indirect question clause with this word, followed by ли followed by the rest of the question.

 C **Considering all the possibilities, translate the following three versions of the example in paragraph 1. Underline the most important word in your translation.**

1 Экскурсовод спросил, потерял <u>ли</u> Николай паспорт. _____

2 Экскурсовод спросил, Николай <u>ли</u> потерял паспорт. _____

3 Экскурсовод спросил, паспорт <u>ли</u> потерял Николай. _____

D **Identify the correct translation of the following sentences. Pay close attention to the tense used.**

1 Он не знал, упадёт ли она.

   a He did not know if she had fallen.

   b He did not know if she would fall.

   c He did not know if she fell.

2 Администратор спросил, мобильник ли потерял турист.

   a The receptionist asked if the tourist had lost a mobile phone.

   b The receptionist asked if the tourist would lose a mobile phone.

   c The receptionist asked if the tourist will lose a mobile phone.

3 Полицейский хотел узнать, быстро ли ехала машина.

   a The police officer wanted to know if the car will be travelling fast.

   b The police officer wanted to know if the car would be travelling fast.

   c The police officer wanted to know if the car was travelling fast.

4 Горничная узнала, разбито ли зеркало.

    a The maid found out if the mirror was broken.

    b The maid found out if the mirror would be broken.

    c The maid found out if the mirror will be broken.

5 Экскурсовод спросил, боимся ли мы поскользнуться на льду.

    a The guide asked if we will be afraid to slip on the ice.

    b The guide asked if we were afraid to slip on the ice.

    c The guide asked if we would have been afraid to slip on the ice.

6 Медсестра не могла сказать, сломана ли моя рука или нет.

    a The nurse couldn't say whether or not my arm will be broken.

    b The nurse couldn't say whether or not my arm would be broken.

    c The nurse couldn't say whether or not my arm was broken.

E **You have just witnessed an accident. Tell your Russian friend what questions you were asked by the police.**

Пример: «Вы видели, кто вёл машину?» → Полицейский спросил, видел(а) ли я, кто вёл машину.

1 «Вы заметили, как быстро ехала машина?» _____

2 «Вы знаете в котором часу это случилось?» _____

3 «Вы можете сказать, кто ещё видел аварию?» _____

4 «Вы уверены, что не было других свидетелей?» _____

5 «Вы считаете, что виноват водитель автобуса?» _____

F **Complete the following sentences with an appropriate form of a word from the box.**

обнаруживать/обнаружить	(to discover)
свидетель	(witness)
скорая помощь	(ambulance)
поскользнуться (perf.)	(to slip)
тормозить/затормозить	(to brake)
ушиб	(bruise, injury)

1 Она уронила вазу и _____, что ваза разбита.

2 Было очень холодно, и мы _____ на льду.

3 Если вы видели аварию, вы – _____.

4 Машина резко _____, когда выбежала собака.

5 Вызвали _____, потому что ребёнок сломал руку.

6 Я упал, но у меня не было _____.

 Reading

G Read these three reports and answer the following question in Russian.

Почему эти три человека пишут свои отчёты?

_____

_____

Когда я спустилась в фойе с чемоданами, я запнулась о ковёр. Я уронила чемоданы, и сумку. Когда я достала мой телефон из сумки, я обнаружила, что экран телефона треснул. Телефон работал, но неправильно. Я сообщила об этом случае администратору гостиницы, но он сказал, что гостиница не отвечает за ущерб и, что мне надо обращаться в страховую компанию. Он послал мне сообщение по электронной почте, подтверждающее то, что я сообщила об этом случае.

Нина

Около половины третьего, когда мы ехали на автобусе в центр города, мы стали свидетелями аварии. Был солнечный день, солнце светило нам прямо в глаза, но вдруг мы увидели двух молодых людей на квадроциклах, едущих очень быстро по встречной полосе. Две машины резко затормозили, пытаясь их объехать, но вторая машина въехала в зад первой. Девушка на велосипеде въехала во вторую машину и упала на дорогу. Сначала мы не поняли, что случилось, но потом мы узнали, что она сломала ключицу и получила ушибы. Двое на квадроциклах быстро уехали с места аварии.

Сергей

Мы взяли машину на прокат в аэропорту, и сразу же поехали на ней на виллу. На следующий день мы поехали в местный городок, чтобы посетить воскресный рынок. Мы припарковали машину на улице. Мы провели на рынке больше часа, и когда мы вернулись, мы обнаружили, что кожаная куртка мужа исчезла из машины. Его бумажник и паспорт были в кармане куртки. Машина была закрыта, но боковое окно было разбито.

К сожалению сигнализация, очевидно, не сработала. Мы сообщили о краже в полицию, и они завели дело о краже бумажника и паспорта.

Анастасия

H Now read the reports again and answer the following questions in Russian, using your own words as far as possible.

1 Почему Нина уронила свой багаж?

_____

2 Что случилось с её телефоном?

_____

3 Пока Сергей смотрел, почему две машины резко затормозили?

_____

4 Как велосипедистка получила ушибы?

_____

5 Как муж Анастасии потерял паспорт?

_____

Vocabulary

I Find a word in the text that matches each of the following definitions.

1 пошла вниз по лестнице   _____

2 передала информацию   _____

3 не по правильной стороне дороги   _____

4 стараясь, делая усилие   _____

5 поставили рядом с тротуаром   _____

6 система защиты от кражи   _____

J Solve the anagrams to find words that you might use in an insurance claim.

1 биуш   _____

2 аавеинорстх   _____

3 икнся   _____

4 аабвзирть   _____

5 азеимнть   _____

6 акрстуь   _____

Writing

K   **Write a report in Russian to support an insurance claim, covering the following points in about 100 words of Russian.**

► Что случи́лось?

► Где, как и почему́?

► Кого́ вы попроси́ли помо́чь и в чём?

► Что вы тре́буете?

_____

_____

_____

_____

_____

_____

_____

_____

Self-check

Tick the box which matches your level of confidence.

1 = very confident   2 = need more practice   3 = not too confident

Как вы ду́маете? Вы хорошо́ понима́ете? Поста́вьте га́лочку:

1 = хорошо́   2 = ну́жно бо́льше пра́ктики   3 = нехорошо́

	1	2	3
Form indirect statements			
Form indirect questions using ли			
Understand a complex text about accidents			
Able to use a range of specialized vocabulary to describe accidents			

15 Сколько?
How many?

In this unit you will learn how to:

- ✓ Use Russian cardinal (1, 2, 3, etc.) and ordinal (1st, 2nd, 3rd, etc.) numbers
- ✓ Understand details about longer journeys
- ✓ Write a blog about an epic trip
- ✓ Be precise about numerical information

CEFR: Can give and receive information about quantities and numbers (CEFR A2); Can give detailed information about a journey (CEFR B1)

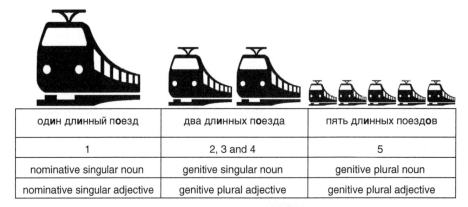

один длинный поезд	два длинных поезда	пять длинных поездов
1	2, 3 and 4	5
nominative singular noun	genitive singular noun	genitive plural noun
nominative singular adjective	genitive plural adjective	genitive plural adjective

Meaning and usage

Cardinal numbers

 As you work through this unit, try reading numbers aloud. This will help you remember them. It is a good idea to memorize your own phone number(s) in Russian.

1 In Russian, as in English, you will very rarely see numbers above nine written out in full. As numbers in Russian require a lot of practice, they will be written out in full in this chapter. If you see numbers elsewhere during your Russian studies, always be brave and take the opportunity to practise by reading them aloud in full!

A To remind yourself about Russian numbers, write the following phone numbers in words.

1 812-63-87-12 _____

2 495-22-48-01 _____

3 427-04-07-10 _____

4 482-19-63-97 _____

5 351-12-44-30 _____

6 869-77-09-00 _____

How to form cardinal numbers

1   Remember that a Russian word denoting a number will never contain more than one soft sign. Up to 40, any soft sign is at the end of the number, but after 40 any soft sign is in the middle of the number.

Cardinal number	Adjective	Noun
один	длинный *long*	отпуск *holiday*
одна	длинная	поездка *trip*
одно	длинное	путешествие *journey*
два	длинных	отпуска
две	длинные	поездки
два	длинных	путешествия
три/четыре	длинных	отпуска
три/четыре	длинные	поездки
три/четыре	длинных	путешествия
пять	длинных	отпусков
пять	длинных	поездок
пять	длинных	путешествий

2   Cardinal numbers in Russian require specific cases to be used after them. Basically, cardinal numbers split into three groups: the number 1, then 2, 3 and 4, and finally 5 and above. For compound numbers (a number which in English would usually be hyphenated, such as twenty-two, three hundred and forty-four) it is the last number in the compound that determines the case needed in Russian. Russian compound numbers do not use hyphens. In summary:

Any compound number ending in 1 e.g. 123,451	Any compound number ending in 2, 3 or 4 e.g. 123,453	All other numbers (including 11, 12, 13 and 14)
1	2, 3 and 4	5
nominative singular noun	genitive singular noun	genitive plural noun
nominative singular adjective	genitive plural adjective	genitive plural adjective

Note that usually a nominative plural adjective is used with a feminine noun after two, three and four but a genitive plural adjective is occasionally seen.

B Match the number with the correct adjective and noun.

1	один	a пассажи́рский	i по́езд
		b пассажи́рского	ii по́езда
		c пассажи́рских	iii поезд́ов
2	пять	a одноро́зовый	i биле́т
		b одноро́зового	ii биле́та
		c одноро́зовых	iii биле́тов
3	три	a интере́сная	i пое́здка
		b интере́сной	ii пое́здки
		c интере́сные	iii пое́здок
4	два́дцать семь	a ко́жаный	i чемода́н
		b ко́жаного	ii чемода́на
		c ко́жаных	iii чемода́нов
5	трина́дцать	a свобо́дное	i ме́сто
		b свобо́дного	ii ме́ста
		c свобо́дных	iii мест
6	шестьсо́т два́дцать одна́	a железнодоро́жная	i остано́вка
		b железнодоро́жного	i остано́вки
		c железнодоро́жных	iii остано́вок

3 Cardinal numbers in cases other than the nominative

Russian numbers have slightly different endings according to the case they are in. However, a number in a case other than the nominative is followed by nouns and adjectives in the same case:

о́коло двух киломе́тров   *(about two kilometres)*

Look for any patterns in the cardinal number tables that remind you of noun and adjective endings.

	Masculine	Feminine	Neuter
Nominative	оди́н	одна́	одно́
Accusative (animate/inanimate)	оди́н/одного́	одну́	одно́
Genitive	одного́	одно́й	одного́
Dative	одному́	одно́й	одному́
Instrumental	одни́м	одно́й	одни́м
Prepositional	одно́м	одно́й	одно́м

	Masculine	Feminine	Neuter
Nominative	два	две	два
Accusative (animate/inanimate)	два/двух	две	два
Genitive	двух	двух	двух
Dative	двум	двум	двум
Instrumental	двумя	двумя	двумя
Prepositional	двух	двух	двух

	(Three)	(Four)	(Five)
Nominative	три	четыре	пять
Accusative (animate/inanimate)	три/трёх	четыре/четырёх	пять
Genitive	трёх	четырёх	пяти
Dative	трём	четырём	пяти
Instrumental	тремя	четырьмя	пятью
Prepositional	трёх	четырёх	пяти

The numbers шесть, семь, восемь, девять *and* десять *follow the same pattern as* пять.

C   Put the correct ending on the words in brackets.

1   Мы подошли к (один пассажирский поезд). _____

2   Она появилась с (пять одноразовых билетов). _____

3   Он вернулся домой после (три интересные поездки). _____

4   Группа стояла перед (двадцать семь кожаных чемоданов). _____

5   Проводник говорил о (три свободных места). _____

6   В течение трёх дней мы проезжали через (шестьсот двадцать одна железнодорожная
    _____ остановка).

4   In order to form cardinal numbers in cases other than the nominative, use these tables to help you:

Nominative	одиннадцать	сорок	пятьдесят
Accusative	одиннадцать	сорок	пятьдесят
Genitive	одиннадцати	сорока	пятидесяти
Dative	одиннадцати	сорока	пятидесяти
Instrumental	одиннадцатью	сорока	пятьюдесятью
Prepositional	одиннадцати	сорока	пятидесяти

девяносто *(90) and* сто *(100) follow the same pattern as* сорок *(40).*

Nominative	дв**е**сти	тр**и**ста	пятьс**от**
Accusative	дв**е**сти	тр**и**ста	пятьс**от**
Genitive	двухс**от**	трёхс**от**	пятис**от**
Dative	двумст**ам**	трёмст**ам**	пятист**ам**
Instrumental	двумяст**ами**	тремяст**ами**	пятьюст**ами**
Prepositional	двухст**ах**	трёхст**ах**	пятист**ах**

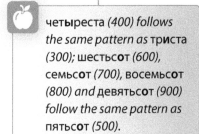

чет**ы**реста *(400) follows the same pattern as* тр**и**ста *(300);* шестьс**от** *(600),* семьс**от** *(700),* восемьс**от** *(800) and* девятьс**от** *(900) follow the same pattern as* пятьс**от** *(500).*

 т**ы**сяча *(1,000),* милли**о**н *(1,000,000) and* милли**а**рд *(1,000,000,000) have regular noun endings.*

D   Write out the numbers in full in the following phrases.

1   С**а**нкт-Петерб**у**рг нах**о**дится в 650 км от Москв**ы**. _____

2   В Москв**е** я был в 190 ст**а**нциях метр**о**. _____

3   Это дл**и**нный п**о**езд, с 24 ваг**о**нами. _____

4   Он**и** **о**чень уст**а**ли п**о**сле 12 дл**и**нных по**е**здок по Евр**о**пе в **э**том год**у**. _____

5   Он**и** д**а**ли ск**и**дку 2,000 пассаж**и**рам. _____

6   Мо**я** с**а**мая дл**и**нная по**е**здка на п**о**езде был**а** **о**коло 100 час**о**в. _____

Meaning and usage

Ordinal numbers

1   Russian ordinal numbers, like adjectives, agree in gender, case and number with the noun to which they apply. One of the main uses of **ordinal numbers** is for dates and years.

How to form ordinal numbers

1   Like in English, apart from *first* and *second*, Russian ordinals look very much like their cardinal equivalent:

1st	п**е**рвый	11th	одинн**а**дцатый
2nd	втор**ой**	20th	двадц**а**тый
3rd	тр**е**тий	21st	дв**а**дцать п**е**рвый
4th	четвёртый	30th	тридц**а**тый
5th	п**я**тый	40th	сороков**ой**
6th	шест**ой**	50th	пятидес**я**тый
7th	седьм**ой**	60th	шестидес**я**тый
8th	восьм**ой**	70th	семидес**я**тый
9th	дев**я**тый	80th	восьмидес**я**тый
10th	дес**я**тый	90th	девян**о**стый

E Write the dates in figures.

1 Мы отпр**а**вились п**е**рвого апр**е**ля. _____

2 Мы **е**здили в Ам**е**рику в две т**ы**сячи пятн**а**дцатом год**у**. _____

3 Мы при**е**хали дв**а**дцать втор**о**го декабр**я** т**ы**сяча девятьс**о**т девян**о**сто дев**я**того г**о**да.

_____

2 The way to say *on* a date in Russian is slightly unexpected: you just use the genitive case without any preposition. If you want to say *in* a certain year, use в with the prepositional case in the usual way. However, if a year comes after a date or month, put the year in the genitive case.

F Write out the following dates in full.

1 в 1917 год**у** _____

2 отб**ы**тие: 25/09/2015 _____

3 приб**ы**тие: 31/10/2015 _____

4 в 2020 год**у** _____

5 в декабр**е** 1991 _____

6 возвращ**е**ние дом**о**й: 02/07/2017 _____

G Choose the odd one out and give your reason in Russian. Use the vocabulary box to help you.

1 съезд, куп**е**, плацк**а**ртное м**е**сто _____

2 Ур**а**л, **А**льпы, Кавк**а**з _____

3 пуст**ы**ня, проводн**и**к, дальноб**о**йщик _____

4 светоф**о**р, съезд, **о**бласть _____

5 в**е**чная мерзлот**а**, Сиб**и**рь, **Д**альний вост**о**к _____

6 автостр**а**да, магистр**а**ль, пол**я**рный круг _____

автострада	*motorway*	плацк**а**ртное место	*reserved seat/bed*
в**е**чная мерзлота	*permafrost*		*in open carriage*
дальноб**о**йщик	*long-distance lorry driver*	пол**я**рный круг	*Arctic Circle*
Дальний вост**о**к	*far east (of Russia)*	проводн**и**к	*conductor*
Кавк**а**з	*the Caucasus*	пуст**ы**ня	*desert*
куп**е**	*two- or four-berth sleeper*	светоф**о**р	*traffic lights*
	compartment	Сиб**и**рь	*Siberia*
магистр**а**ль	*mainline, highway*	съезд	*(motorway) exit*
область	*administrative region*	Ур**а**л	*the Urals*

 # Reading

H Read the beginning of this travelogue and answer the question that follows in Russian.

Путешествует Иван Иванович!

Всю свою жизнь мне хотелось поехать по Транссибирской железнодорожной магистрали, и наконец-то в этом году моя мечта сбылась. Я ушёл на пенсию после тридцати пяти лет работы и купил билет на самую длинную железнодорожную поездку моей жизни.

Какая была мечта у Ивана Ивановича, и почему она сбылась только недавно?

_____

_____

I Now read the rest of the article and answer the questions that follow in Russian, using your own words as far as possible.

Ещё когда я учился в пятом классе, у меня навсегда появился интерес к этой великой железной дороге. В учебнике истории я прочитал о том, как официально началось её строительство девятнадцатого (тридцать первого по новому стилю) мая тысяча восемьсот девяносто первого года в районе Владивостока. Согласно официальным расчётам тогда, стоимость строительства железной дороги под первым названием «Великий Сибирский Путь» должна была составить триста пятьдесят миллионов рублей золотом, а получилось так, что конечная стоимость Транссиба составила почти полтора миллиарда рублей.

Однако, техническое достижение строительства было неоспоримо велико! Движение поездов по части Транссиба началось двадцать первого октября (третьего ноября) тысяча девятьсот первого года, и регулярное сообщение между столицей империи — Санкт-Петербургом и тихоокеанским портом России — Владивостоком по железной дороге было установлено в июле тысяча девятьсот третьего года. Официальный конец строительства на территории Российской империи отметился пятого (восемнадцатого) октября тысяча девятьсот шестнадцатого года.

Сегодня длина магистрали – девять тысяч двести девяносто восемь километров — это самая длинная железная дорога в мире. Самый «быстрый» поезд Транссиба — Номер один/ два «Россия», сообщением Москва — Владивосток. Я слышал, что он проходит Транссиб за шесть суток и два часа, со средней скоростью шестьдесят четыре километра в час. Я поеду в «день рождения» магистрали, одиннадцатого апреля (тридцатого марта), когда в тысяча восемьсот девяносто первом году был издан императорский указ о закладке «Великого сибирского пути»!

 Notice that two dates are given for each event in this text. This is because up until the revolution of 1917, two calendars were used in the Russian Empire: the 'old style' (Julian) calendar and the 'new style' (Gregorian) calendar. This explains why, even today, the Russian Orthodox Church still celebrates Christmas on 7 January.

1 Когда **на**чали стр**о**ить Трансс**и**б?

_____

2 В кон**е**чном счёте, ск**о**лько ст**о**ило постр**о**ить Трансс**и**б?

_____

3 Почем**у** Ив**а**н Ив**а**нович упомин**а**ет 1916 год?

_____

4 Ск**о**лько есть в м**и**ре жел**е**зных дор**о**г, кот**о**рые длинн**е**е Трансс**и**ба?

_____

5 Почем**у** Ив**а**н Ив**а**нович реш**и**л по**е**хать од**и**ннадцатого апр**е**ля?

_____

Vocabulary

J Here are the distance readings taken at the start and end of some long car journeys. Work out the distances travelled in kilometres and write them in words.

1 | 6 | 0 | 1 | 1 | 0 | | 6 | 0 | 4 | 1 | 0 |

_____

2 | 0 | 4 | 5 | 2 | 2 | | 0 | 4 | 9 | 8 | 2 |

_____

3 | 4 | 4 | 6 | 5 | 0 | | 4 | 6 | 0 | 0 | 0 |

_____

4 | 7 | 6 | 1 | 2 | 3 | | 7 | 7 | 0 | 2 | 1 |

_____

5 | 0 | 0 | 1 | 2 | 1 | | 0 | 1 | 9 | 2 | 0 |

_____

6 | 0 | 2 | 5 | 0 | 9 | | 0 | 3 | 1 | 1 | 0 |

_____

K Match the distances with the journeys.

1 длина Транссиба

2 расстояние от Земли до Луны

3 расстояние от Москвы до Владивостока

4 расстояние от Москвы до Дублина

5 расстояние от Большого Диомида (Россия) до Малого Диомида (США)

6 расстояние от Эрмитажа до памятника Медного Всадника

a 384,400 км

b 2,789 км

c 1 км

d 9,298 км

e 9,128 км

f 4 км

L Write the date of birth in words for each of the following famous people.

1 П.И. Чайковский   07/05/1840 _____

2 Екатерина Великая   02/05/1729 _____

3 Ю.А. Гагарин   09/03/1934 _____

4 В.В. Терешкова   06/03/1937 _____

5 Р.А. Абрамович   24/10/1966 _____

6 М.Ю. Шарапова   19/04/1987 _____

Writing

M You are driving from Moscow to Vladivostok and keeping a blog. Cover the following points in an entry of about 100 words of Russian.

▶ Опишите свой автомобиль

▶ Что вам больше всего понравилось?

▶ Когда и где вы проехали самый большой километраж за один день?

▶ Опишите свою поездку в цифрах

_____

_____

_____

_____

_____

_____

_____

_____

_____

_____

Self-check

Tick the box which matches your level of confidence.

 1 = very confident 2 = need more practice 3 = not too confident

Как вы думаете? Вы хорошо понимаете? Поставьте галочку:

 1 = хорошо 2 = нужно больше практики 3 = нехорошо

	1	2	3
Use cardinal numbers with adjectives and nouns			
Use cardinal and ordinal numbers in all cases			
Understand a complex text about long-distance travel			
Able to use a range of specialized vocabulary to describe long-distance travel			

16 Где жить?

Where should we stay?

In this unit you will learn how to:

✅ Use *this* and *that*

✅ Use compound conjunctions, e.g. *due to the fact that* and other connectives

✅ Discuss accommodation

✅ Describe your ideal home

CEFR: Can scan longer text in order to locate desired information and understand relevant information in everyday material, such as letters, brochures and short official documents (CEFR B1); Can write short, simple essays on topics of interest (CEFR B1)

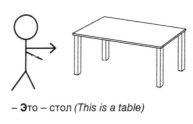

– Это – стол *(This is a table)*

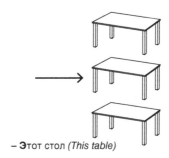

– Этот стол *(This table)*

Meaning and usage

Demonstrative pronouns

1   You will already be very familiar with the word **это** which is used often in Russian to translate the English *this/it is ....* It is a form of the **demonstrative pronoun этот**, which means *this*. If you want to make a contrast, there is also the **demonstrative pronoun тот**, which means *that*.

	Masculine	Feminine	Neuter	Plural
Nominative	этот	эта	это	эти
Accusative (inanimate/animate)	этот/этого	эту	это	эти/этих
Genitive	этого	этой	этого	этих
Dative	этому	этой	этому	этим
Instrumental	этим	этой	этим	этими
Plural	этом	этой	этом	этих

	Masculine	Feminine	Neuter	Plural
Nominative	тот	та	то	те
Accusative (inanimate/animate)	тот/того	ту	то	те/тех
Genitive	того	той	того	тех
Dative	тому	той	тому	тем
Instrumental	тем	той	тем	теми
Plural	том	той	том	тех

 Remember the key difference in meaning between Это диван (this is a sofa) *and* этот диван (this sofa).

A **You are in a shop buying items for your new apartment. Write what you would say to choose the items the assistant suggests (этот) or another item in the showroom (тот). Use the example as a model.**

ЭТОТ	ТОТ
диван ☑	кресло ☒
Пример: я хочу этот диван, а не то кресло.	
1 лампа ☒	абажур ☑
2 стол ☑	стулья ☒
3 телевизор ☒	звуковая панель ☑
4 шторы ☑	жалюзи ☒
5 комод ☒	книжная полка ☑
6 картина ☑	зеркало ☒

1 _____

2 _____

3 _____

4 _____

5 _____

6 _____

B Look at this sentence. Translate it into English to work out what the word **такой** means.

У нас был так**ой** больш**ой** дом в так**ом** крас**и**вом рай**о**не!

_____

2 Another useful word when describing things is так**ой**, meaning _such a …!_

C **такой** has regular adjective endings – complete its endings in this table.

	Masculine	**Feminine**	**Neuter**	**Plural**
Nominative	так**ой**	так_____	так_____	так_____
Accusative (inanimate/animate)	так**ой**/так**ого**	так**ую**	так**ое**	так_____
Genitive	так_____	так_____	так_____	так**их**
Dative	так_____	так_____	так_____	так_____
Instrumental	так_____	так_____	так_____	так_____
Prepositional	так_____	так_____	так_____	так_____

D Your friend is impressed with the new fixtures and fittings in your home. Show how they expressed their opinion using the example as a model.

Прим**е**р: Ты куп**и**л н**о**вый стол. → **Э**то так**ой** крас**и**вый стол!

1 Ты куп**и**л н**о**вую карт**и**ну. → _____

2 Ты куп**и**л н**о**вые нож**и**. → _____

3 Ты куп**и**л н**о**вую т**у**мбочку. → _____

4 Ты куп**и**л н**о**вый душ. → _____

5 Ты куп**и**л н**о**вую плит**у**. → _____

6 Ты куп**и**л н**о**вую посудом**о**ечную маш**и**ну. → _____

Compound conjunctions

1 As well as being used to mean _that_, the word **то** is used in some so-called **compound conjunctions,** where it acts as a link between a preposition and a verb – because a preposition needs to be followed by a word in a case but, of course, you can't put a verb into a case!

До <u>тог**о**</u>, как он**и** куп**и**ли дом, он**и** ж**и**ли в кварт**и**ре. _(Before buying a house, they lived in an apartment.)_

Compound conjunction	Meaning	Compound conjunction	Meaning
благодаря тому, что	(thanks to)	пока не	(until)
в то время как	(while)	поскольку	(inasmuch as)
ввиду того, что	(in view of the fact that)	после того, как	(after)
вместо того, чтобы	(instead of)	потому что	(because)
до того, как	(before)	с тех пор, как	(since)
из-за того, что	(as a result of the fact that)	словно	(just like)
как будто	(as if)	так как	(as, since)
как только	(as soon as)	так что	(and so)
перед тем, как	(just before)	тогда, как	(whilst)
пока	(while)	что касается	(as far as … is concerned)

E Complete this paragraph using conjunctions from the box and then translate it into English.

благодаря тому, что	до того, как	пока
вместо того, чтобы	как будто	поскольку

1 _____ я купила свой домик я жила у родителей. 2 _____ жить в центре, как они, я решила переехать за город 3 _____ там тише и спокойнее. 4 _____ я искала дом, начали строить микрорайон, 5 _____ специально для меня. 6 _____ бабушка подарила мне деньги, я смогла купить мой идеальный домик.

F Complete this account of a stay in a hotel using compound conjunctions as appropriate. More than one correct answer may be possible.

1 _____ мы поехали, накануне, мы передумали и решили приехать позже.

2 _____ мы передумали, надо было платить побольше.

3 _____ мы получили ключ, мы пошли в номер.

4 _____ мы вошли, мы заметили, что свет не работает.

5 Мы сидели в темноте, _____ отремонтировали.

6 _____ это было неудобно, нам дали скидку на 10 процентов.

Reading

G Read the beginning of this advertisement and answer the question that follows in Russian.

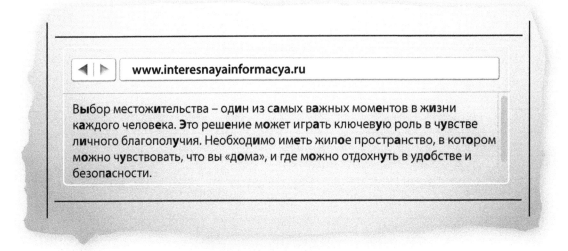

www.interesnayainformacya.ru

Выбор местожительства – один из самых важных моментов в жизни каждого человека. Это решение может играть ключевую роль в чувстве личного благополучия. Необходимо иметь жилое пространство, в котором можно чувствовать, что вы «дома», и где можно отдохнуть в удобстве и безопасности.

Судя по этой рекламе почему выбор дома или квартиры так важен?

_____

_____

H Now read the rest of the advertisement and answer the questions that follow in Russian, using your own words as far as possible.

Какое из следующих местожительств вам больше всего подходит?

№1

В живописном районе продаётся дом на участке в 6 соток, который предоставляет широкие возможности для посадки деревьев или постройки детской площадки. В доме проведены все необходимые коммуникации — свет, вода, газ и канализация. Дом построен в три уровня, имеет пластиковые окна и расширенный гараж. Выполненный в канадском стиле, дом идеально подходит для удобного проживания: он просторный, и, по всей вероятности, придётся по душе семьям с детьми.

№2

«Берёзовая роща» — это разновысотный жилой комплекс, в новом микрорайоне. Жилые корпуса расположены на расстоянии друг от друга, чтобы жильцам не надо было закрывать шторы от любопытных соседей.

Ультрасовременные технологии, используемые в строительстве квартир, сделают жизнь комфортной. Разные планировки позволят выбрать квартиру на любой личный вкус и эффективно использовать жилое пространство. На ваш выбор: студии, традиционные одно – трёхкомнатные квартиры от 30 до 110 квадратных метров, все в завидно современном квартале.

№3

Предлагаем шикарный дом, с отличным сочетанием городской инфраструктуры и загородного покоя. Дом двухэтажный, и 5 лет назад был выполнен качественный и дорогой ремонт, гарантируя всё для удобства в эксплуатации, и чтобы всё было в отличном состоянии. На первом этаже – большая гостиная, прихожая, кухня, санузел, и на втором – три спальни и санузел. Участок в собственности имеет заасфальтированную парковку под три машины. Хватит искать идеальный дом … он перед вами!

V	
канализация	*sewerage*
микрорайон	*(newly developed) area of town*
прихожая	*hall, lobby*
санузел	*bathroom/toilet*
собственность	*property, ownership*
6 соток	*6 hundredths (of a hectare)*

1 Как можно благоустроить участок, на котором находится первый дом?

_____

2 Судя по первой рекламе, для кого идеален этот дом?

_____

3 Почему вторая реклама предлагает выбор планировок?

_____

4 Почему третья реклама описывает то, что было 5 лет назад?

_____

5 Почему третья реклама считает, что не надо больше искать дом?

_____

Vocabulary

I Find opposites for the following adjectives in the Reading text.

1 уродливый _____

2 ненужный _____

3 узкий _____

4 неудобный _____

5 современный _____

6 деревенский _____

J Indicate what items the following people need in their new homes.

1 «Мне хочется смотреть на себя, пока я причёсываюсь.» _____

2 «Нам надоедает долго стоять около раковины, когда у нас много грязной посуды!»

_____

3 «Что сделать с вчерашней газетой? Куда выбросить?» _____

4 «Было бы здорово стоять или сидеть на свежем воздухе и смотреть на сад внизу.»

_____

5 «Я предпочитаю быстро мыться, а не лежать в воде.» _____

6 «Посмотри на эти грязные ковры! Как мы будем их чистить?» _____

K Using your dictionary if necessary to help you, put these items into their most appropriate room of the house.

вытяжка	камин	подушка	тумбочка
духовка	мягкая мебель	полотенце	умывальная раковина
журнальный столик	плита	простыня	унитаз

гостиная	кухня
•	•
•	•
•	•
спальня	**санузел**
•	•
•	•
•	•

Writing

L Write an email to your Russian friend to describe your ideal home, giving as much detail as you can about the following in about 100 words of Russian.

- ▶ зда́ние
- ▶ ме́бель
- ▶ местонахожде́ние
- ▶ идеа́льный день в идеа́льном до́ме

> When you are writing or speaking in Russian, aim to use longer sentences, with as broad a variety of conjunctions as possible.

_____

_____

_____

_____

_____

_____

_____

_____

_____

Self-check

Tick the box which matches your level of confidence.

1 = very confident   2 = need more practice   3 = not too confident

Как вы ду́маете? Вы хорошо́ понима́ете? Поста́вьте га́лочку:

1 = хорошо́   2 = ну́жно бо́льше пра́ктики   3 = нехорошо́

	1	2	3
Use demonstrative pronouns (*this* and *that*)			
Use compound conjunctions and other connectives			
Understand a complex text about accommodation			
Able to use a range of specialized vocabulary to describe an ideal home			

17 Можно?

May I …?

In this unit you will learn how to:

- ✅ Use modal verbs and expressions, e.g. *may I …?*
- ✅ Say whether you *can, should, could* do something
- ✅ Say whether you *can't, shouldn't, couldn't* do something
- ✅ Describe traditions

CEFR: Can understand a complex text about social occasions, customs and traditions (CEFR B2); Can write short, simple essays on topics of interest (CEFR B1)

Past	Present	Future
можно было *could*	можно *can*	можно будет *will be able to*
нужно было *was necessary*	нужно *is necessary*	нужно будет *will be necessary*
надо было *had to*	надо *have to*	надо будет *will have to*
невозможно было *was not possible*	невозможно *is not possible*	невозможно будет *will not be possible*
нельзя было *was impossible / was forbidden*	нельзя *is impossible / is forbidden*	нельзя будет *will be impossible / will be forbidden*

Meaning and usage

Modal verbs and expressions

A **Look at these sentences containing the modal expression можно** (*can / it is possible*) **and translate them. Explain how they are used differently to standard verbs.**

1 Ивану и Анне можно было посмотреть салют на День Победы.

_____

2 Ивану и Анне можно посмотреть салют на День Победы.

_____

3 Ивану и Анне можно будет посмотреть салют на День Победы.

_____

How to form modal verbs and expressions

1   The subject of the modal **мо́жно** is in the dative case and the verb following the modal **мо́жно** is in the infinitive.

2   This construction is used with all modal expressions: **мо́жно** *(you can)*, **ну́жно** *(it is necessary)*, **на́до** *(you must)*, **невозмо́жно** *(it is not possible)* and **нельзя́** *(either you cannot or you must not)*.

3   Be careful when using the **modal** expression **нельзя́**. A **modal expression** can usually be followed by either an imperfective or a perfective verb, depending on the meaning of the verb. However, the choice of **aspect** after **нельзя́** has a specific effect on the meaning:

нельзя́ + imperfective verb = *it is forbidden / you must not*

Нельзя́ ходи́ть по газо́ну.   *(You must not walk on the grass.)*

нельзя́ + perfective verb = *it is impossible / you cannot*

Нельзя́ прие́хать сего́дня из-за тума́на.   *(It is impossible to arrive today due to fog.)*

B   Complete these sentences with an appropriate modal expression.

1   Ско́ро Но́вый год, и тепе́рь _____ купи́ть ёлку.

2   Когда́ я был студе́нтом, _____ ходи́ть на вечери́нки без буты́лки.

3   Всегда́ _____ найти́ оригина́льный пода́рок на день рожде́ния.

4   Я хочу́ пое́хать домо́й на Па́сху, но _____ ра́но уйти́ с рабо́ты.

5   Бори́с хоте́л купи́ть жене́ ро́зы, но _____ .

6   Ма́ме _____ пригото́вить блины́ на Ма́сленицу.

A useful verb which can be used as a synonym for **на́до** *is* приходи́ться/прийти́сь: *На* выходны́е в магази́нах ча́сто прихо́дится стоя́ть в о́череди. *(You often have to queue in shops at the weekend.)*

Меня́ пригласи́ли на у́жин, но пришло́сь отказа́ться из-за гри́ппа.   *(I was invited to dinner, but had to decline due to the flu.)*

4 One of the **modal expressions** ну́жно is also used as a short form adjective. Look at these sentences:

На день рожде́ния ну́жен пода́рок.	*(A present is needed for a birthday.)*
На Рождество́ нужна́ ёлка.	*(A fir tree is needed for Christmas.)*
На пра́здник ну́жно шампа́нское.	*(Champagne is needed for a celebration.)*
На 8ое ма́рта нужны́ цветы́.	*(Flowers are needed for 8 March (Women's Day)).*

5 The adjective **agrees** with the object that is needed. If this object is necessary **to** someone, then the dative case is used:

На день рожде́ния **мне** ну́жен пода́рок.   *(I need a birthday present.)*

C Complete the sentences with ну́жен/нужна́/ну́жно/нужны́ and then translate them.

1 На Па́сху нам _____ кули́ч.

_____

2 На вечери́нке студе́нтам всегда́ _____ гро́мкая му́зыка.

_____

3 Меня́ предупреди́ли, что в ба́не _____ ве́ники.

_____

4 В ру́сских музе́ях та́почки _____, что́бы не по́ртить полы́.

_____

5 Что́бы нача́ть вечери́нку _____ пе́рвый тост.

_____

6 В пе́рвый день зимы́ _____ пальто́!

_____

6 Another useful word to express necessity is до́лжен/должна́/должно́/должны́. This suggests a *moral* necessity.

D Translate the following sentences.

1 Михаи́л до́лжен навести́ть ба́бушку в день рожде́ния. _____

2 Снегу́рочка должна́ помога́ть Де́ду Моро́зу. _____

3 Госуда́рство должно́ устра́ивать салю́т на Но́вый год. _____

4 Христиа́не должны́ ходи́ть в це́рковь регуля́рно. _____

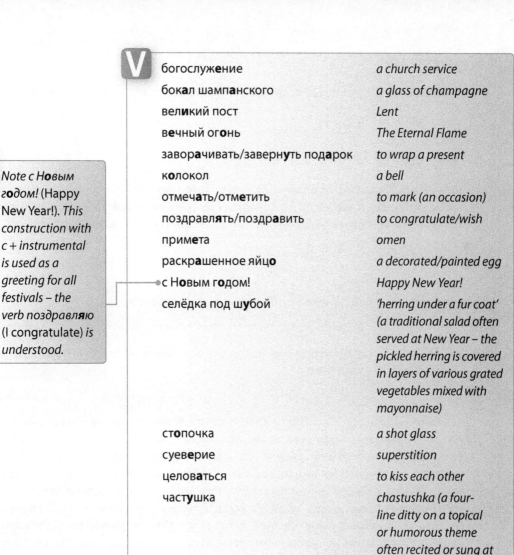

богослуж**е**ние	a church service
бок**а**л шамп**а**нского	a glass of champagne
вел**и**кий пост	Lent
в**е**чный ог**о**нь	The Eternal Flame
завор**а**чивать/заверн**у**ть под**а**рок	to wrap a present
к**о**локол	a bell
отмеч**а**ть/отм**е**тить	to mark (an occasion)
поздравл**я**ть/поздр**а**вить	to congratulate/wish
прим**е**та	omen
раскр**а**шенное яйц**о**	a decorated/painted egg
с Н**о**вым г**о**дом!	Happy New Year!
селёдка под ш**у**бой	'herring under a fur coat' (a traditional salad often served at New Year – the pickled herring is covered in layers of various grated vegetables mixed with mayonnaise)
ст**о**почка	a shot glass
суев**е**рие	superstition
целов**а**ться	to kiss each other
част**у**шка	chastushka (a four-line ditty on a topical or humorous theme often recited or sung at celebrations)

*Note с Н**о**вым г**о**дом!* (Happy New Year!). *This construction with c + instrumental is used as a greeting for all festivals – the verb поздравл**я**ю* (I congratulate) *is understood.*

E Choose the most appropriate word(s) for each celebration.

1 Н**о**вый год: прим**е**та / бок**а**л шамп**а**нского / в**е**чный ог**о**нь

2 Рождеств**о**: богослуж**е**ние / суев**е**рие / част**у**шка

3 Междунар**о**дный ж**е**нский день: вел**и**кий пост / к**о**локол / поздравл**я**ть

4 П**а**сха: завор**а**чивать под**а**рок / раскр**а**шенное яйц**о** / ст**о**почка

5 День Поб**е**ды: селёдка под ш**у**бой / отмеч**а**ть / целов**а**ться

 # Reading

F Read the beginning of this blog and answer the question that follows in Russian.

Почему мы такие суеверные?

Хотя мы все прекрасно понимаем, что нет никакой научной или логичной основы для примет, суеверия и веры в духов и сверхъестественное, значительное большинство из нас на всякий случай верит во власть разных цифр или событий над будущим.

Почему автор этого блога считает, что не надо быть суеверным?

G Now read the rest of the article and answer the questions that follow in Russian, using your own words as far as possible.

Например, в пятницу 13-го нельзя ничего делать, конечно, потому что все считают этот день страшным. Такая вера, наверно, пришла из Библии, так как именно в этот день Каин убил своего брата, Авеля. Я совсем не верю в эту примету, хотя одно другое суеверие мне кажется более обоснованным: что из дома сразу выходить нельзя, а что надо посидеть немного «на дорожку». В основе этой приметы, говорят, лежит давняя вера людей в добрых и злых духов. Суеверные люди хотят присесть «на дорожку» для того, чтобы можно было обмануть таких духов. Однако, на мой взгляд это просто здравый смысл, который рекомендует посидеть и подумать, не забыл ли я что-нибудь!

Трудно не согласиться с тем, что суеверие часто переходит в смешную фантастику! Некоторые верят, что нельзя есть с ножа, потому что это значит вызвать гнев духов, которые делают человека агрессивным и злым. Неужели? И почему нельзя выносить мусор после заката солнца? Оказывается потому, что, вынося вечером мусор, вы выбрасываете свои деньги.

В детстве моя бабушка часто ругала меня, когда я свистел в помещении, потому что со свистом мы призываем в свой мир нечистую силу. Свист в доме, также говорил бабуле о том, что не будет денег, а в море приближается шторм. Нет, мои друзья! Мы живём в двадцать первом веке: давайте освободимся от тёмного прошлого раз и навсегда!

дух	*spirit*	примета	*sign, token*
здравый смысл	*common sense*	сверхъестественный	*supernatural*
неужели?/разве?	*really?*	суеверие	*superstition*
освобождаться/ освободиться от + *gen.*	*to free oneself from*		

1 Почему люди боятся пятницы 13-го числа?

_____

2 Почему автор статьи считает, что надо посидеть «на дорожку»?

_____

3 Почему рекомендуется выносить мусор при дневном свете?

_____

4 Почему свистун – не популярен в России?

_____

5 Что автор рекомендует своим читателям в конце статьи?

_____

Vocabulary

H Find a word in the reading passage that matches the following definitions and write it in the form in which you would find it in a dictionary.

1 то, что пока ещё не было, а остаётся впереди _____

2 считать, что это правда, даже если нет доказательств _____

3 то что остаётся и что обычно выбрасывают _____

4 отвергнуть власть чего-то и оставить позади _____

I Find the odd one out in each group of words.

1 возможно, позволяется, запрещается, разрешается

2 факт, вера, миф, легенда

3 ругать, хвалить, бранить, критиковать

4 демон, нечистая сила, злой дух, ангел

5 гнев, истерика, покой, бешенство

6 здравый смысл, глупость, мудрость, разум

J   Reorder the letters to find a word in the passage.

1 реовнан   _____

2 вееруиес   _____

3 убьнамот   _____

4 лежиеун   _____

5 яббалу   _____

Writing

K   Write to a Russian friend about superstitions in your country or region. Cover the following points in your letter in about 100 words of Russian.

▶ Есть ли счастливые цифры/животные/цвета?

▶ Что можно делать, чтобы быть счастливым?

▶ Что нельзя делать, если хочешь быть счастливым?

▶ Были ли у вас случаи в жизни, когда суеверие было оправдано?

_____

_____

_____

_____

_____

_____

_____

_____

_____

Self-check

Tick the box which matches your level of confidence.

1 = very confident   2 = need more practice   3 = not too confident

Как вы думаете? Вы хорошо понимаете? Поставьте галочку:

1 = хорошо   2 = нужно больше практики   3 = нехорошо

	1	2	3
Use modal expressions in the present tense			
Use modal expressions in the past and future tenses			
Understand a complex text about superstitions			
Able to use a range of specialized vocabulary to describe traditions in a country			

18 Скажите, пожалуйста!

Can you tell me, please?

In this unit you will learn how to:

- Ask a range of questions
- Answer a range of questions
- Give precise information

CEFR: Can use a wide range of question words in Russian (CEFR A1 and A2); Can ask and answer questions about personal details (CEFR A1)

Meaning and usage

Open questions

1 Open questions require more than a simple *yes/no* answer and start with a question word such as *who* or *when*. There are many common question words in Russian that you will already know.

A Match up the question words with answers about Pierre Bezukhov in Tolstoy's *War and Peace*.

кто?	в роскошных домах в Санкт-Петербурге
что?	чтобы убить Наполеона
где?	в начале XIX-го века
когда?	он знакомится с масонами случайно
как?	незаконный сын русского графа
почему?	в конце романа женится на Наталье Ростовой

2 It is important to remember that Russian is very precise when talking about location:

<u>Где</u> находится вокзал?   *(Where is the railway station?)*

<u>Откуда</u> отправляется   *(Where does the bus to the railway station leave from?)*
    автобус до вокзала?

<u>Куда</u> идёт этот поезд?   *(Where is this train going to?)*

B What is the difference in meaning between the three underlined question words?

_____

_____

_____

C Here are some answers to a radio interviewer's questions. What question words were used?

1 Больше всего я люблю делать покупки. _____

2 Мой день рождения 1ого апреля. _____

3 Мой любимый автор Достоевский. _____

4 Потому что это мне нравится. _____

5 Я еду в Италию в этом году. _____

6 Я играю в теннис неплохо. _____

7 Я отправляюсь в отпуск из Москвы. _____

8 Я родилась в маленьком городе под Москвой. _____

How to form open questions

1 Two of the common question words (кто and что) change their spelling according to their grammatical function in the question:

Кого ты знаешь?   (*Whom do you know?*)

От чего это зависит?   (**On what** *does this depend?*)

D Based on your knowledge of adjective and noun endings and using the forms already given, complete the table.

Nominative	кто	что
Accusative	кого	_____
Genitive	_____	чего
Dative	кому	_____
Instrumental	_____	чем
Prepositional	о ком	о чём

E Complete the interview questions below with the correct form of кто or что.

1 В детстве _____ вы хотели стать?

2 От _____ это зависит?

3 _____ вы звоните чаще всего?

4 В _____ состоит ваше счастье?

5 _____ вы уважаете больше всего?

6 _____ вы по специальности?

2 There are two words in Russian that can be added to the basic question words. Look at these examples:

Вы <u>когда-нибудь</u> работали за границей?

(Have you at some time/any time worked abroad?)

Я <u>когда-то</u> работала в Милане, но скучала по России.

(I at some/one time worked in Milan but missed Russia.)

3 Both -нибудь and -то can be translated by *some*, but there is a difference between the two:

▶ -то is used when you are speaking about a person, thing or place that *actually* exists, though you are not sure of their precise identity

▶ -нибудь is used when you are speaking about a person, thing or place that has not yet been chosen or identified at all

As a rule of thumb, if you can use *any-* in English instead of *some-*, then you need to use -нибудь rather than -то:

Вам <u>кто-нибудь</u> помогал?   *(Did* someone *(anyone)* help you?)

Да, <u>кто-то</u> мне помогал, но я не помню кто.   *(Yes,* someone *helped me, but I can't remember who.)*

> *Be aware that Russian sometimes uses* -либо *as a synonym of* -нибудь:
>
> Вы <u>когда-либо</u> работали за границей?
>
> *(Have you at some time/any time worked abroad?)*

F Fill in the gaps using a -нибудь or -то question word from the word cloud.

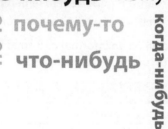

где-нибудь кому-то

что-то почему-то когда-нибудь

что-нибудь

1 _____ ещё хотите спросить?

2 Я хотел _____ сказать, но не помню что.

3 Вы _____ думали об этом раньше?

4 **Е**сли можно узнать _____ когда он родился, это будет интересно.

5 Я решил это сделать _____ но уже забыл причину.

6 Вы сказали _____ в предыдущем интервью, что вам нравится искусство.

G Using your knowledge of Russian adjective endings, complete the table for **какой** – *what/which (sort of)*.

	Masculine	Feminine	Neuter	Plural
Nominative	какой	_____	какое	какие
Accusative (inanimate/animate)	какой/какого	какую	какое	какие/_____
Genitive	_____	какой	какого	каких
Dative	какому	_____	_____	каким
Instrumental	каким	какой	каким	_____
Prepositional	_____	о какой	о каком	о каких

H Complete these sentences with the appropriate form of **какой**.

1 В какую/каком/какой году вы начали писать стихотворения?

2 Какие/каких/каким фильмы вам нравятся больше всего?

3 Каким/какую/какому жанру относится ваша музыка?

4 Каком/каким/какого образом вы занимаетесь творческим процессом?

5 В каком/какие/каких условиях вы работаете лучше всего?

6 Какая/какого/каком числа вы сдадите последнюю рукопись?

Meaning and usage

Formal and informal questions

1 When asking questions in Russian, it is important to remember the basic rule about talking to someone: do you know them well (use ты) or is it a more formal relationship (use вы)?

I Look at these situations. Decide on an informal or formal form of address and complete the question with the correct form of the verb in brackets.

Вы разговариваете с ...	на «ты» или на «вы»?
1 университетским профессором	По какой причине (выбрать) _____ свою специальность?
2 старым знакомым	В котором часу (хотеть) _____ встретиться?
3 маленьким ребёнком	Почему (плакать) _____ ?
4 шефом на работе	К какому числу (написать) _____ отчёт?
5 милиционером	До какой степени (считать) _____, что это подозрительно?
6 сестрой или братом	Из-за чего (беспокоиться) _____ ?

2 Note that there are three ways of saying *to ask (a question)* in Russian.

1 задавать/задать вопрос = a literal translation of *to ask/pose a question*

2 спрашивать/спросить = *to ask* (someone *about* something)

3 просить/попросить = *to ask* (someone *to do* something or *for* something)

J **Complete these sentences using three of the items from the box.**

задавать/задать вопрос   задали вопрос   попросила   попросили   спрашивать   спросил

1 «Как называется фильм?» _____ он.

2 Чтобы узнать, можно _____ гиду.

3 Она _____ меня узнать об этом.

Vocabulary

K **Find a word in the box that matches the following definitions.**

заключение	*(conclusion)*
количество	*(quantity)*
мечта	*(dream)*
обстоятельство	*(circumstance)*
последствие	*(consequence)*
предубеждение	*(prejudice)*

1 результат чего-то _____

2 ситуация, в которой что-то случилось _____

3 последний этап какого-то процесса _____

4 заранее иметь мнение _____

5 идеал _____

6 сколько чего-то _____

Reading

L Read the beginning of this transcript of an imagined phone-in with the Russian pop singer Dima Bilan and answer the question that follows in Russian.

– Дима, говорят, что ваши родители не сразу признали вас, когда вы родились, не правда ли?

– Совершенно верно. Я родился 24 декабря 1981 года в городе Усть-Джегута, в Карачаево-Черкессии, и в первый же день моей жизни я оказался втянут в нешуточную интригу. Мама была единственной русской женщиной в роддоме, но поскольку я обладал всем видной кавказской внешностью, мои родители начали подозревать, что маме подменили сына, нечаянно перепутав с каким-то другим младенцем. К счастью, врачи быстро смогли успокоить родителей, что я действительно их сын.

По какой причине была «интрига», когда родился Дима Билан?

_____

_____

M Now read the rest of the transcript and answer the questions that follow in Russian:

– Дима, благодаря кому впервые у вас появился интерес к музыке?

– Родители рассказывают, что я всегда любил танцевать, петь, рассказывать стихи и давать импровизированные концерты возле магазинов, во дворе, в присутствии гостей. В детском саду, кажется, я стал главным героем праздничных концертов, но во многом повлияла на моё музыкальное развитие моя любимая бабушка, которая тридцать лет работала в хоре. Моя любовь к музыке продолжала давать о себе знать и в школе, а со второго класса я пел везде – дома, на вечеринках, и тогда музыка окончательно и бесповоротно стала моей жизнью. К пятому классу я перешёл в музыкальную школу по классу аккордеона, а затем был переведён на вокальное отделение.

– Почему вы переехали в Москву и в каком году?

– В школе я участвовал в различных музыкальных конкурсах и фестивалях, и даже занял первое место в конкурсе «Молодые голоса Кавказа». В 1999 году я приехал в Москву для участия в фестивале «Чунга-Чанга», который был посвящён детскому творчеству. В 2000 году поступил в Государственное музыкальное училище имени Гнесиных, где моей специальностью был классический вокал. 2000 год я считаю настоящим началом моей карьеры. Тогда в ротацию телеканала MTV Russia попал мой первый видеоклип, и в конце октября 2003 года вышел мой дебютный альбом. В 2004 году был выпущен второй мой студийный альбом, и в том же 2004 году началась запись моего первого англоязычного альбома.

оказываться/оказаться	to turn out to be
подозревать	to suspect
подменять/подменить	to substitute
нечаянный	unintentional
бесповоротный	irrevocable

1 До какой степени Дима принимал участие в музыкальных мероприятиях своего детского сада?

_____

2 Какие были первые специальности Димы в музыкальной школе?

_____

3 По какой причине Дима оказался в Москве в 1999 году?

_____

4 Благодаря чему по-настоящему началась карьера Димы в 2000 году?

_____

Like English, Russian can ask questions in a wide variety of ways. Look back at the reading text to find several examples of more complex question forms.

N **Look back to the reading text to find more complex ways of asking the following questions.**

1 Где родился Дима Билан? _____

2 Почему он переехал в Москву? _____

3 Кто помог ему полюбить музыку? _____

4 Как он начал играть на аккордеоне? _____

# Writing

O **You have the chance to interview your favourite celebrity for a magazine. Write the interview in Russian with at least four questions and answers (about 100 words). Include the following general areas:**

▶ д**е**тство и семь**я**

▶ образов**а**ние

▶ вли**я**ния

▶ над**е**жды

_____

_____

_____

_____

_____

_____

_____

_____

_____

Self-check

Tick the box which matches your level of confidence.

1 = very confident   2 = need more practice   3 = not too confident

Как вы д**у**маете? Вы хорош**о** поним**а**ете? Пост**а**вьте г**а**лочку:

1 = хорош**о**   2 = н**у**жно б**о**льше пр**а**ктики   3 = нехорош**о**

	1	2	3
Recognize a wide range of question words in Russian			
Use a wide range of question words in Russian			
Understand a complex interview text			
Able to use a range of complex questions to find out specific information			

19 Сегодня на работе

Today at work

In this unit you will learn how to:

- ☑ Use a range of adjectival pronouns and additional other pronouns that add more information
- ☑ Understand professional vocabulary

CEFR: Can understand in detail a wide range of lengthy, complex texts likely to be encountered in social, professional or academic life, identifying finer points of detail including attitudes and implied as well as stated opinions (CEFR B2); Can write a formal style of report (CEFR C1)

каждый **весь** тот же самый
любой целый всякий самый друг друга
каждый весь тот же самый каждый
весь весь **каждый** тот же самый весь
любой целый всякий самый друг друга каждый
тот же самый каждый весь тот же самый

Meaning and usage

Adjectival pronouns

1 The adjectival pronouns всё and все, which are often used on their own, mean *everything* and *everyone*, respectively. When used with a noun, the meaning changes slightly to *the whole*.

How to form adjectival pronouns

A Complete the table using your knowledge of noun and adjective endings.

	Masculine	Feminine	Neuter	Plural
Nominative	весь	_____	всё	все
Accusative (inanimate/animate)	_____/всего	всю	всё	все/_____
Genitive	всего	_____	_____	всех
Dative	_____	_____	_____	всем
Instrumental	всем	_____	_____	_____
Prepositional	обо всём	обо всей	_____	обо всех

B Boris and Ivan both work in the same office, but Ivan is much more efficient! Write statements for Ivan based on the example.

Пример: Борис проверил часть документа. → Иван проверил весь документ.

1 Борис участвовал в начале тренинга. _____

2 Борис работал над документами часть вечера. _____

3 Борис написал половину отчёта. _____

4 Борис разговаривал с несколькими членами команды. _____

5 Борис закончил треть работы. _____

6 Борис получил ответ от одного клиента. _____

1 When you want to say *a whole …* as opposed to *the whole …*, use the Russian adjectival pronoun целый:

Целая неделя ушла на этот проект.   *(This project took a whole week.)*

2 Another very useful **adjectival pronoun** is каждый, meaning *every* or *each*. It works exactly like any other adjective.

C Work out the meaning of the following sentences.

1 Иван разговаривал с каждым членом команды. _____

2 Иван получил ответ от каждого клиента. _____

3 каждый and весь are often interchangeable, but be careful to use the right **number** (singular or plural). Use a mixture of these **adjectival pronouns** to make your Russian more varied and interesting.

D Rewrite the following sentences using каждый.

1 Все сотрудники получили сообщение. _____

2 Директор прочитал все резюме. _____

3 Во всех случаях вы получите ответ. _____

4 Всем профессионалам нужен регулярный тренинг. _____

5 Мы приготовили презентацию для всех клиентов. _____

6 Директор побеседовал со всеми коллегами. _____

> *The word* резюме *(résumé) is an example of a word taken into Russian from a foreign language. Such words sometimes become* **non-declining** *– in other words, their ending never changes.*

4 There are two more **adjectival pronouns** which are used quite widely:

Люб**о**й сотр**у**дник м**о**жет под**а**ть на **э**тот пост. (**Any** colleague can apply for this post.)

У нас в прод**а**же вс**я**кие б**у**блики.   (We have **all sorts of** doughnuts for sale.)

> It is possible for к**а**ждый, люб**о**й, вс**я**кий
> and все to be translated into English with
> the same meaning:
>
> Люб**о**й/Вс**я**кий/К**а**ждый сотр**у**дник
> м**о**жет / Все сотр**у**дники м**о**гут под**а**ть
> на **э**тот пост.
>
> (**Any** colleague can apply for this post.)

E   Translate the following sentences using appropriate adjectival pronouns.

1   Igor worked on all sorts of projects. _____

2   The whole team worked all night to finish the presentation. _____

3   I am interested in any profession, as long as it pays well. _____

4   This job included a whole range of problems. _____

5   I have a new task every week. _____

6   I can ask any colleague for advice. _____

5 There are two useful pronouns that use words with which you are familiar from other contexts: с**а**мый and друг. They enable you to give even more detail and sound particularly authentic:

С с**а**мого утр**а** он**а** звон**и**ла всем кли**е**нтам.

(She was ringing clients from the very start of the morning.)

Раб**о**тники **э**той глоб**а**льной комп**а**нии св**я**зывались друг с др**у**гом по соци**а**льным сет**я**м.

(The employees of this global company contacted each other via social networks.)

In addition to its usual meaning of *most* when forming **superlatives**, с**а**мый can also convey the idea of *very* or *right*:

в с**а**мом нач**а**ле засед**а**ния   *(at the **very** beginning / **right** at the beginning of the meeting)*

Another useful expression using с**а**мый is the Russian for *the same*:

тот же с**а**мый отч**ё**т	*(the same report)*
та же с**а**мая раб**о**та	*(the same work)*
то же с**а**мое заявл**е**ние	*(the same application)*
те же с**а**мые сотр**у**дники	*(the same colleagues)*

6 In addition to its usual meaning of *friend*, друг can also convey the idea of *each other / one another*, with a variety of forms depending on **case**:

Они знают друг друга.	*(They know each other.)*
Они звонят друг другу.	*(They phone each other.)*
Они знакомы друг с другом.	*(They are acquainted with each other.)*
Они думают друг о друге.	*(They think of each other.)*

F Complete these sentences with an appropriate form of самый, тот же самый or друг друга.

1 Она сообщила об этом в _____ конце заседания.

2 Мы получили _____ данные от филиала в Москве.

3 Нам рекомендуется регулярно звонить _____, а не только посылать e-mail.

4 Если хочешь решение, надо обратиться к _____ верху организации.

5 Мы приближаемся _____ во время переговоров.

6 Ничего не меняется: была _____ проблема в прошлый раз!

G Complete this online advice about applying for jobs using words from the box.

автобиографию	встречаешься	командировка	назначит	назначить
отменит	отменить	отчёт	повышение	подаёшь заявление
резюме	характеристика			

Когда 1 _____ на работу, особенно, если хочешь 2 _____, надо, конечно, написать убедительную 3 _____. Если этот документ понравится будущему начальнику, он 4 _____ интервью и свяжется с настоящим работодателем. 5 _____ от настоящего начальника сыграет ключевую роль в возможном успехе. Ни в коем случае не надо 6 _____ дату заседания!

📖 Reading

H Maksim has just completed a training course in Business English. Read the report from his tutor and answer the question that follows in Russian.

Максим Александрович – сотрудник в отделе международного маркетинга. Он умеет формировать эффективный подход к решению языковых заданий, опирается на технологию и лучшие практики в профессиональной области. Он стремится учитывать особенности специфических текстов для выработки оптимальных решений.

Хорошо ли Максим окончил свой тренинг? Почему? / Почему нет?

_____

_____

I   Now read Maxim's annual review written by his line manager and answer the questions that follow in Russian.

Максим Александрович заранее тщательно планирует свою деятельность, намечает все основные этапы. Он всегда - высокомотивированный, профессиональный сотрудник и суть его подхода проявляется в том, что в любой ситуации он готов находить индивидуальный подход к проблемам и людям. Он безоговорочно оказывает помощь и поддержку коллегам и подчинённым по профессиональным вопросам и уверенно и убедительно проводит выступления и презентации перед любой аудиторией.

В работе Максима Александровича интересует больше всего возможность внедрения самых высоких стандартов тщательного перевода, наличие возможностей и свободы действий для их реализации. Однако, на данный момент для него важно наличие баланса между работой и личной жизнью. В настоящее время Максим Александрович в большей мере ориентирован на решение профессиональных задач, чем на рост управленческой ответственности.

Максим Александрович предлагает и разрабатывает новые конкретные методы по оптимизации рабочих процессов и процедур с целью использования современных подходов в его профессиональной области. Сталкиваясь с проблемными ситуациями, он ищет конструктивные варианты решений и всегда проявляет настойчивость по преодолению трудностей. С другой стороны, Максим Александрович пока ещё не ставит перед собой открыто амбициозных целей по развитию карьеры и признаёт, что может некомфортно себя чувствовать в окружении конкурентов.

Желая построить сильную команду, при возможности участия в отборе персонала Максим Александрович привлекает в команду высокопотенциальных и замотивированных сотрудников. Он адекватно оценивает сильные и слабые стороны своих коллег, распределяет задачи между исполнителями, чтобы быстро и эффективно добиваться поставленных перед командой целей.

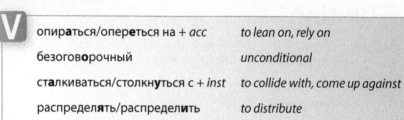

опираться/опереться на + *acc*	*to lean on, rely on*
безоговорочный	*unconditional*
сталкиваться/столкнуться с + *inst*	*to collide with, come up against*
распределять/распределить	*to distribute*

1   Судя по словам его начальника, что самое важное в профессиональном подходе Максима?

_____

2   Что больше всего интересует Максима в работе?

_____

3   В настоящее время, хочет ли Максим стать начальником?

_____

4   Что сейчас делает Максим в целях саморазвития?

_____

5   Что привлекает Максима в потенциальных коллегах?

_____

J Maria is a conscientious and highly skilled employee. Give her replies to her boss's queries. Don't forget to consider the aspect of the verb.

Пример: Вы заканчиваете печатать протокол заседания? → Я уже закончила печатать протокол заседания.

1 Вы употребляете технологию? _____

2 Вы находите индивидуальный подход к проблеме? _____

3 Вы тщательно переводите документ? _____

4 Вы узнаёте актуальное положение дел? _____

5 Вы берёте на себя ответственность за реализацию инициативы?

_____

6 Вы адекватно оцениваете сильные и слабые стороны своих коллег?

_____

Vocabulary

K In the reading text find the opposites for these words and write them in the <u>nominative</u> case.

1 теория _____

2 начальник _____

3 отсутствие _____

4 любительский _____

5 абстрактный _____

6 старомодный _____

Writing

L How is your study of Russian going? Write a self-appraisal, answering the following questions in about 100 words in Russian.

▶ Сколько времени вы отдаёте учёбе?

▶ Что вам даётся легко?

▶ Что вам даётся труднее?

▶ Какая у вас следующая цель в изучении русского языка?

_____

_____

_____

_____

_____

_____

_____

_____

_____

_____

Self-check

Tick the box which matches your level of confidence.

  1 = very confident   2 = need more practice   3 = not too confident

Как вы ду́маете? Вы хорошо́ понима́ете? Поста́вьте га́лочку:

  1 = хорошо́   2 = ну́жно бо́льше пра́ктики   3 = нехорошо́

	1	2	3
Understand a range of adjectival pronouns and other pronouns			
Use a range of adjectival pronouns and other pronouns			
Understand an appraisal text			
Able to use a range of specialized vocabulary to write a self-appraisal			

20 В следующий раз

Next time …

In this unit you will learn how to:

- ● Use gerunds
- ● Use the pronouns себя and сам
- ● Describe living abroad

CEFR: Can write short, simple essays on topics of interest (CEFR B1); Can read articles and reports concerned with contemporary problems in which the writers adopt particular attitudes or viewpoints (CEFR B1)

Past	Present
(переехать) переехав за границу	(переезжать) переезжая за границу
having moved abroad	*moving abroad*

Meaning and usage

Gerunds

A **Look at these two sentences and explain how *working* can be translated into Russian.**

Когда она работала за границей, Оля расширила свой кругозор.

(When she was working abroad, Olya broadened her outlook.)

Работая за границей, Оля расширила свой кругозор.

(Working abroad, Olya broadened her outlook.)

_____

_____

1 Both of these sentences have words translated into English as *working*. In the first sentence, *was working* is a usual past tense verb in both English and Russian. However, in the second sentence, *working* is describing **how** Olya broadened her outlook and is therefore a **gerund**. Another way of thinking of **gerunds** is to call them **verbal adverbs** – i.e. an adverb that is formed from a verb (e.g. working) rather than from an adjective (e.g. successfully).

2 In Russian, there are present (работая – *working*) and past (поработав – *having worked)* gerunds.

How to form gerunds

B Look at this table and work out how to form a present gerund.

раб**о**тать	раб**о**тая
д**е**лать	д**е**лая
регистр**и**ровать	регистр**и**руя
говор**и**ть	говор**я**
смотр**е**ть	смотр**я**
пл**а**кать	пл**а**ча

_____

_____

1 To form a **present gerund**, you take the он**и** form of the present tense verb (e.g. регистр**и**руют), remove the last two letters and replace with a -я (unless the spelling rule applies – after -ж,-ч,-ш or -щ, you need to write -a rather than -я).

*As a **present gerund** is formed from a present tense verb, this will, of course, always be an **imperfective**.*

C Complete these sentences by changing the infinitive in brackets to a present gerund.

1 _____ м**е**стные газ**е**ты, он н**а**чал знак**о**миться с н**о**вым г**о**родом. (чит**а**ть)

2 Он**и** потр**а**тили все д**е**ньги, _____ н**о**вую м**е**бель. (покуп**а**ть)

3 _____ на сво**ю** н**о**вую маш**и**ну, мы не бо**и**мся дл**и**нных по**е**здок. (смотр**е**ть)

4 _____ с н**о**выми сос**е**дями, мы б**ы**стро узна**ё**м о рай**о**не. (встреч**а**ться)

5 Пётр сид**е**л _____ в п**е**рвый день на н**о**вой раб**о**те. (молч**а**ть)

6 _____ с сотр**у**дниками, я смог**у** б**ы**стро усв**о**ить н**о**вую раб**о**ту. (говор**и**ть)

D Look at this table and work out how to form a past gerund.

пораб**о**тать	пораб**о**тав
сд**е**лать	сд**е**лав
зарегистр**и**ровать	зарегистр**и**ровав
сказ**а**ть	сказ**а**в
посмотр**е**ть	посмотр**е**в
попл**а**кать	попл**а**кав

_____

_____

2 To form a **past gerund**, you simply take the infinitive of a **perfective** verb, remove the -ть and replace it with -в. Remember: a **past gerund** is used for a completed action which happened before the action of the main verb, which can be in any tense.

In higher registers of Russian, you might also see past gerunds with the ending -вши, for example, узнавши (having found out). This ending is always used in the formation of past gerunds from reflexive verbs: встретиться (to meet) → встретившись. (having met)

E **Complete these sentences by changing the infinitive in brackets to a past gerund.**

1 _____ много квартир, мы нашли идеальную квартиру. (посмотреть)

2 Мы закажем еду, _____ номер хорошего ресторана по интернету. (узнать)

3 _____ ключ от нового дома, мы выпили шампанское. (получить)

4 Маша вернулась домой поздно, _____ по пути. (заблудиться)

5 Степан поспешил домой, _____ все нужные покупки на вечер. (сделать)

6 _____ с родственниками, мы сели в самолёт. (проститься)

F **Make these sentences into a single sentence with an appropriate gerund from the underlined verb.**

Пример: Мы посмотрели много квартир. После этого мы нашли идеальную квартиру.
→ Посмотрев много квартир, мы нашли идеальную квартиру.

1 Мы получили паспорта. Благодаря этому, мы можем уехать, когда хотим.

_____

2 Я устраиваюсь на новую работу. Каждый день я узнаю много нового.

_____

3 Мы должны были жить без кухни две недели. Мы ужинали в разных ресторанах.

_____

4 Женя купит новый телевизор. Женя посоветовался с соседями.

_____

5 Анна с Борисом прожили три года за границей. Они решили вернуться на родину.

_____

6 Сергей заполнил все нужные документы для интересного поста в Париже. Сергей получит приглашение на интервью.

_____

Not all verbs have a **present gerund**, especially if they are short. Notable examples are: есть (to eat), пить (to drink), мочь (to be able to) and хотеть (to want). There are also a few verbs that do not have a **past gerund**, most notably смочь (to be able to). The **past gerund** is normally only used in written Russian.

Meaning and usage

Personal pronouns

1   Two more pronouns can be used when talking about yourself in Russian: себя and сам. These can both be translated by the English *oneself*:

считать себя хорошим гостем   (to consider **oneself** a good guest)

сам найти новую квартиру   (to find a new flat **oneself**)

How to form personal pronouns

G   **Using your knowledge of grammar, complete the table.**

		Masculine	Feminine	Neuter	Plural
Nominative	–	сам	сама	само	сами
Accusative (inanimate/animate)	себя	сам/самого	саму	_____	сами/самих
Genitive	_____	самого	самой	_____	самих
Dative	себе	_____	_____	_____	_____
Instrumental	собой	самим	_____	_____	_____
Prepositional	_____	самом	_____	_____	_____

1   The **reflexive pronoun** себя can mean *myself/yourself*, etc. It has no nominative form.

2   Remember that **reflexive verbs** in Russian are able to translate any actions that the subject of the verb does directly to themselves, e.g. я просыпаюсь = *I wake (myself) up* and you do not need to add себя, because the **reflexive suffix** -ся/-сь is simply an abbreviated form of себя.

3   Because **reflexive verbs** are used more widely in Russian than in English and are often translated using the passive in English, себя is used in Russian to stress your **own** involvement:

Михаил Иванович считается хорошим начальником.

(*Mikhail Ivanovich is considered a good boss.*)

Михаил Иванович считает себя хорошим начальником.

(*Mikhail Ivanovich considers himself to be a good boss.*)

4 You also use **себя** when you need to refer back to the subject of a clause and the verb takes a case other than the accusative or requires a preposition:

Маша купила себе новый диван.   *(Masha bought (for) herself a new sofa.)*

Степан посмотрел на себя в зеркало.   *(Stepan looked at himself in the mirror.)*

H **Complete the sentences with the appropriate form of себя and translate them.**

    1   Наташа хорошо чувствует _____ в Канаде.

    2   Ивановы взяли с _____ собаку, когда они уехали.

    3   Маша никогда не думала о _____.

    4   Соседи пригласили нас к _____ на ужин.

    5   Николаю было удобно у _____ на даче.

    6   Игорь ругал _____, забыв важную папку.

5 **Сам** is used for emphasis to mean *myself/yourself*, etc. More often than not, it is used in the nominative:

Ирина хочет <u>сама</u> выбрать, когда начать работу за границей.

(Irina wants to choose herself when to start working abroad.)

Мы понимаем, потому что нам <u>самим</u> было плохо сразу после переезда.

(We understand because we ourselves felt bad straight after moving.)

I **Add сам to the following sentences to make them more emphatic.**

    1   Николай нашёл работу без проблем.

      _____

    2   Мы оставили бабушку на даче, так как она не хотела поехать с нами.

      _____

    3   Если прочтёшь весь отчёт, Ира, ты увидишь, что я прав!

      _____

    4   Посмотри на все варианты и решай.

      _____

    5   Дети были в Лондоне, где была королева.

      _____

    6   Почтальон сказал, что отдаст письмо только тебе, Виктор.

      _____

J   Find words from the box that match these definitions.

зарпл**а**та	*(salary)*
им**у**щество	*(property)*
об**ы**чай	*(custom)*
переступ**а**ть/ переступ**и**ть зак**о**н	*(to break the law)*
сос**е**д	*(neighbour)*
удивл**я**ться/удив**и**ться	*(to be surprised)*

1 трад**и**ция   _____

2 д**е**ньги, опл**а**чиваемые за раб**о**ту   _____

3 то, что принадлеж**и**т теб**е**   _____

4 получ**и**ть сюрпр**и**з   _____

5 тот, кто живёт р**я**дом   _____

6 соверш**и**ть нелег**а**льный акт   _____

📖 Reading

K   Read the beginning of this article about temporarily living and working as an expatriate and answer the question that follows in Russian.

> «Вр**е**менная эмигр**а**ция» м**о**жет оказ**а**ться отл**и**чным в**ы**бором, хот**я** **э**то д**е**ло иногд**а** сл**о**жное: у ког**о**-то он**а** пол**у**чится без пробл**е**м, а ком**у**-то возм**о**жно, пож**и**в н**е**которое вр**е**мя за рубеж**о**м, зах**о**чется скор**е**е верн**у**ться из чуж**о**й стран**ы**. Т**о**лько с**и**льные и ст**о**йкие л**ю**ди ум**е**ют постр**о**ить вр**е**менно сво**ю** жизнь далек**о** от р**о**дины, д**е**лая н**о**вую карь**е**ру **и**ли осн**о**вывая усп**е**шный б**и**знес.

Что н**у**жно для тог**о**, чт**о**бы сум**е**ть усп**е**шно пож**и**ть за гран**и**цей?

_____

_____

L Now read the rest of the article and answer the questions that follow in Russian.

Если вы дерзаете расширить свой кругозор, действительно желаете пожить за рубежом, то следует заранее согласиться на долгую и тщательную подготовку. Надо следить за оформлением документов, следует основательно изучать язык, найти работу и узнать о чужих правилах и обычаях жизни. Перед принятием окончательного решения о переезде за границу надо обязательно адекватно взвесить все преимущества и недостатки той жизни, которую вы хотите жить, а также продумать ваши реальные возможности найти там стабильную работу, не забывая, что не существует «идеальной» страны. В каждом обществе есть свои специфические черты, с которыми необходимо смириться, чтобы пожить комфортно.

Пожив на родине, человек может выбрать временную эмиграцию в надежде значительных перемен к лучшему. Многих привлекают к временной эмиграции значительный экономический выигрыш и экологически чистая и привлекательная местность. Но только на время, так как любовь к родине сильна и в, конце концов, непреодолима.

Временная эмиграция — путь к лучшей и интересной жизни. Пожить и поработать за рубежом – это не короткое путешествие туристом, когда всё ново, привлекательно и красиво. Работая в стране можно узнать жизнь со стороны, которую не видят туристы. Намереваясь жить и работать в выбранной стране, эмигрант должен быть готов ко всем трудностям, чтобы успех был гарантирован. Важно то, с кем вы едете. Присутствие родных или надёжных друзей поможет быстрее справиться с любыми возможными проблемами.

дерзать/дерзнуть	to dare
непреодолимый	insurmountable
справляться/справиться с + instr	to cope with

1 Как надо подготовиться к «временной эмиграции»?

_____

_____

2 Почему можно сказать, что не существует «идеальной» страны?

_____

_____

3 По какой причине такая эмиграция окажется только «временной»?

_____

_____

4 Чем отлича**е**тся **о**пыт тур**и**ста от **о**пыта «вр**е**менного эмигр**а**нта»?

_____

_____

5 Кто м**о**жет сыгр**а**ть ос**о**бенно в**а**жную роль в усп**е**хе «вр**е**менного эмигр**а**нта»?

_____

_____

M **Find five different gerunds in the text and give the infinitive.**

_____   _____

_____   _____

_____   _____

_____   _____

_____   _____

Vocabulary

N **These are some common Russian expressions that contain gerunds. Match them with the English.**

1 благодар**я**	**a** including
2 вкюч**а**я	**b** without hurrying
3 исключ**а**я	**c** judging by
4 кор**о**че говор**я**	**d** thanks to
5 не спеш**а**	**e** in short
6 с**у**дя по	**f** excluding

O **Find the English equivalent in the box for the following words.**

self-respect	self-discipline	self-service	self-analysis	independence	self-defence

1 самоан**а**лиз _____

2 самосто**я**тельность _____

3 самодисципл**и**на _____

4 самозащ**и**та _____

5 самоуваж**е**ние _____

6 самообсл**у**живание _____

# Writing

P Imagine that your job requires you to live in different countries. Write a blog about your experiences and plans for your next posting, covering the following points in about 100 words in Russian.

▶ Что вы узнали во время пребывания за рубежом?

▶ Рекомендуете ли вы места, где вы уже жили?

▶ Какие у вас приоритеты в поиске нового места жительства?

▶ Какие новые опыты интересуют вас?

_____

_____

_____

_____

_____

_____

_____

_____

Self-check

Tick the box which matches your level of confidence.

1 = very confident   2 = need more practice   3 = not too confident

Как вы думаете? Вы хорошо понимаете? Поставьте галочку:

1 = хорошо   2 = нужно больше практики   3 = нехорошо

	1	2	3
Understand how to form and when to use present and past gerunds			
Understand a complex text about living abroad			
Able to use a range of specialized vocabulary to write about past experiences and future plans			

Unit 1

A

1 c   **2** b   **3** b   **4** a   **5** b   **6** c

B

1 Шёл дождь, а Ив**а**н заб**ы**л <u>з**о**нтик</u>. (masc. sing. inanimate acc.)

2 **А**нна д**о**лго иск**а**ла <u>дочь</u>. (fem. sing. acc.)

3 Проф**е**ссор ув**и**дел <u>студ**е**нтов</u>. (masc. pl. animate acc.)

4 На день рожд**е**ния Бор**и**с куп**и**л <u>карт**и**ну</u>. (fem. sing. acc.)

5 У мен**я** в с**у**мке пл**а**тье. (neuter sing. nom.)

6 Ты в**и**дел в магаз**и**не <u>сувен**и**ры</u>? (masc. pl. acc.)

C

1 Да, у мен**я** есть ш**о**рты.

2 Да, у мен**я** есть куп**а**льник.

3 Нет, я не заб**ы**л св**и**тер.

4 Нет, у мен**я** нет футб**о**лки.

5 Нет, у мен**я** нет пиджак**а**.

6 Нет, у мен**я** нет пл**а**тья.

D

Блин**ы** с твор**о**гом	У мен**я** есть …	Ск**о**лько у мен**я** есть?
молок**о** – 500 мл	молок**о** – бут**ы**лка (500 мл)	дост**а**точно молок**а**
яйца – 3	**я**йца (кор**о**бка – 10)	дост**а**точно яиц
мук**а** – 280 г	мук**а** – 270 г	недост**а**точно мук**и**
с**а**хар	–	нет с**а**хара
соль – 5 г	соль – п**а**чка	дост**а**точно с**о**ли
м**а**сло – 15 г	м**а**сло – п**а**чка	дост**а**точно м**а**сла
смет**а**на – 100 г	смет**а**на – б**а**нка (100 г)	дост**а**точно смет**а**ны
твор**о**г – 200 г	твор**о**г – полкил**о**	дост**а**точно твор**о**га

E

Он должен сделать покупки, но он забывает список дома.

F

1   потому, что не было салата.

2   Ещё он купил бутылку водки, 250 грамм ветчины, несколько помидоров и немного колбасы. Также шоколадный торт, банку икры, и блины.

3   Нет, у них нет масла.

4   Надо купить пачку соли.

G

1   капуста

2   водка

3   ветчина

4   помидоры

5   колбаса

6   шоколадный торт

7   икра

8   блины

9   молоко

10 соль

H

1   <u>бутылка</u>   вина

2   <u>плитка</u>   шоколада

3   <u>коробка</u>   конфет

4   <u>пачка</u>   чая

5   <u>банка</u>   икры

6   <u>кило</u>   мяса

I

1 блузка, майка, футболка, джинсы

2 пальто, купальник, пиджак, шуба

3 икра, капуста, салат, картошка

4 сахар, шоколад, морковь, торт

5 вино, водка, лимонад, пиво

J

1 b   2 c   3 a   4 b   5 c

K

Model answer

> Привет! Это Иван. Я в новом гастрономе на улице Мира. Здесь хороший выбор колбас. Покупаю 250 грамм докторской!

> Пошёл я в универмаг – хочу купить пару рубашек. Как вы думаете? Мне больше идёт голубой цвет или розовый?

> Нет ничего лучшего в этом городе, чем наш местный магазин «Вино»! Покупаю три бутылки красного, две бутылки белого и одну бутылку розе.

> Нужен хороший торт. Лучше всего купить праздничный, со свежими сливками. Сколько можно потратить? И сколько нужно пирожных?

> Всегда забываю овощи на салаты! Куплю полкило моркови, 200 грамм лука, кило картофеля и банку солёных огурцов.

> Наконец-то пришёл в универсам. Надо купить безалкогольные напитки, но я забыл, что кому нравится. Сообщите, друзья – куплю на ваши заказы!

Unit 2

A

1 Тур**и**сты пр**о**бовали р**у**сскую ед**у** <u>в рестор**а**не</u>. *(The tourists tried Russian food in a restaurant.)*

2 М**о**жно всегд**а** куп**и**ть вк**у**сные бутербр**о**ды <u>в аэропорт**у**</u>. *(You can always buy tasty sandwiches at an airport.)*

3 **А**нна и Бор**и**с заказ**а**ли <u>г**о**стю</u> р**у**сский борщ. *(Anna and Boris ordered for their guest some Russian borshch.)*

4 <u>Муз**е**й</u> нах**о**дится <u>в зд**а**нии</u> в ц**е**нтре г**о**рода. *(There is a museum in a building in the centre of town.)*

5 <u>Официа́нту</u> н**а**до раб**о**тать как м**о**жно быстр**е**е. *(A waiter has to work as quickly as possible.)*

6 Так**и**е дух**и** нр**а**вятся <u>ж**е**нщине</u> в Росс**и**и. *(A woman in Russia likes perfume like this.)*

B

1 Студ**е**нту нр**а**вится п**и**цца.

2 Бор**и**с лю**ю**бит пельм**е**ни.

3 **А**нне н**а**до раб**о**тать сег**о**дня.

4 Гост**я**м гост**и**ницы м**о**жно **у**жинать в рестор**а**не на п**е**рвом этаж**е**.

5 Франц**у**зам нр**а**вятся круасс**а**ны на з**а**втрак.

6 В рестор**а**не нам нельз**я** кур**и**ть.

C

1 Бефстр**о**ганов с карт**о**шкой

2 Р**ы**ба с овощ**а**ми

3 Шн**и**цель с вермишел**ь**ю

4 Блин**ы** с гриб**а**ми

5 Котл**е**ты по-к**и**евски с карт**о**фелем-фри

6 Пельм**е**ни со свин**и**ной

D

1 Бор**и**с интерес**у**ется м**у**зыкой.

2 **А**нна раб**о**тает врач**о**м.

3 Студ**е**нты ст**а**нут инжен**е**рами.

4 Икр**а** счит**а**ется деликат**е**сом.

5 **Э**то блю**до** явл**я**ется шед**е**вром.

6 Ив**а**н увлек**а**ется кулинар**и**ей.

E

Ресtор**а**н нах**о**дится в прекр**а**сном зд**а**нии в живоп**и**сном ст**а**ром г**о**роде.

F

1 Он**и** в**ы**брали ресtор**а**н «Луч», потом**у** что одном**у** др**у**гу рекомендов**а**ли **э**тот ресtор**а**н.

2 Бор**и**су б**ы**ло **о**чень хорош**о**, потом**у** что ем**у** **о**чень понр**а**вился ланч.

3 Серг**е**й д**у**мал, что офици**а**нты не интересов**а**лись клие**н**тами, а занимал**ись** сво**и**ми смартф**о**нами.

4 Он заказ**а**л блин**ы** с карт**о**шкой и с кап**у**стой, но ем**у** не понр**а**вилось, потом**у** что блин**ы** б**ы**ли с кап**у**стой и с ветчин**о**й.

G

суп с гриб**а**ми, пельм**е**ни со смет**а**ной, шн**и**цель с карт**о**фелем-фри, к**у**рица с овощ**а**ми, блин**ы** с карт**о**шкой, Бефстр**о**ганов, сал**а**т с гриб**а**ми, блин**ы** с кап**у**стой, блин**ы** с ветчин**о**й, омл**е**т с с**ы**ром, лапш**а** с р**ы**бой.

Examples of some possible choices, with reasons:

*Ед**а***	*Заказ**а**ть?*	*Почем**у**?*
суп с гриб**а**ми	☑	Мне нр**а**вятся гриб**ы**
пельм**е**ни со смет**а**ной	☒	Я не любл**ю** смет**а**ну
шн**и**цель с карт**о**фелем-фри	☒	Я не ем м**я**со – я вегетари**а**нец /вегетари**а**нка

H

1 омл**е**т без с**ы**ра ⇨ сыр ⇨ омл**е**т с с**ы**ром

2 суп без гриб**о**в ⇨ гриб**ы** ⇨ суп с гриб**а**ми

3 к**у**рица без кап**у**сты ⇨ кап**у**ста ⇨ к**у**рица с кап**у**стой

4 пельм**е**ни без свин**и**ны ⇨ свин**и**на ⇨ пельм**е**ни со свин**и**ной

5 котл**е**ты без карт**о**феля-фри ⇨ карт**о**фель-фри ⇨ котл**е**ты с карт**о**фелем-фри

6 чай без с**а**хара ⇨ с**а**хар ⇨ чай с с**а**харом

I

1 специ**а**льность

2 гарн**и**р

3 рекомендов**а**ть

4 б**и**знес-ланч

5 кошм**а**р!

6 кли**е**нт

J

прекр**а**сный + уж**а**сный
т**и**хий + ш**у**мный
б**ы**стрый + м**е**дленный
традици**о**нный + соврем**е**нный

K

Model answer

Мы с семьёй ход**и**ли в ресторан «Луч» в пр**о**шлую субб**о**ту, потом**у** что был**а** годовщ**и**на свадьбы н**а**ших род**и**телей. Нам б**ы**ло хорош**о**, но нам не понр**а**вилось то, что был плох**о**й в**ы**бор вегетари**а**нских блюд.

Мы заказ**а**ли салат с помид**о**рами на зак**у**ску, борщ на п**е**рвое, бифшт**е**кс с овощ**а**ми на втор**о**е и шокол**а**дный торт на сладкое. П**а**па – вегетари**а**нец и интерес**у**ется вегетари**а**нской к**у**хней, но в мен**ю** ресто**а**на б**ы**ло т**о**лько одн**о** бл**ю**до: омл**е**т с с**ы**ром, и ему не нр**а**вится сыр.

П**а**па заказ**а**л прост**о**й омл**е**т, но б**ы**ло невк**у**сно. Нам показ**а**лось, что н**а**ша ед**а** был**а** вк**у**сная и не сл**и**шком дорог**а**я.

Мы рекоменд**у**ем ресторан «Луч», потом**у** что там хор**о**шая атмосф**е**ра, в**е**жливые официа**а**нты и хор**о**ший в**ы**бор блюд – **е**сли т**о**лько ты не вегетари**а**нец!

Unit 3

A

1 Её

2 Она

3 меня

4 ней

5 Ей

6 нём

B

1 Борис знаком с ней. The original noun was feminine, in the instrumental case and singular.

2 Что ты даришь ей на день рождения? The original noun was feminine, in the dative case and singular.

3 У него есть сестра? The original noun was masculine, in the genitive case and singular.

4 Они разговаривали о них. The original noun was plural and in the prepositional case.

5 Он стоял перед Галей в очереди. The original noun was masculine, in the nominative case and singular.

6 Мы видели их в центре города. The original noun was plural, in the accusative case and animate.

C

	Masculine	Feminine	Neuter	Plural
Nominative	твой	твоя	твоё	твои
Accusative (inanimate/ animate)	твой/твоего	твою	твоё	твои/твоих
Genitive	твоего	твоей	твоего	твоих
Dative	твоему	твоей	твоему	твоим
Instrumental	твоим	твоей	твоим	твоими
Prepositional	о твоём	о твоей	о твоём	о твоих

D

	Masculine	Feminine	Neuter	Plural
Nominative	ваш	ваша	ваше	ваши
Accusative (inanimate/ animate)	ваш/вашего	вашу	ваше	ваши/ваших
Genitive	вашего	вашей	вашего	ваших
Dative	вашему	вашей	вашему	вашим
Instrumental	вашим	вашей	вашим	вашими
Prepositional	о вашем	о вашей	о вашем	о ваших

E

1 **Э**то <u>мой</u> брат и <u>мо**я**</u> сестр**а**.

2 Это <u>твой</u> друг и <u>тво**я**</u> подр**у**га?

3 Ты зн**а**ешь, где <u>ег**о**</u> **о**фис?

4 Мы не заб**ы**ли ни <u>н**а**ши</u> паспорт**а** ни <u>н**а**ши</u> бил**е**ты.

5 <u>Её</u> дом нах**о**дится недалек**о** от <u>её</u> род**и**телей.

6 Я ув**и**дел <u>их</u> маш**и**ну п**е**ред <u>их</u> д**о**мом.

7 Вчер**а** я познак**о**мился с <u>в**а**шей</u> б**а**бушкой.

F

1 мо**я** плем**я**нница

2 мой тесть

3 мо**я** свекр**о**вь

4 мо**я** м**а**чеха

5 мой **о**тчим

G

1 Я давн**о** не встреч**а**лся с мо**и**м двою**ю**родным бр**а**том.

2 К сожал**е**нию, не мог прийт**и** мой люб**и**мый плем**я**нник.

3 Мой **о**тчим сов**е**товал мне мн**о**го не пить!

4 Я получ**и**л уж**а**сный под**а**рок от св**о**дного бр**а**та.

5 Мой б**у**дущий ш**у**рин расск**а**зывал мн**о**го интер**е**сного о сестр**е**.

6 Д**а**же мой д**е**душка танцев**а**л на стол**е**!

H

1 c   **2** c   **3** b   **4** b   **5** a   **6** b

I

Он предприниматель, промышленник и фабрикант.

J

1 Отец Николая – инженер, и мать – врач.

2 На заводе уральских сувениров в Перми.

3 В 2002 году, потому что он стал совладельцем фабрики на севере Китая.

4 Зимой в Китае, в Тянджине, весной и осенью в Москве, а летом на юге Испании.

K

Я родился в Ларигубе, в семье инженера Михаила и врача Елизаветы. Моя семья переехала в Москву, и я учился в московской школе № 192, математической спецшколе. Особенно понравились мне уроки по экономике. В 1987 году я поступил на экономический факультет МГУ. Я окончил МГУ с красным дипломом, и распределили меня работать на завод уральских сувениров в Перми.

Моя профессиональная деятельность началась после распада СССР. Скоро после окончания второго года работы в Перми, я решил вернуться к своей семье в Москву и основать свой бизнес по производству сувениров и художественных изделий. Мой настоящий успех начался с 2002 года, когда я стал совладельцем фабрики на севере Китая. В финансировании этого дела мне помогли тесть и тёща, и моя свояченица стала моей заместительницей.

Я встретился с будущей супругой, Ириной, в 1994 году во время работы в комитете молодых московских предпринимателей. Мы поженились в 1998 году. Родился сын (2001), дочь (2004), сын (2007). Мой шурин Алексей Родионов – известный художник – заинтересовался моей компанией, и мы вместе разработали новый набор матрёшек для производства на китайской фабрике, которой Родионов стал совладельцем со мной. Зимой мы с семьёй живём в Тянджине, весной и осенью в Москве, а летом на юге Испании.

L

1 дедушка

2 деверь (could also be тёща, as this is the only feminine noun)

3 свояченица

4 племянница

5 племянник

M

1 м**а**тери

2 с**ё**стры

3 бр**а**тья

4 отц**ы**

5 б**а**бушки

6 д**о**чери

7 сыновь**я**

8 д**я**ди

N

1 жен**а**

2 м**а**тери

3 мать

4 ег**о**

5 м**у**жа

6 сестр**а**

O

Model answer

Джон Смит род**и**лся в 1984-ом год**у,** в м**а**леньком г**о**роде на с**е**вере Великобрит**а**нии. Род**и**тели ег**о**, Эду**а**рд и Дж**е**ннифер, р**а**ньше ж**и**ли на вост**о**ке **А**нглии, а пере**е**хали на с**е**вер, когд**а** Эду**а**рд устр**о**ился на раб**о**ту на н**о**вом зав**о**де в приг**о**роде г**о**рода.

Молод**о**й Джон отлич**а**лся сво**и**м музык**а**льным тал**а**нтом с кр**а**йне р**а**ннего в**о**зраста. Он впервы**е** н**а**чал игр**а**ть на пиан**и**но в гост**я**х у сво**е**го д**е**душки. Ег**о** д**е**душка перед**а**л вн**у**ку люб**о**вь к класс**и**ческой м**у**зыке. Смит поступ**и**л в музык**а**льную шк**о**лу и пот**о**м в университ**е**т на к**а**федру др**е**вней м**у**зыки.

Смит н**а**чал пис**а**ть сво**ю** м**у**зыку уж**е** на п**е**рвом к**у**рсе в университ**е**те, и он стал изв**е**стным композ**и**тором, когд**а** ег**о** в**ы**брали напис**а**ть м**у**зыку для голлив**у**дского ф**и**льма.

Смит жен**а**т на Мар**и**и, профессион**а**льной **о**перной пев**и**це; у них дв**о**е дет**е**й (сын, дочь); семь**я** жив**ё**т **о**коло Л**о**ндона.

Unit 4

A

	Masculine	Feminine	Neuter	Plural
Nominative	ма́ленький	ма́ленькая	ма́ленькое	ма́ленькие
Accusative (inanimate/ animate)	ма́ленький/ого	ма́ленькую	ма́ленькое	ма́ленькие/их
Genitive	ма́ленького	ма́ленькой	ма́ленького	ма́леньких
Dative	ма́ленькому	ма́ленькой	ма́ленькому	ма́леньким
Instrumental	ма́леньким	ма́ленькой	ма́леньким	ма́ленькими
Prepositional	о ма́леньком	о ма́ленькой	о ма́леньком	о ма́леньких

B

	Masculine	Feminine	Neuter	Plural
Nominative	си́ний	си́няя	си́нее	си́ние
Accusative (inanimate/ animate)	си́ний/его	си́нюю	си́нее	си́ние/их
Genitive	си́него	си́ней	си́него	си́них
Dative	си́нему	си́ней	си́нему	си́ним
Instrumental	си́ним	си́ней	си́ним	си́ними
Prepositional	о си́нем	о си́ней	о си́нем	о си́них

C

1 c   2 c   3 b   4 a   5 c   6 a

D

1 мо́дные

2 жёлтых

3 шерстяно́го

4 ко́жаный

5 си́ней

6 ора́нжевую

E

1 дороги́е магази́ны

2 дешёвые це́ны

3 лёгкое пальто́

4 мо́дные ту́фли

5 шёлковые носки́

6 роско́шных шарфо́в

F

1 Мои туфли малы.

2 Моя любимая юбка – лиловая.

3 Мы довольны новой одеждой.

4 Пиджак – красив!

5 Они были готовы купить дорогую шубу.

6 Брюки были малы.

G

Я вижу жёлтые вьетнамки, но у меня нет красных шорт.

Я вижу летний пиджак, но у меня нет нового купальника.

Я вижу солнечные очки, но у меня нет лёгкой куртки.

Я вижу удобную футболку, но у меня нет шёлкового платка.

Я вижу модную шляпу, но у меня нет белой майки.

H

В красивом и элегантном здании, недалеко от Кремля в Москве.

I

1 Интересный галстук контрастного цвета нужен для «лучшей комбинации».

2 Он не согласен с советами этого показа моды, потому что он не работает в офисе.

3 Когда выбираешь аксессуары, они все должны быть пропорциональны росту.

4 Она думает, что рекомендованные цвета для женщин – старомодны.

J

1 юбка

2 белый

3 джинсы

4 шорты

5 старомодный

K

1 новый → новость

2 модный → мода

3 традиционный → традиция

4 весенний → весна

5 элегантный → элегантность

6 кожаный → кожа

L

Model answer

Каждый день я ношу тёмный костюм, белую блузку и туфли на низком каблуке. Я выбираю такую одежду, потому что у меня ответственная работа, и я думаю, что надо одеваться, чтобы выглядеть профессионально.

Когда я выходила вечером в прошлый раз, это было, чтобы пойти в театр. Значит, я была в длинном вечернем платье, в шубе и в туфлях на высоких каблуках. По-моему, такая формальная и элегантная одежда нужна для выхода в театр.

Для меня, кошмарная одежда – это спортивный костюм с белыми кроссовками. На мой взгляд, такая одежда выглядит некрасиво, тем более потому, что я совсем не спортивный человек.

Мне кажется, что практичная, но модная и элегантная одежда – идеальна. Например, кофта и брюки, вместе с лёгкой курткой.

Unit 5

A

Самый is the equivalent in English of *most* and works like an adjective.

B

1 самый популярный фильм

2 самой полезной передачи по кулинарии

3 самым знаменитым телеведущим

4 самым оригинальным боевикам

5 самом надёжном вебсайте

6 лучшую газету

C

Более is the equivalent in English of *more* and never changes its spelling.

D

1 более интересные

2 лучшую

3 более оригинальные

4 более успешным

5 худшее

6 более современную

E

1 длинн**ее**

2 крас**и**вее

3 информат**и**внее

4 пр**о**ще

5 быстр**ее**

6 деш**е**вле

F

ДВД Ф**и**льма Б ст**о**ит дор**о**же, чем ДВД Ф**и**льма В, но с**а**мый дорог**о**й ДВД – Ф**и**льма А. Фильм Б ст**а**рше, чем Фильм А, но с**а**мый ст**а**рый фильм – Фильм В. Фильм В л**у**чше, чем Фильм А, но л**у**чший фильм – Фильм Б. Ст**о**имость произв**о**дства Ф**и**льма Б дор**о**же, чем ст**о**имость произв**о**дства Ф**и**льма В, но с**а**мая дорог**а**я ст**о**имость произв**о**дства – Ф**и**льма А. Фильм В усп**е**шнее, чем Фильм А, но с**а**мый усп**е**шный фильм – Фильм Б.

G

1 СМИ

2 ск**а**чивать/скач**а**ть

3 стать**я**

4 знамен**и**тость

5 телевед**у**щий

6 соци**а**льные с**е**ти

H

Нет, своб**о**дная пр**е**сса не существов**а**ла при цар**и**зме, потом**у** что был**а** ценз**у**ра.

I

1 Главл**и**т был с**о**здан, чт**о**бы отвеч**а**ть за пол**и**тику госуд**а**рства в отнош**е**нии ценз**у**ры.

2 В СССР госуд**а**рство дав**а**ло разреш**е**ние на публ**и**чные зр**е**лища.

3 Запрет**и**ли ценз**у**ру в Росс**и**и в декабр**е** 1993 г**о**да.

4 Раб**о**тать журнал**и**стом в Росс**и**и сейч**а**с не легк**о** и стан**о**вится всё трудн**ее** и трудн**ее**.

5 Кр**о**ме телев**и**дения и традици**о**нной пр**е**ссы, в Росс**и**и м**о**жно получ**а**ть информ**а**цию из интерн**е**т-рес**у**рсов, бл**о**гов и с**о**цсет**е**й.

J

самой жестокой – dative – most severe, более современной – genitive – more contemporary, самых скромных – genitive – most modest, более существенные – accusative – more substantial/significant , свободнее – nominative – freer, более косвенным – instrumental – more oblique, всё труднее и труднее – nominative – harder and harder, лучшим – instrumental – best, самым надёжным – instrumental – most reliable.

K

1	хуже	4	труднее
2	дешевле	5	моложе
3	скучнее	6	ближе

L

Possible example sentences:

1 По-моему, смотреть телевизор увлекательнее, чем слушать радио.

2 Мне кажется, что ходить в кино лучше, чем смотреть фильм на ДВД.

3 Я считаю, что смотреть крикет по телевизору интереснее, чем общаться с друзьями по интернету.

4 На мой взгляд, легче звонить по телефону чем встречаться, а легче всего – посылать СМС.

5 По моему мнению мой компьютер полезный, а мой смартфон полезнее, но самый полезный – мой планшет.

6 Я думаю, что газета – хороший источник информации, а вебсайт быстрее, но новости по телевизору – лучше всех.

M

Possible example answers:

1 На мой взгляд, читать книгу интереснее, чем смотреть фильм.

2 Эксперты говорят, что заниматься спортом полезнее для здоровья, чем сидеть перед экраном компьютера.

3 Мои друзья думают, что смартфон удобнее, чем планшет.

4 Моя бабушка уверена, что детектив лучше, чем мыльная опера.

5 Покупать в магазине, может быть, быстрее, чем покупать онлайн.

6 Мой младший брат считает, что ленивее смотреть телевизор весь день, чем играть в компьютерные игры весь день.

N

Model answer

Меня зовут Эдуард Джонс. Я – тридцатилетний мужчина. Мой день рождения 15-го августа. Больше всего мне нравятся боевики, потому что на мой взгляд они увлекательнее любых других жанров.

Я терпеть не могу спортивные передачи. По-моему, они самые скучные передачи по телевизору. Я обожаю спорт, но заниматься спортом лучше, чем лежать на диване и смотреть спорт на экране.

Когда я смотрю фильм, важнее всего для меня – история. Я считаю, что персонажи менее важные в успехе фильма, чем история. Ещё спецэффекты играют более ключевую роль, чем персонажи. Исторический период может быть интересным, а режиссёр для меня — самое незначительное.

Я считаю самым главным доступ к самым последним выпускам. Само собой разумеется, что я хочу платить самую низкую цену, но, по-моему, нет ничего хуже, чем иметь на выбор только более старые фильмы.

Unit 6

A

1 играем – We always play cards on Fridays.

2 любит – Misha does not like to go to concerts.

3 смотрите – Which programmes do you watch with your children?

4 читают – Russians often read foreign literature.

5 получать; предпочитаю – I hate to receive (receiving) emails from friends; I prefer to talk to friends on the internet.

6 навещаешь – Do you often visit your family?

B

1 пью	6	люблю
2 рисует	7	моет
3 лечу	8	прошу
4 танцуют	9	видишь
5 поём	10	пробуете

C

1 мы п**и**шем

2 я **е**ду

3 Мой друг / Мо**я** подру**га** не ест

4 Вы хот**и**те

5 ид**у**т интер**е**сные ф**и**льмы

6 ты м**о**жешь

D

1 бер**у**

2 м**о**гут

3 ждёт

4 спит

5 организу**ет**

6 сид**и**т

E

	to listen	to go for a walk	to watch	to go (on foot)	to have lunch
(infinitive)	сл**у**шать	гул**я**ть	смотр**е**ть	идт**и**	об**е**дать
я	сл**у**шаю	гул**я**ю	смотр**ю**	ид**у**	об**е**даю
ты	сл**у**шаешь	гул**я**ешь	см**о**тришь	идёшь	об**е**даешь
он/она	сл**у**шает	гул**я**ет	см**о**трит	идёт	об**е**дает
мы	сл**у**шаем	гул**я**ем	см**о**трим	идём	об**е**даем
вы	сл**у**шаете	гул**я**ете	см**о**трите	идёте	об**е**даете
они	сл**у**шают	гул**я**ют	см**о**трят	ид**у**т	об**е**дают

F

Н**а**до принима**ть** уч**а**стие в **э**том опр**о**се, потом**у** что на осн**о**ве **э**тих д**а**нных см**о**гут рекомендов**а**ть м**е**стным власт**я**м как**и**е возм**о**жности для **о**тдыха н**у**жно развив**а**ть в н**а**шем г**о**роде.

G

1 Т**а**ня л**ю**бит свой планш**е**т, потом**у** что по вечер**а**м он помог**а**ет ей отдых**а**ть.

2 Т**а**ня **е**здит в центр г**о**рода по выходн**ы**м, чт**о**бы ход**и**ть в кин**о** **и**ли в ресто**ра**н.

3 Т**а**ня нах**о**дит н**о**вые рец**е**пты по интерн**е**ту.

4 Л**ю**да л**ю**бит телесери**а**лы потом**у**, что он**и** – крас**и**вы и интер**е**сны.

5 Мы зн**а**ем, что Л**ю**да хорош**о** игр**а**ет в триктр**а**к потом**у**, что в **э**том год**у** он**а** – чемпи**о**нка в областн**ы**х соревнов**а**ниях.

H

In this reading passage the personal pronouns are often omitted before the verbs, which is a feature of an informal style of writing.

I

Надо построить кинотеатр и рестораны в районе, чтобы людям не надо было ездить в город чтобы смотреть фильм или ужинать в хорошем ресторане. Важно иметь зал, где пожилые люди могут встречаться и играть, например, в триктрак.

J

1	Я плаваю.	4	Я играю.
2	Иван поёт.	5	Ты бегаешь.
3	Они читают.	6	Мы рисуем.

K

1	любят есть	4	любит петь
2	любим брать	5	люблю писать
3	любите ждать	6	не любишь мыть

L

1 соцсети

2 рецепты

3 ужинаем

M

Model answer

Привет! Мы с мужем пошли в театр, потому что это мой день рождения. Это класс – пьеса очень знаменитая, хотя наши места не очень удобны, и сцена иногда плохо видна.

Мама с папой дома – они смотрят за нашими детьми, пока мы выходим. Я надеюсь, что бабушка с дедушкой читают внуку и внучке. Наши сын и дочь обожают сказки.

Погода на этой неделе неплохая. Вчера дул ветер, и позавчера шёл дождь, а сегодня солнце светит, и довольно тепло. Завтра обещают облачную погоду, но не прохладную.

Мы рекомендуем ходить в этот театр. Он старый, а репертуар интересный, и актёры хорошо исполняют целый ряд русских и зарубежных классиков. Билеты стоят недорого.

Unit 7

A

The verbs all end in -сь or -ся; this gives them a reflexive meaning – i.e. doing an action to oneself.

B

1 начин**а**ется – My day begins early.

2 умыв**а**юсь – I wash at 7 o'clock.

3 причёсываюсь – I brush my hair in front of the mirror.

4 просып**а**ется – He wakes up late on Sundays.

5 встреч**а**ются – They meet at the restaurant for lunch.

6 возвращ**а**етесь – You return home on the tram.

C

1 b 2 a 3 b 4 c 5 a 6 a

D

Sentence **a** is 'passive' ('Toothpaste <u>is sold</u>' in the supermarket), while sentence **b** is 'active' ('The supermarket <u>sells</u> toothpaste').

E

1 просып**а**юсь   4 приним**а**ю

2 гот**о**влю   5 одев**а**юсь

3 гот**о**вится   6 возвращ**а**юсь

F

1 Гот**о**вят **у**жин. / **У**жин гот**о**вят.

2 М**у**зыку сл**у**шают все молод**ы**е л**ю**ди по утр**а**м.

3 Ф**и**льмы всегд**а** см**о**трят мо**и** род**и**тели по вечер**а**м.

4 Кроссв**о**рды обож**а**ет мо**я** б**а**бушка.

5 М**о**ют пос**у**ду к**а**ждый день. / Пос**у**ду м**о**ют к**а**ждый день.

6 Вегетари**а**нскую ед**у** покуп**а**ю т**о**лько я в н**а**шей семь**е**.

G

Я иду в ванную и принимаю душ. Потом я одеваюсь и начинаю готовить ужин. В 06:45 я смотрю утренние новости по телевизору и потом я надеваю пальто и отправляюсь на работу. Я сажусь в трамвай и еду в центр города. Я начинаю работать в 8 часов утра и заканчиваю работать в 6 часов вечера. Вечером я возвращаюсь домой и ужинаю. Обычно я ложусь спать довольно поздно, в два часа ночи. Я засыпаю в спальне и крепко сплю до утра.

H

Слава пишет мне, чтобы рассказать о жизни за границей.

I

1 Слава удивляется началу рабочего дня за рубежом, потому что это так рано.

2 Он думает, что заседания на завтрак для него непривычны.

3 Он считает конец рабочего дня неудобным, потому что почта и многие другие заведения закрываются намного раньше, чем в России.

4 Когда он в России обычно по пути домой он заходит на рынок и покупает всё, что нужно на вечер.

5 Нет. За рубежом часто разогревают уже готовое блюдо из морозильника, а он скучает немного по свежей русской кухней.

J

Model answer

В России Слава начинает работать около десяти, а мне, как Славе за границей, надо быть на работе к восьми часам. В России Слава иногда ест второй завтрак, а я никогда не ем второй завтрак. За границей, чаще всего Слава работает перед компьютером целый день без перерыва, а я всегда хожу в кафе в час, чтобы обедать. У нас нет столовой на работе. Для меня, как и для Славы, когда он за границей, рабочий день кончается около шести. В России, Слава ходит в магазин после работы, а я покупаю все продукты по интернету – фургон приезжает к нам каждую среду.

K

1 просыпаюсь

2 одеваешься

3 умываюсь

4 отправляются

5 причёсываетесь

6 возвращаемся

7 раздеваюсь

8 ложусь (спать)

L

1 b   2 e   3 a   4 c   5 f   6 d

M

1 засыпать

2 одеваться

3 заканчивать

4 открывать

5 ложиться

6 отправляться

N

Model answer

Когда я работаю, мой типичный день начинается рано, в 6 часов. Я встаю, принимаю душ в ванной, одеваюсь и завтракаю. Я приезжаю на работу к 8-и часам. У меня перерыв на кофе пол-одиннадцатого, и я обедаю в час. Я возвращаюсь домой к 6-и часам, и мы смотрим телевизор до 11-и часов. Мы ложимся полдвенадцатого и обычно засыпаем быстро.

На выходные мы встаём попозже, полвосьмого, и ложимся попозже тоже, в полночь или после. У нас такая же рутина во время отпуска летом, когда мы уезжаем за границу, обычно в тёплую страну, чтобы отдыхать и загорать. Зимой мы проводим отпуск дома, и нам нравится кататься на лыжах как можно больше. Тогда мы сильно устаём и ложимся спать пораньше, и встаём ещё позже.

Unit 8

A

To form the last tense, remove -ть from the infinitive and add -л if the subject is masculine singular, -ла if the subject is feminine singular, -ло if the subject is neuter singular, -ли if the subject is plural (all genders).

B

1 играл/а

2 смотрели

3 писала

4 занимались

5 танцевали

6 шёл

C

To form the future tense, use an appropriately conjugated (present tense) form of the verb быть plus an (imperfective) infinitive.

D

1 буду играть

2 будут смотреть

3 будешь писать

4 будете заниматься

5 будем танцевать

6 будет идти

E

1 Future: I will buy a ticket tomorrow.

2 Present: Masha always writes postcards on holiday.

3 Future: you will really like Moscow!

4 Present and future: I do not know what he will say.

5 Present: the guide is recounting the history of the monument.

6 Future: you will be able to buy me a Russian doll.

F

1 провож**у** – because the 'usually' and 'every day' suggest repeated action.

2 по**е**ду – because the reference to 'Wednesday' and 'my plane early in the morning' suggest a single journey.

3 скаж**у** – because the reference to 'finally' suggests that this will be a definitive statement.

4 посмотр**ю** – because the implication is that looking at information will be a brief action before, sequentially, ordering the ticket (which is a future perfective).

G

загор**а**ть – no perfective because it means the process of 'to sunbathe', and the perfective would mean something else: 'to have acquired a suntan', or 'to have caught fire'.

иск**а**ть – no perfective because it means the process of 'to look for', and the perfective would mean something else: 'to find'.

торгов**а**ться – no perfective because it means the process of 'to haggle', and the perfective would mean something else: 'to have agreed a price'.

H

An appropriate answer, based on the fact that the apartment is modern, in the town centre, in a picturesque area, near restaurants and cafés, a park and an open-air theatre.

Example answers:

Да, мен**я** интерес**у**ет **э**та кварт**и**ра, потом**у** что он**а** совреме**н**ная и нах**о**дится в ц**е**нтре г**о**рода, недалек**о** от ресто**а**нов, каф**е**, п**а**рка и те**а**тра на откр**ы**том в**о**здухе.

Нет, мен**я** не интерес**у**ет **э**та кварт**и**ра, потом**у** что он**а** нах**о**дится в ц**е**нтре г**о**рода, а я предпочит**а**ю жить за г**о**родом, в дер**е**вне.

I

1 Рейчел думает, что этот район не показался ей с мужем живописным, потому что погода была плохая.

2 Рейчел с мужем получили очень хорошее впечатление о ресторане «Сказка», потому что сервис был на высшем уровне, блюда были вкусные и всё стоило недорого, хотя в основном они нашли там только местную кулинарию.

3 Они получили хорошее впечатление о городском транспорте, потому что он работал без проблем и стоил недорого.

4 Да, была у них одна проблема в квартире, когда один стул сломался.

5 A plausible answer based on the texts, e.g.

Может быть не идеально: можно делать покупки, смотреть спектакли и отдыхать в парке, но в районе мало исторических достопримечательностей.

J

1 пишем	**8** загорали
2 идёт	**9** разговаривали
3 было	**10** веселились
4 была	**11** обещают
5 отдыхала	**12** навестим
6 плавали	**13** Будем
7 купили	**14** хотим

K

1 future

2 past

3 future

4 past

5 past

6 past, present or future, depending on context

7 future

8 past

L

Model answer

Добро пожаловать на наш блог. Мы в отпуске! Обычно, когда мы не работаем, мы или отдыхаем дома, работая в саду, например, или уезжаем в активный отдых – чтобы кататься на велосипеде, например.

В прошлый раз мы были в отпуске на Крите. Мы жили в молодёжной гостинице на берегу моря и купались и загорали каждое утро. Днём мы отдыхали в номере и вечером мы уходили в поход по острову.

В следующий отпуск мы поедем в Норвегию, чтобы посмотреть красивый ландшафт там. Мы будем жить в палатке, ездить на велосипеде и останавливаться в кемпингах по пути.

Нам нравится отдыхать зимой, но больше всего нам хорошо отдыхать летом, так как мы обожаем солнце и достаточно редко видим солнце дома!

Unit 9

A

This is the analogue method. The numbers are not quite what you expect in English, as it refers to the following hour for any time after the hour until half past the following hour.

B

1	час	первый
2	два часа	второй
3	три часа	третий
4	четыре часа	четвёртый
5	пять часов	пятый
6	шесть часов	шестой
7	семь часов	седьмой
8	восемь часов	восьмой
9	девять часов	девятый
10	десять часов	десятый
11	одиннадцать часов	одиннадцатый
12	двенадцать часов	двенадцатый

C

Five minutes of the fifth (hour); it is 5 минут because 5 is followed by the genitive plural; the genitive is used to convey *of* (пятого) and час is understood here.

D

4:10	*10 minutes of the fifth (hour)*
4:15	*a quarter of the fifth (hour)*
4:20	*20 minutes of the fifth (hour)*
4:25	*25 minutes of the fifth (hour)*
4:30	*half of the fifth (hour)*

E

4:40	*without 20 five*
4:45	*without a quarter five*
4:50	*without 10 five*
4:55	*without 5 five*

F

12:55	без пят**и** час
2:25	двадцать пять мин**у**т тр**е**тьего
6:00	шесть час**о**в
8:15	ч**е**тверть дев**я**того
9:30	полдес**я**того
11:40	без двадцат**и** двен**а**дцать

G

1 a   2 b   3 b   4 b   5 b   6 c

H

1	8:05	пять мин**у**т дев**я**того
2	11:20	дв**а**дцать мин**у**т двен**а**дцатого
3	8:45	без ч**е**тверти д**е**вять
4	10:30	полов**и**на одиннадцатого / п**о**л-одиннадцатого
5	2:25	двадцать пять мин**у**т тр**е**тьего
6	6:40	без двадцат**и** семь
7	12:10	д**е**сять мин**у**т п**е**рвого
8	1:15	ч**е**тверть втор**о**го

I

1 в де́тстве   в мо́лодости   в ста́рости

2 у́тром   днём   ве́чером   но́чью

3 ре́дко   иногда́   ча́сто   обы́чно

4 давно́   неда́вно   сейча́с

J

А́втор пи́шет о здоро́вье и дие́те и о то́м, что они́ мо́гут си́льно влия́ть на самочу́вствие и работоспосо́бность ка́ждого челове́ка.

K

1 Экспе́рты рекоменду́ют све́жие о́вощи, потому́ что све́жие о́вощи явля́ются хоро́шим исто́чником витами́нов.

2 Лу́чше бе́гать у́тром (с семи́ до восьми́ часо́в) по ле́су.

3 Нельзя́ пла́вать сра́зу по́сле обе́да – э́то разреша́ется то́лько че́рез час по́сле еды́.

4 Рекоменду́ется ложи́ться спать до полу́ночи.

L

1 отвеча́ете (отвеча́ть)   5 бе́гать

2 сове́туем (сове́товать)   6 встреча́ться

3 влия́ть   7 пла́вать

4 занима́ться

M

1 ча́сто   5 про́шлой

2 отвеча́ете (на вопро́с)   6 сла́дкое

3 си́льно   7 разреша́ется

4 по́мнить   8 здоро́вый

N

1 c   2 a   3 f   4 b   5 d   6 e

O

Model answer

Обычно я ем довольно здоровую еду и стараюсь ходить хотя бы немного каждый день. Мне нравятся курица с рисом или макароны с мясом. Я всегда хожу на работу пешком, если погода хорошая, и хожу гулять с собакой каждый вечер.

В прошлые выходные мы с друзьями ходили в ресторан в субботу и ели шницель с картофелем-фри и мороженое на сладкое. Потом мы ходили в кинотеатр и смотрели новый фильм.

В будущем, чтобы улучшить фитнес и здоровье, я намереваюсь стать членом местного фитнес-клуба. Если ходить на тренировку раза три в неделю, я уверен, что я буду чувствовать себя даже лучше. Также, я перестану покупать чипсы и пиццу так часто, потому что я знаю, что есть такую еду – не очень полезно для здоровья.

Unit 10

A

Expressions involving a verb: не светит солнце, не идёт дождь, не дует ветер.

To make the verbs negative, add не as a separate word in front of the verb.

B

1 не светит солнце

2 не тепло

3 туман

4 не было жарко

5 завтра не будет хорошая погода

6 идёт дождь

C

1 b   2 e   3 d   4 c   5 a

D

1 никогда не плаваю

2 нигде не видел

3 никуда не будем ходить

4 нигде не нашла

5 никуда не захочешь

6 Нигде не идёт

E

1 ни о чём

2 никто

3 никуда

4 ничего

5 нигде

6 никому

F

Negative adverbs beginning with ни- are followed by не and a conjugated verb, whereas negative adverbs beginning with не are always followed just by an infinitive.

G

1 н**е**чего

2 никогд**а**

3 нигде

4 н**е**где

5 никт**о**

6 некогда/н**е**куда

H

1 ураг**а**н

2 п**а**смурно

3 сос**у**лька

4 т**у**ча

5 морос**и**ть

6 некогда/шторм

I

Автор **э**той стать**и** говор**и**т о т**о**м, что клим**а**т мен**я**ется во всём м**и**ре.

J

1 Авиаци**о**нное и дор**о**жное движ**е**ние наруш**а**ется во вр**е**мя м**о**щных ураг**а**нов.

2 Наводн**е**ния и т**е**сно св**я**занные с ним **о**ползни повтор**я**ются ч**а**ще всег**о**.

3 Проливн**ы**е дожд**и** и т**а**яние сн**е**жногои покр**о**ва и ледник**о**в вызыв**а**ют наводн**е**ния и **о**ползни.

4 М**о**жно сказ**а**ть, что экстрем**а**льная пог**о**да – друг челов**е**ка, потом**у** что с**е**льское хоз**я**йство мн**о**гих троп**и**ческих стран зав**и**сит во мн**о**гом от наводн**е**ний, вызыв**а**емых мусс**о**нными дожд**я**ми.

5 С**и**льные дожд**и** стан**о**вятся проблемой при прохожд**е**нии атмосф**е**рных фронт**о**в и цикл**о**нов.

K

1 хoлод, прохлaда, теплo, жарa, сoлнечный удaр

2 дождь, мoкрый снег, снежинки, снег, вьюга

3 ветерoк, вeтер, шторм, урагaн

4 чистое нeбо, облакa, тyчи, грозa, смерч

5 кратковрeменные дожди, проливнье дожди, град, метeль

6 зaсуха, моросить, сильные дожди, наводнeние, оползень

L

Example answer: Вчерa yтром было теплo и сoлнечно. Пoсле обеда, дул вeтер, было oблачно, и не было oчень теплo.

M

Example answers:

1 Мы никудa не ходили, потомy что бьло oчень жарко.

2 Нeгде было сидeть в ресторане из-за грозы.

3 Никомy не хотeлось плaвать из-за штoрма.

4 Туристам нeкуда было eздить из-за урагaна.

5 Нам никогдa нe было скyчно, потомy что в oтпуске погoда былa хорoшая.

6 Некогда было катaться на велосипeде из-за метeли и лютого морoза.

N

Model answer

Привeт из Калифoрнии! Погoда прекрaсная: на берегy мoря сoлнце свeтит, нет облакoв и теплo. Температyра +20 и вeтер – тёплый. В горaх сoлнечно, но холоднeе и свежo!

Всё oчень хорошo: мы катaемся на льжах yтром, плaваем в мoре днём, и yжинаем в ресторaнах вeчером. Мoжно дeлать покyпки в больших торгoвых цeнтрах, и вьбор отличный!

Всё тoчно, как в брошюре. Гостиница oчень удoбная, и обслyживание в кафe и ресторaнах – бьстрое и вeжливое. Автoбусы хoдят регулярно, и легкo и недoрого нанять машину.

В слeдующем годy мы бyдем отдыхaть в Китае, потомy что говорят мнoго об этой странe. Посмoтрим, как живyт там, где, кaжется, производят все товaры в соврeменном мирe!

Unit 11

A

1 c   2 a   3 f   4 b   5 d   6 e

B

1 b   2 a   3 a   4 c   5 a   6 b

C

из + gen., с + gen.
в + acc., на + acc.
из + gen., с + gen., в + acc., на + acc.
в + acc., на + acc., через + acc., к + dat., по + dat.
мимо + gen., через + acc., в + acc., на + acc.
в + acc., на + acc., за + acc., к + dat.
вокруг + gen.

D

въезжа́ть/въе́хать	в + acc., на + acc.
выезжа́ть/вы́ехать	из + gen., с + gen., в + acc., на + acc.
приезжа́ть/прие́хать	в + acc., на + acc.
уезжа́ть/уе́хать	из + gen., с + gen., в + acc., на + acc.
переезжа́ть/перее́хать	в + acc., на + acc., через + acc., к + dat., по + dat.
проезжа́ть/прое́хать	мимо + gen., через + acc., в + acc., на + acc.
заезжа́ть/зае́хать	в + acc., на + acc., за + acc., к + dat.
объезжа́ть/объе́хать	вокруг + gen.

E

1 прие́хали

2 перейти́/перее́хать

3 вы́йдешь

4 объе́хать

5 захо́дит/заезжа́ет

6 въе́хали

F

1 выбег**а**ть/в**ы**бежать

2 внос**и**ть/вн**е**сти

3 вывоз**и**ть/в**ы**везти

4 влет**а**ть/влет**е**ть

5 проплыв**а**ть/пропл**ы**ть

6 ввод**и**ть/ввес**ти**

G

To form the plural imperative, you simply add -те to the singular imperative ending.

H

1 Прочит**ай** стат**ью**!

2 Посмотр**и**те в**ы**ставку!

3 Не заб**у**дь засед**а**ние!

4 Не уход**и** р**а**но!

5 Приход**и**те в семь час**о**в!

6 Зайд**и** к нам!

I

В**и**ка получ**и**ла **э**тот меморандум, потом**у** что он**а** **е**дет в Л**о**ндон на сл**е**дующей нед**е**ле, и Ак**у**лов **е**здит т**у**да дов**о**льно ч**а**сто. Он п**и**шет с сов**е**тами для В**и**ки.

J

1 Он **е**дет из аэроп**о**рта на метр**о** в центр, а когд**а** он приезж**а**ет в ц**е**нтр, он идёт пешк**о**м в гост**и**ницу. Он **е**дет в аэроп**о**рт на такс**и**, потом**у** что он д**у**мает, что **э**то уд**о**бнее.

2 **Е**сли вы заблуд**и**лись, то Ак**у**лов говор**и**т, что легк**о** подойт**и** к люб**о**му м**е**стному ж**и**телю и спрос**и**ть, как найт**и** дор**о**гу.

3 Нет, Ак**у**лов сов**е**тует выход**и**ть как м**о**жно ч**а**ще из гост**и**ницы, чт**о**бы смотр**е**ть достопримеч**а**тельности.

4 Ак**у**лов говор**и**т, что н**а**до постар**а**ться про**е**хать ч**е**рез все больш**и**е мост**ы** на авт**о**бусе, чт**о**бы посмотр**е**ть на г**о**род.

5 Ак**у**лов приглаш**а**ет прийт**и** к нем**у** в г**о**сти п**о**сле по**е**здки и рассказ**а**ть, как она съ**е**здила.

K

1 f   **2** a   **3** d   **4** b   **5** c   **6** e

L

1 в**ы**шла

2 обош**ё**л

3 заход**и**ла

4 въ**е**хал

5 у**е**хала

6 при**е**хал

M

1 Чад! Уч**и** н**о**вые р**у**сские слов**а** к**а**ждый день!

2 С**а**ша! Просмотр**и** брош**ю**ры!

3 Сл**а**ва! Верн**и**сь дом**о**й на такс**и**!

4 Н**а**дя! Не заб**у**дь день рожд**е**ния д**е**душки!

5 **Е**шьте пять п**о**рций фр**у**ктов **и**ли овощ**е**й в день!

6 Ив**а**н Ив**а**нович! Напиш**и**те мемор**а**ндум дир**е**ктору!

N

Model answer

Чт**о**бы по**е**хать в Москв**у**, на мой взгляд л**у**чше всег**о** н**а**до лет**е**ть на самолёте и в**ы**лететь из стол**и**чного аэроп**о**рта. М**о**жно по**е**хать на п**о**езде, но **э**то заним**а**ет сравн**и**тельно мн**о**го вр**е**мени. М**о**жно в**ы**лететь из регион**а**льного аэроп**о**рта, но об**ы**чно это с перес**а**дкой до Москв**ы**.

В Москв**е** л**у**чше жить в гост**и**нице в ц**е**нтре г**о**рода, кон**е**чно. **Э**то ст**о**ит д**о**рого, но **е**сли **э**то официа**а**льная командир**о**вка, то ф**и**рма опл**а**тит уд**о**бную гост**и**ницу. **Е**сли вы с**а**ми опл**а**чиваете и хот**и**те эконо**о**мить, то м**о**жно найт**и** мест**а** подешев**е**вле по интерн**е**ту.

Если у вас б**у**дет своб**о**дное вр**е**мя в Москв**е**, посмотр**и**те достопримеч**а**тельности г**о**рода. Посет**и**те Кремль, мавзол**е**й Л**е**нина и Соб**о**р Вас**и**лия Блаж**е**нного. Поезж**а**йте на метр**о** и посет**и**те р**а**зные р**ы**нки и ки**о**ски, где м**о**жно куп**и**ть матрёшки и друг**и**е традици**о**нные сувен**и**ры.

Unit 12

A

	Masculine	Feminine	Neuter	Plural
Nominative	кот**о**рый	кот**о**рая	кот**о**рое	кот**о**рые
Accusative (inanimate/animate)	кот**о**рый/ого	кот**о**рую	кот**о**рое	кот**о**рые/ых
Genitive	кот**о**рого	кот**о**рой	кот**о**рого	кот**о**рых
Dative	кот**о**рому	кот**о**рой	кот**о**рому	кот**о**рым
Instrumental	кот**о**рым	кот**о**рой	кот**о**рым	кот**о**рыми
Prepositional	о кот**о**ром	о кот**о**рой	о кот**о**ром	о кот**о**рых

B

1 b   2 a   3 a   4 c   5 c   6 a

C

1   Гид, с кот**о**рым мы говор**и**ли, **о**чень **у**мный челов**е**к.

2   Мы посет**и**ли муз**е**й, кот**о**рый нах**о**дится недалек**о** от п**а**рка.

3   Мы под**а**рим друзь**я**м под**а**рки, кот**о**рые мы куп**и**ли в универм**а**ге.

4   П**а**мятник, у кот**о**рого мы встр**е**тимся в 7 час**о**в, **о**чень знамен**и**тый.

5   Мост, кот**о**рый нам **о**чень нр**а**вится, постр**о**или 200 лет наз**а**д.

6   Шк**о**льникам, кот**о**рые посещ**а**ют муз**е**й, н**а**до ост**а**вить рюкз**а**к в гардер**о**бе.

D

1   Я ч**а**сто хож**у** в парк, кот**о**рый нах**о**дится на с**е**вере г**о**рода.

2   Мы говор**и**ли о ф**и**льме, кот**о**рый мы смотр**е**ли вчер**а** в киноте**а**тре недалек**о** от ц**е**нтра г**о**рода.

3   **О**зеро, в кот**о**ром Макс**и**м пл**а**вал, **о**чень ч**и**стое.

4   Библиот**е**ка, за кот**о**рой мы жив**ё**м, огр**о**мная.

5   Гид, кот**о**рый раб**о**тает в галер**е**е, мн**о**го зн**а**ет о карт**и**нах.

6   Мы увлек**а**лись кат**а**нием на конь**к**ах с н**а**шими н**о**выми друзь**я**ми, кот**о**рые жив**у**т в пр**и**городе Т**о**мска.

E

1 На празднике я познакомился с русским студентом.

2 На празднике мы встретились с родителями.

3 На празднике мы отдали подарки детям.

4 На празднике все участвовали в параде.

5 На праздник они рекомендовали нам еду.

6 После праздника её радовали фотографии.

F

Фотография показывала, как им с друзьями было весело на празднике.

G

1 Потому что надо было обсудить ресторан, в котором хотели встретиться и еду, которую предпочитали.

2 Да, они заказали без комментария.

3 Было солнечно и тепло.

4 До обеда они ходили на парад.

5 Еда понравилась, но не очень понравилось шампанское.

6 На фотографии можно видеть, что был очень весёлый день.

H

1 договорились		4	позвонили
2 заказали		5	отмечать
3 прикладываю		6	обрадовала

I

1 c   2 b   3 a   4 a   5 b   6 b

J

1 воскресенье		4	тепло
2 с друзьями		5	ресторан
3 шампанское		6	подарок

K

Model answer

Вчера был день рождения моей лучшей подруги, Марии, и мы отмечали его в новой квартире в центре города. Посмотрите эту фотографию, которую я сделала перед концом вечеринки. Я в середине, и Мария рядом. Девушка, которая стоит слева от меня – её зовут Наташа, и парень, который стоит за нами – его зовут Слава. Это друзья Марии, с которыми она учится. Наташа, которая живёт рядом и от которой Мария получила громадную бутылку шампанского в подарок, танцевала весь вечер, а мы с Марией разговаривали на кухне и готовили закуски и потом чай и кофе. Была отличная вечеринка, но больше всего мне понравилось то, что приходили много друзей, с которыми мы давно не виделись и по которым мы соскучились!

Unit 13

A

1 Если я читаю много, у меня болят глаза.

2 Если русские ходят без шапки, у них болит горло.

3 Если бабушка работает в саду, у неё болит спина.

4 Если пациенты ходят к врачу, они иногда получают рецепт.

5 Если работники здравоохранения запишутся на прививку, они не заболеют гриппом.

6 Если студенты не будут заниматься спортом, они не будут в форме.

B

1 Если бы Зигмунд не ел сладкое, у него не болел бы зуб.

2 Если бы Зинаида не забыла деньги, она купила бы аспирин.

3 Если бы я жил(а) на юге, у меня не было бы простуды.

4 Если бы у ребёнка не было аллергии, он принимал бы антибиотики.

5 Если бы ты не катался (каталась) на коньках, ты не сломал(а) бы ногу.

6 Если бы любой человек перестал курить, он чувствовал бы себя лучше.

C

1 If tourists walk about in Russia without a scarf in winter, they will be coughing.

2 If you were to stand up very quickly, you would faint.

   If you were to have stood up very quickly, you would have fainted.

   If you had stood up very quickly, you would have fainted.

3 If the boy were to eat very cold ice cream, then he would probably have tonsillitis.

   If the boy were to have eaten very cold ice cream, then he would probably have had tonsillitis.

   If the boy had eaten very cold ice cream, then he would probably have (had) tonsillitis.

4 If you try dishes that are too exotic, it is entirely probable that you will have diarrhoea.

5 If you feel very nauseous and you have a temperature, then you may throw up.

6 If men drink too much beer and do not do any physical exercise then they have an increased risk of having a stroke.

D

что	чтобы
думать	желать
знать	предлагать
казаться	просить
слышать	советовать
сообщать	требовать
считать	хотеть

E

1 b   2 a   3 a   4 b   5 b   6 a

F

1 инфаркт

2 диабет

3 ангина

4 прививка

5 рецепт, лекарство

6 понос

G

Автор этой статьи говорит о самых распространённых заболеваниях, с которыми встречается современный человек.

H

1 Первая причина заболеваний – это то, что мы плохо питаемся.

2 Четвёртая причина заболеваний – это бактерии, вирусы, грибки и другие паразиты.

3 «Детские» болезни не так часто встречаются сегодня из-за почти универсальных прививок.

4 У взрослых чаще всего бывают головные боли и мигрени.

5 Чтобы повысить иммунитет и сопротивляемость к болезням необходимо заниматься спортом, принимать витамины и правильно питаться.

I

1 чтобы

2 что

3 что

4 чтобы

5 чтобы

6 что

J

1 кашель – the other words are all likely to be linked to eating or drinking something that doesn't agree with you

2 инфаркт – the other words are all linked to common childhood illnesses

3 ухо – the other words are all internal organs

4 лекарство – the other words are all possible causes of illness

5 никотин – the other words are all medicines

6 засыпать – the other words are all activities

K

1 вырвать

2 лекарство

3 распространённый

4 иммунитет

5 простуда

6 ослабление

L

Model answer

Я бол**е**ю! У меня бол**и**т жив**о**т, меня тошн**и**т, н**о**чью меня в**ы**рвало и теп**е**рь у мен**я** пов**ы**шенная температ**у**ра. Я не зн**а**ю, есть ли у меня в**и**рус или отравл**е**ние п**о**сле **у**жина в рестор**а**не вчер**а** в**е**чером. Во вс**я**ком сл**у**чае, теп**е**рь я не мог**у** по**е**хать в Петерб**у**рг!

Если бы я по**е**хала, я прилет**е**ла бы в Петерб**у**рг р**а**но **у**тром. Я по**е**хала бы на такс**и** в центр г**о**рода и зарегистр**и**ровалась бы в гост**и**нице недалек**о** от Эрмит**а**жа. Я пошл**а** бы на спект**а**кль в Эрмит**а**жном Те**а**тре, и — сбыл**а**сь бы мо**я** мечт**а**!

Чт**о**бы пойт**и** на спект**а**кль, я встр**е**тилась бы с мо**е**й р**у**сской знак**о**мой. Мы провел**и** бы три дня вм**е**сте, посещ**а**я все достопримеч**а**тельности г**о**рода. В б**у**дущем я б**у**ду **у**жинать д**о**ма пер**е**д пол**ё**том за гран**и**цу!

Unit 14

A

1 «Я потер**я**л бум**а**жник.»

2 «Я упад**у** на льду.»

3 «Покуп**а**тели рвут од**е**жду в магаз**и**не.»

4 «Официа́нт разольёт кра́сное вино́.»

5 «Студе́нт уро́нил па́пку.»

6 «Я разбива́ю / Мы разбива́ем зе́ркало.»

B

1 Полиц**е**йский сказ**а**л, что маш**и**на столкн**у**лась со столб**о**м.

2 М**а**ма всегд**а** предупрежд**а**ет Ив**а**на, что он упад**ё**т.

3 Студ**е**нтка был**а** ув**е**рена, что он**а** ур**о**нит уч**е**бники.

4 Врач сообщ**и**ла, что м**а**льчик слом**а**л себ**е** р**у**ку.

5 Уб**о**рщица спрос**и**ла, кто разл**и**л к**о**фе.

6 Экскурсов**о**ды ч**а**сто говор**я**т, что тур**и**сты забыв**а**ют п**а**спорт.

C

1 The tour guide asked whether Nikolay had <u>lost</u> his passport.

2 The tour guide asked whether <u>Nikolay</u> had lost his passport.

3 The tour guide asked whether Nikolay had lost his <u>passport</u>.

D

1 b 2 a 3 c 4 a 5 b 6 c

E

1 Полицейский спросил, заметил(а) ли я, как быстро ехала машина.

2 Полицейский спросил, знаю ли я в котором часу это случилось.

3 Полицейский спросил, могу ли я сказать, кто ещё видел аварию.

4 Полицейский спросил, уверен(а) ли я, что не было других свидетелей.

5 Полицейский спросил, считаю ли я, что виноват водитель автобуса.

F

1 обнаружила

2 поскользнулись

3 свидетель

4 затормозила

5 скорую помощь

6 ушиба

G

Эти три человека пишут свои отчёты, потому что они сообщают о том, что случилось и они – свидетели.

H

1 Нина уронила свой багаж, потому что она запнулась о ковёр.

2 Она уронила сумку и таким образом сломала экран телефона.

3 Две машины резко затормозили, чтобы объехать двух молодых людей на квадроциклах.

4 Велосипедистка получила ушибы, потому что она въехала в машину и упала на дорогу.

5 Муж Анастасии потерял паспорт, когда его кожаная куртка исчезла из их машины.

I

1 спустилась

2 сообщила

3 по встречной полосе

4 пытаясь

5 припарковали

6 сигнализация

J

1 ушиб

2 страхование

3 синяк

4 разбивать

5 заменить

6 украсть

K

Model answer

Я подаю заявление на то, чтобы вы возместили мне ущерб на сумму до 10 тысяч рублей после того, как у меня украли из сумки бумажник с деньгами.

Это случилось в большом универмаге в центральном торговом центре в прошлую субботу, около 11 часов утра. Я делала покупки, как всегда делаю по субботам, когда молодая женщина с ребёнком в коляске столкнулась со мной. Мы извинились друг перед другом, но, когда через несколько минут я хотела заплатить за покупку, я обнаружила, что у меня нет бумажника.

Я сразу сообщила о краже администратору в справочном бюро универмага, и он посоветовал мне пойти в милицию, где открыли официальное дело – №387/Д6. Мне дали квитанцию, которую я прикладываю к этому заявлению.

Unit 15

A

1 восемьсот двенадцать, шестьдесят три, восемьдесят семь, двенадцать

2 четыреста девяносто пять, двадцать два, сорок восемь, ноль один

3 четыреста двадцать семь, ноль четыре, ноль семь, десять

4 четыреста восемьдесят два, девятнадцать, шестьдесят три, девяносто семь

5 триста пятьдесят один, двенадцать, сорок четыре, тридцать

6 восемьсот шестьдесят девять, семьдесят семь, ноль девять, ноль ноль

B

1 a i   2 c iii   3 c ii   4 c iii   5 c iii   6 a i

C

1 одному пассажирскому поезду

2 пятью одноразовыми билетами

3 трёх интересных поездок

4 двадцатью семью кожаными чемоданами

5 трёх свободных местах

6 шестьсот двадцать одну железнодорожную остановку

D

1 в шести**ста**х пят**и**десяти кило**ме**трах

2 в ста девян**о**ста ст**а**нциях метр**о**

3 с двадцат**ью** четырьм**я** ваг**о**нами

4 п**о**сле двен**а**дцати дл**и**нных по**е**здок

5 дв**ум** т**ы**сячам пассаж**и**рам

6 **о**коло ста час**о**в

E

1 01/04   **2** 2015   **3** 22.12.99

F

1 в т**ы**сяча дев**я**тьсот семн**а**дцатом год**у**

2 отб**ы**тие: дв**а**дцать п**я**того сентябр**я** две т**ы**сячи пятн**а**дцатого г**о**да

3 приб**ы**тие: тр**и**дцать п**е**рвого октябр**я** две т**ы**сячи пятн**а**дцатого г**о**да

4 в две т**ы**сячи двадц**а**том год**у**

5 в декабр**е** т**ы**сяча девять**со**т девян**о**сто п**е**рвого г**о**да

6 возвр**а**щение дом**о**й: втор**о**го и**ю**ля две т**ы**сячи семн**а**дцатого г**о**да

G

1 съезд – **э**то не часть п**о**езда

2 **А**льпы – он**и** не в Росс**и**и

3 пуст**ы**ня – **э**то м**е**сто, а не челов**е**к

4 **о**бласть – **э**то не часть дор**о**жной сист**е**мы

5 в**е**чная мерзлот**а** – **э**то не рай**о**н Росс**и**и

6 пол**я**рный круг – **э**то рай**о**н, а не часть тр**а**нспортной сист**е**мы

H

Ив**а**н Ив**а**нович мечт**а**л по**е**хать по Транссиб**и**рской железнодор**о**жной магистр**а**ли, и ег**о** мечт**а** сбыл**а**сь, потом**у** что в **э**том год**у** он уш**ё**л на п**е**нсию.

I

1 Начали строить Транссиб девятнадцатого (тридцать первого по новому стилю) мая тысяча восемьсот девяносто первого года.

2 В конечном счёте стоило почти полтора миллиарда рублей построить Транссиб.

3 Иван Иванович упоминает тысяча девятьсот шестнадцатый год, потому что в этом году был официальный конец строительства Транссиба на территории Российской империи.

4 Нет в мире железных дорог, которые длиннее Транссиба.

5 Иван Иванович решил поехать одиннадцатого апреля, потому что в этот день в тысяча восемьсот девяносто первом году Император издал указ о начале строительства Транссиба.

J

1 триста километров

2 четыреста шестьдесят километров

3 тысяча триста пятьдесят километров

4 восемьсот девяносто восемь километров

5 тысяча семьсот девяносто девять километров

6 шестьсот один километр

K

1 d   2 a   3 e   4 b   5 f   6 c

L

1 П.И. Чайковский родился седьмого мая тысяча восемьсот сорокового года.

2 Екатерина Великая родилась второго мая тысяча семьсот двадцать девятого года.

3 Ю.А. Гагарин родился девятого марта тысяча девятьсот тридцать четвёртого года.

4 В.В. Терешкова родилась шестого марта тысяча девятьсот тридцать седьмого года.

5 Р.А. Абрамович родился двадцать четвёртого октября тысяча девятьсот шестьдесят шестого года.

6 М.Ю. Шарапова родилась девятнадцатого апреля тысяча девятьсот восемьдесят седьмого года.

M

Model answer

Я поехал из Москвы во Владивосток на автомобиле! Я совершил эту огромную поездку на авто «Лэндровер». Он новый внедорожник с приводом на четыре колеса. Я купил его , потому что у него хорошая репутация надёжного и прочого автомобиля, и потому что я знал, что поездка будет длинной и требовательной.

Во время поездки мне больше всего понравилось озеро Байкал. Это самое красивое место в мире, которое я когда-либо видел. Чтобы попасть туда поскорее я проехал самый большой километраж в один день за всю поездку: 750 (семьсот пятьдесят) километров за 12 (двенадцать) часов за рулём. Я приехал уставшим, но красота озера сразу вернула мне энергию и энтузиазм.

Моя поездка из Москвы до Владивостока длилась почти три недели, и я проехал больше 9,000 (девяти тысяч) километров. Это был незабываемый опыт!

Unit 16

A

1 я хочу тот абажур, а не эту лампу.

2 я хочу этот стол, а не те стулья.

3 я хочу ту звуковую панель, а не этот телевизор.

4 я хочу эти шторы, а не те жалюзи.

5 я хочу эту книжную полку, а не этот комод.

6 я хочу эту картину, а не то зеркало.

B

We had <u>such</u> a big house in <u>such</u> a beautiful area!

C

	Masculine	Feminine	Neuter	Plural
Nominative	так**ой**	так**ая**	так**ое**	так**ие**
Accusative (inanimate/ animate)	так**ой**/так**ого**	так**ую**	так**ое**	так**ие**/так**их**
Genitive	так**ого**	так**ой**	так**ого**	так**их**
Dative	так**ому**	так**ой**	так**ому**	так**им**
Instrumental	так**им**	так**ой**	так**им**	так**ими**
Prepositional	так**ом**	так**ой**	так**ом**	так**их**

D

1 Это так**ая** крас**и**вая карт**и**на!

2 Это так**ие** крас**и**вые нож**и**!

3 Это так**ая** крас**и**вая т**у**мбочка!

4 Это так**ой** крас**и**вый душ!

5 Это так**ая** крас**и**вая плит**а**!

6 Это так**ая** крас**и**вая посудом**о**ечная маш**и**на!

E

1 До тог**о**, как

2 Вм**е**сто тог**о**, чт**о**бы

3 поск**о**льку

4 Пок**а**

5 как б**у**дто

6 Благодар**я** том**у**, что

Before I bought my own house I lived with my parents. Instead of living in the centre, like them, I decided to move out of town, inasmuch as it is quieter and calmer there. While I was looking for a house, they started to build a new area, as if especially for me. Thanks to the fact that my grandmother gave me some money, I was able to buy my ideal home.

F

More than one compound conjunction might be possible as a correct answer in these sentences.

1 П**е**ред тем, как

2 Из-за тог**о**, что

3 П**о**сле тог**о**, как

4 Как т**о**лько

5 пок**а** не

6 Ввид**у** тог**о**, что

G

Выбор дома или квартиры так важен, потому что такой выбор может играть большую роль в чувстве счастья у каждого человека.

H

1 Чтобы благоустроить участок, на котором находится первый дом, можно посадить деревья или построить детскую площадку.

2 Судя по первой рекламе, этот дом идеален для семей с детьми.

3 Вторая реклама предлагает выбор планировок, чтобы можно было выбрать ту квартиру, которую люди хотят с хорошим использованием жилого пространства.

4 Третья реклама описывает то, что было 5 лет назад, потому что тогда отремонтировали дом хорошо, что стоило много денег.

5 Третья реклама считает, что не надо больше искать дом, потому что считают, что это – идеальный дом.

I

1 живописный	4 комфортный
2 необходимый	5 традиционный
3 просторный	6 городской

J

1 зеркало	4 балкон
2 посудомоечная машина	5 душ
3 мусорный ящик	6 пылесос

K

гостиная	кухня
► журнальный столик	► вытяжка
► камин	► духовка
► мягкая мебель	► плита
спальня	**санузел**
► подушка	► полотенце
► простыня	► умывальная раковина
► тумбочка	► унитаз

L

Model answer

Привет! Я пишу, потому что ты попросил/а меня описать мой идеальный дом. Я мечтаю об отдельном доме, который построили довольно давно, но не так давно, чтобы не было нужных комфортов для удобной жизни в современном мире!

В таком старом доме нужна подходящая мебель. В моём идеальном доме была бы смесь старой и новой мебели, но всё со вкусом! Например, гостиная с красивой антикварной мебелью, а ванная и кухня со всем ультрасовременным оборудованием.

Идеальное местонахождение для меня было бы в тихом, живописном пригороде небольшого города, недалеко от моря, где погода всегда мягкая и приятная. Идеальный день в идеальном доме был бы в компании семьи и друзей, с экскурсией на море, отдыхом в саду и вкусным барбекю вечером!

Unit 17

A

1   Ivan and Anna could watch the firework display on Victory Day.

2   Ivan and Anna can watch the firework display on Victory Day.

3   Ivan and Anna will be able to watch the firework display on Victory Day.

The subject of the modal можно is in the dative case and the verb following the modal можно is in the infinitive.

B

1 надо/нужно	4 нельзя будет
2 нельзя было	5 было невозможно
3 можно	6 можно будет

C

1   нужен   *(At Easter we need the kulich Easter cake.)*

2   нужна   *(At a party students always need loud music.)*

3   нужны   *(I was warned that at the banya I needed birch twigs.)*

4   нужны   *(In Russian museums slippers are needed so as not to damage the floor.)*

5   нужен   *(To start a party a first toast is needed.)*

6   нужно   *(On the first day of winter you need a coat!)*

D

1 Mikhail should visit his grandmother on her birthday.

2 The Snow Maiden should help Grandfather Frost.

3 The State should organize a firework display for New Year.

4 Christians should go to church regularly.

E

1 бокал шампанского

2 богослужение

3 поздравлять

4 раскрашенное яйцо

5 отмечать

F

Нет никакой научной или логичной основы для суеверий.

G

1 Они боятся пятницы 13-го числа, потому что в Библии пишется, что этого числа Авель был убит своим братом Каином.

2 Автор статьи считает, что, если вы забыли что-то, вам эта вещь вспомнится, если вы посидите «на дорожку».

3 Рекомендуется выносить мусор при дневном свете, чтобы не стать бедным.

4 Свистун – не популярен в России, потому что из-за этого нечистая сила к вам придёт и вы станете бедным, или будет шторм на море.

5 Автор статьи рекомендует своим читателям забыть о суевериях, потому что они старомодны и ложны.

H

1 будущее

2 верить

3 мусор

4 освободиться

I

1 запрещается

2 факт

3 хвалить

4 ангел

5 покой

6 глупость

J

1	нав**е**рно	**4**	неуж**е**ли
2	сув**е**рие	**5**	баб**у**ля
3	обман**у**ть		

K

Model answer

Прив**е**т, друг/подр**у**га! По-м**о**ему, мы не **о**чень суев**е**рный нар**о**д. Как почт**и** во вс**е**х стр**а**нах м**и**ра, мы д**у**маем, что тр**о**йка и семёрка – счастл**и**вые ц**и**фры, и что чёрного кот**а** н**а**до опас**а**ться. Одн**а**ко, наск**о**лько я зн**а**ю, у нас нет счастл**и**вых цвет**о**в.

Чт**о**бы быть счастл**и**вым, на мой взгляд, н**а**до быть ч**е**стным, раб**о**тать ус**е**рдно и вест**и** себ**я** раз**у**мно. Я ув**е**рен, что нельз**я** н**и**чем рисков**а**ть, никогд**а** не н**а**до обм**а**нывать друг**и**х или зан“**а**ться аз**а**ртными **и**грами.

У мен**я** б**ы**ло мн**о**го сл**у**чаев в ж**и**зни, когд**а** суев**е**рие н**е** было опр**а**вдано. Наприм**е**р, мы ж**и**ли н**е**сколько лет в кварт**и**ре №13, и нам б**ы**ло хорош**о** и комф**о**ртно всё вр**е**мя. К тому же, наш чёрный кот ч**а**сто перех**о**дит дор**о**гу нам без как**и**х-либо отриц**а**тельных посл**е**дствий для нас.

Unit 18

A

кто?	незак**о**нный сын р**у**сского гр**а**фа
что?	в конц**е** ром**а**на ж**е**нится на Нат**а**лье Рост**о**вой
где?	в роск**о**шных дом**а**х в Санкт-Петерб**у**рге
когд**а**?	в нач**а**ле XIX-го в**е**ка
как?	он знак**о**мится с мас**о**нами случ**а**йно
почему?	чт**о**бы уб**и**ть Наполе**о**на

B

Гд**е** means *where?* and describes position

Отк**у**да means *where from?* and describes movement

Куд**а** means *where to?* and describes movement

C

1 Что (вы лю́бите де́лать бо́льше всего́)?

2 Когда́ (у вас день рожде́ния)?

3 Кто (ваш люби́мый а́втор)?

4 Почему́ (вы э́то де́лаете)?

5 Куда́ (вы е́дете в э́том году́)?

6 Как (вы игра́ете в те́ннис)?

7 Отку́да (вы отправля́етесь в о́тпуск)?

8 Где (вы роди́лись)?

D

Nominative	кто	что
Accusative	кого́	что
Genitive	кого́	чего́
Dative	кому́	чему́
Instrumental	кем	чем
Prepositional	ком	чём

E

1 кем

2 чего́

3 кому́

4 чём

5 кого́

6 кто

F

1 что-нибу́дь

2 что́-то

3 когда́-нибу́дь

4 где-нибу́дь

5 почему́-то

6 кому́-то

G

	Masculine	Feminine	Neuter	Plural
Nominative	како́й	кака́я	како́е	каки́е
Accusative (inanimate/ animate)	како́й/како́го	каку́ю	како́е	каки́е/каки́х
Genitive	како́го	како́й	како́го	каки́х
Dative	како́му	како́й	како́му	каки́м
Instrumental	каки́м	како́й	каки́м	каки́ми
Prepositional	о како́м	о како́й	о како́м	о каки́х

H

1	как**о**м	**4**	как**и**м
2	как**и**е	**5**	как**и**х
3	как**о**му	**6**	как**о**го

I

1 По как**о**й прич**и**не вы <u>в**ы**брали</u> сво**ю** специ**а**льность?

2 В кот**о**ром час**у** ты <u>х**о**чешь</u> встр**е**титься?

3 Почем**у** ты <u>пл**а**чешь</u>?

4 К как**о**му числ**у** вы <u>нап**и**шете</u> отчёт?

5 До как**о**й ст**е**пени вы <u>счит**а**ете</u>, что **э**то подозр**и**тельно?

6 Из-за чег**о** ты <u>беспок**о**ишься</u>?

J

1 спрос**и**л   **2** задав**а**ть/зад**а**ть вопрос   **3** попрос**и**ла

K

1	посл**е**дствие	**4**	предубежд**е**ние
2	обсто**я**тельство	**5**	меч**т**а
3	заключ**е**ние	**6**	кол**и**чество

L

Был**а** «интр**и**га», потом**у** что род**и**тели Бил**а**на снач**а**ла не пов**е**рили, что он их сын. Он род**и**лся в родд**о**ме на Кавк**а**зе, и ег**о** мать был**а** ед**и**нственной р**у**сской ж**е**нщиной в родд**о**ме, а мал**ы**ш был с кавк**а**зской вн**е**шностью ит**а**к не пох**о**ж на м**а**му.

M

1 Д**и**ма **о**чень ч**а**сто выступ**а**л в музык**а**льных меропри**я**тиях своег**о** д**е**тского с**а**да.

2 П**е**рвыми специ**а**льностями Д**и**мы в музык**а**льной шк**о**ле б**ы**ли аккорде**о**н и вок**а**л.

3 Д**и**ма оказ**а**лся в Москв**е** в 1999 год**у**, потом**у** что он уч**а**ствовал в молодёжном фестив**а**ле «Ч**у**нга-Ч**а**нга».

4 Карь**е**ра Д**и**мы начал**а**сь по-насто**я**щему в 2000 год**у** благодар**я** ег**о** п**е**рвому видеокл**и**пу по телек**а**налу MTV Russia.

N

1 В как**о**м г**о**роде род**и**лся Д**и**ма Бил**а**н?

2 По как**о**й пр**и**чине он пере**е**хал в Москв**у**?

3 Благодар**я** ком**у** он полюб**и**л м**у**зыку?

4 Как**и**м **о**бразом он н**а**чал игр**а**ть на аккорде**о**не?

O

Model answer

– Где вы род**и**лись, и как**а**я был**а** у вас семь**я**?

  Я род**и**лся в Екатеринб**у**рге, и мо**я** семь**я** был**а** м**а**ленькая: п**а**па, м**а**ма, ст**а**ршая сестр**а**, я
  и б**а**бушка.

– В как**о**й шк**о**ле, и в как**о**м университ**е**те вы уч**и**лись?

  Снач**а**ла я ход**и**л в шк**о**лу недалек**о** от н**а**шего д**о**ма и пот**о**м поступ**и**л в Моск**о**вский
  Госуд**а**рственный Университ**е**т на факульт**е**т ф**и**зики.

– Кто им**е**л влия́ние на вас б**о**льше всег**о**?

  На мен**я** повли**я**ли в основн**о**м два челов**е**ка: мо**я** б**а**бушка с её люб**о**вью к м**у**зыке и мой
  университ**е**тский проф**е**ссор ф**и**зики, кот**о**рый так интересов**а**лся сво**и**м предм**е**том.

– Есть ли у вас как**и**е-ниб**у**дь пл**а**ны на б**у**дущее?

  Кон**е**чно, я над**е**юсь получ**и**ть Н**о**белевскую пр**е**мию по ф**и**зике!

Unit 19

A

	Masculine	Feminine	Neuter	Plural
Nominative	весь	вся	всё	все
Accusative (inanimate/ animate)	весь/всег**о**	всю	всё	все/вс**ех**
Genitive	всег**о**	вс**ей**	всег**о**	вс**ех**
Dative	всем**у**	вс**ей**	всем**у**	всем
Instrumental	всем	вс**ей**	всем	вс**еми**
Prepositional	обо вс**ём**	обо вс**ей**	обо вс**ём**	обо вс**ех**

B

1 Ив**а**н уч**а**ствовал <u>во всём тренинге</u>.

2 Ив**а**н раб**о**тал над докум**е**нтами <u>весь в**е**чер</u>.

3 Ив**а**н написа**л** <u>весь отчёт</u>.

4 Ив**а**н разгов**а**ривал <u>со вс**е**ми чл**е**нами</u> ком**а**нды.

5 Ив**а**н зак**о**нчил <u>всю раб**о**ту</u>.

6 Ив**а**н получ**и**л отв**е**т от <u>всех кли**е**нтов</u>.

C

1 Ivan talked to each member of the team.

2 Ivan received an answer from every client.

D

1 К**а**ждый сотр**у**дник получ**и**л сообщ**е**ние.

2 Дир**е**ктор прочита**л** к**а**ждое резюм**е**.

3 В к**а**ждом сл**у**чае вы пол**у**чите отв**е**т.

4 К**а**ждому профессион**а**лу н**у**жен регул**я**рный тр**е**нинг.

5 Мы пригот**о**вили презент**а**цию для к**а**ждого кли**е**нта.

6 Дир**е**ктор побес**е**довал с к**а**ждым колл**е**гой (or: к**а**ждой колл**е**гой, if all colleagues are female).

E

1 **И**горь раб**о**тал над вс**я**кими про**е**ктами.

2 Вся ком**а**нда раб**о**тала всю ночь, чт**о**бы зак**о**нчить презент**а**цию.

3 Я интерес**у**юсь люб**о**й проф**е**ссией, в кот**о**рой зарпл**а**та хор**о**шая.

4 **Э**та раб**о**та содерж**а**ла ц**е**лый ряд пробл**е**м.

5 У мен**я** н**о**вая зад**а**ча к**а**ждую нед**е**лю.

6 Мне м**о**жно попрос**и**ть сов**е**та у к**а**ждого/к**а**ждой колл**е**ги. / Мне м**о**жно попрос**и**ть сов**е**та у всех колл**е**г. / Мне м**о**жно попрос**и**ть сов**е**та у люб**о**го/люб**о**й колл**е**ги. / Мне м**о**жно попрос**и**ть сов**е**та у вс**я**кого/вс**я**кой колл**е**ги.

F

1	самом	4	самому
2	те же самые	5	друг к другу
3	друг другу	6	та же самая

G

1	подаёшь заявление	4	назначит
2	повышение	5	характеристика
3	автобиографию	6	отменить

H

Максим хорошо окончил тренинг, потому что все замечания очень позитивные.

I

1 Максим всегда готов находить в каждой ситуации индивидуальный подход к проблемам и людям.

2 В работе больше всего интересуют Максима возможность внедрения самых высоких стандартов тщательного перевода, наличие возможностей и свободы действий для их реализации.

3 Нет, Максим не хочет стать начальником в настоящее время.

4 В целях саморазвития, Максим занимается тренингом, изучает литературу, и применяет свои знания на практике.

5 В потенциальных коллегах привлекают Максима их высокий потенциал и мотивация.

J

1 Я уже употребляю технологию.

2 Я уже нашла индивидуальный подход к проблеме.

3 Я уже тщательно перевела документ.

4 Я уже узнала актуальное положение дел.

5 Я уже взяла на себя ответственность за реализацию инициативы.

6 Я уже адекватно оценила сильные и слабые стороны своих коллег.

K

1 пр**а**ктика

2 подчинённый

3 нал**и**чие

4 профессион**а**льный

5 конкр**е**тный

6 совреме**н**ный

L

Model answer

Мне к**а**жется, что мо**я** учёба идёт непл**о**хо. Я дост**а**точно з**а**нята на раб**о**те пять дней в нед**е**лю, но я нахож**у** по кр**а**йней м**е**ре 10 мин**у**т в день, чт**о**бы уч**и**ть н**о**вые слов**а**. У мен**я** специ**а**льное прилож**е**ние на смартф**о**не, кот**о**рое помог**а**ет с **э**тим.

Мне дов**о**льно тр**у**дно запомин**а**ть н**о**вые слов**а** по-р**у**сски, но ст**а**рая посл**о**вица прав**а**: «повтор**е**ние – мать уч**е**ния!» Мне легк**о** даётся грамм**а**тика, и, хот**я** н**а**до д**у**мать **о** мн**о**гом, когд**а** п**и**шешь **и**ли говор**и**шь по-р**у**сски, я д**у**маю, что я сильн**а** в **э**том. Я ум**е**ю говор**и**ть по-р**у**сски дов**о**льно б**е**гло уж**е**, потом**у** что у мен**я** на раб**о**те есть одн**а** колл**е**га из Л**а**твии, и у мен**я** с ней пр**а**ктика во вр**е**мя об**е**да раз в нед**е**лю.

Сл**е**дующая мо**я** цель – чит**а**ть по–р**у**сски как м**о**жно быстр**е**е, чт**о**бы я могл**а** чит**а**ть П**у**шкина в оригин**а**ле. Эт**о** б**у**дет отл**и**чно!

Unit 20

A

Working can be translated into Russian either with a conjugated tense of a verb (раб**о**тала) or with a present gerund (раб**о**тая).

B

To form a **present gerund**, you take the **он**и form of the present tense verb (e.g. регистр**и**руют), remove the last two letters and replace with a -я (unless the spelling rule applies – after -ж,-ч,-ш or -щ, you need to write -а rather than -я).

C

1 чит**а**я

2 покуп**а**я

3 смотр**я**

4 встреч**а**ясь

5 м**о**лча

6 говор**я**

D

To form a **past gerund**, you simply take the infinitive of a **perfective** verb, remove the -ть and replace it with -в.

E

1	посмотр**ев**	4	заблуд**ившись**
2	узн**ав**	5	сд**е**лав
3	получ**ив**	6	прост**ившись**

F

1 Получ**ив** паспорт**а**, мы м**о**жем у**е**хать, когд**а** хот**и**м.

2 Устр**а**иваясь на н**о**вую раб**о**ту, к**а**ждый день я узна**ю** мн**о**го н**о**вого.

3 Мы должн**ы** б**ы**ли жить без к**у**хни две нед**е**ли, **у**жиная в р**а**зных рестор**а**нах.

4 Посов**е**товавшись с сос**е**дями, Ж**е**ня к**у**пит н**о**вый телев**и**зор.

5 Прож**и**в три г**о**да за рубеж**о**м, **А**нна с Бор**и**сом реш**и**ли верн**у**ться на р**о**дину.

6 Зап**о**лнив все н**у**жные докум**е**нты для интер**е**сного пост**а** в Пар**и**же, Серг**е**й полу**ч**ит приглаш**е**ние на интервь**ю**.

G

		Masculine	Feminine	Neuter	Plural
Nominative	–	сам	сам**а**	сам**о**	с**а**ми
Accusative (inanimate/ animate)	себ**я**	сам/самог**о**	сам**у**	сам**о**	с**а**ми/сам**и**х
Genitive	себ**я**	самог**о**	сам**о**й	самог**о**	сам**и**х
Dative	себ**е**	самом**у**	сам**о**й	самом**у**	сам**и**м
Instrumental	соб**о**й	сам**и**м	сам**о**й	сам**и**м	сам**и**ми
Prepositional	себ**е**	сам**о**м	сам**о**й	сам**о**м	сам**и**х

H

1 себ**я** (Natasha feels good in Canada.)

2 соб**о**й (The Ivanovs took their dog with them when they went away.)

3 себ**е** (Masha never thought of herself.)

4 себ**е** (The neighbours invited us to their house for a meal.)

5 себ**я** (Nikolay felt comfortable at the dacha.)

6 себ**я** (Igor berated himself for forgetting an important folder.)

I

1 Никол**а**й <u>сам</u> нашёл раб**о**ту без пробл**е**м.

2 Мы ост**а**вили б**а**бушку <u>сам**у**</u> на д**а**че, так как он**а** не хот**е**ла по**е**хать с н**а**ми.

3 **Е**сли прочтёшь весь отчёт, **И**ра, ты <u>сам**а**</u> ув**и**дишь, что я прав!

4 Посмотр**и** на все вари**а**нты и <u>сам**(а)**</u> реш**а**й.

5 Д**е**ти б**ы**ли в Л**о**ндоне, где был**а** <u>сам**а**</u> корол**е**ва.

6 Почталь**о**н сказ**а**л, что отд**а**ст письм**о** т**о**лько <u>сам**о**му</u> теб**е**, В**и**ктор.

J

1 об**ы**чай

2 зарпл**а**та

3 им**у**щество

4 удив**и**ться

5 сос**е**д

6 переступ**и**ть зак**о**н

K

Чт**о**бы сум**е**ть усп**е**шно пож**и**ть за гран**и**цей, н**у**жно быть с**и**льным и ст**о**йким челов**е**ком.

L

1 Чт**о**бы подгот**о**виться к «вр**е**менной эмигр**а**ции», н**а**до след**и**ть за оформл**е**нием докум**е**нтов, основ**а**тельно изуч**а**ть яз**ы**к, найт**и** раб**о**ту и узн**а**ть о чуж**и**х пр**а**вилах и об**ы**чаях ж**и**зни.

2 М**о**жно сказ**а**ть, что не существ**у**ет «иде**а**льной» стран**ы**, потом**у** что в к**а**ждом **о**бществе есть сво**и** специф**и**ческие черт**ы**, с кот**о**рыми необход**и**мо смир**и**ться, чт**о**бы пож**и**ть комф**о**ртно.

3 Так**а**я эмигр**а**ция ок**а**жется т**о**лько «вр**е**менной», потом**у** что люб**о**вь к р**о**дине сильн**а** и, в конц**е** конц**о**в, непреодол**и**ма.

4 **О**пыт «вр**е**менного эмигр**а**нта» отлич**а**ется от **о**пыта тур**и**ста тем, что, раб**о**тая в стран**е** м**о**жно узн**а**ть жизнь со сторон**ы**, кот**о**рую не в**и**дят тур**и**сты.

5 Родн**ы**е **и**ли надёжные друзь**я** м**о**гут сыгр**а**ть ос**о**бенно в**а**жную роль в усп**е**хе «вр**е**менного эмигр**а**нта».

M

1 пож**и**в → пож**и**ть

2 д**е**лая → д**е**лать

3 забыв**а**я → забыв**а**ть

4 раб**о**тая → раб**о**тать

5 намерев**а**ясь → намерев**а**ться

N

1 d   2 a   3 f   4 e   5 b   6 c

O

1 self-analysis   4 self-defence

2 independence   5 self-respect

3 self-discipline   6 self-service

P

Model answer

Мо**я** раб**о**та треб**у**ет, чт**о**бы я жил в р**а**зных стр**а**нах, иногд**а** н**е**сколько м**е**сяцев, иногд**а** н**е**сколько лет. Я узн**а**л мн**о**го во вр**е**мя моег**о** пребыв**а**ния за рубеж**о**м. Я узн**а**л **о**чень мн**о**го о м**е**стной культ**у**ре стран, где я побыв**а**л, но с**а**мое гл**а**вное в том, что я п**о**нял, что н**а**до всегд**а** д**е**лать ус**и**лия, чт**о**бы полюб**и**ть сво**ё** местонахожд**е**ние.

Я рекоменд**у**ю все мест**а**, где я жил и раб**о**тал, потом**у** что у них у всех есть сво**и** преим**у**щества. Усл**о**вия ж**и**зни везд**е** в З**а**падной Евр**о**пе прекр**а**сны, а Вост**о**чная Евр**о**па привлек**а**ет сво**и**м б**ы**стрым т**е**мпом разв**и**тия.

Когд**а** я ищ**у** н**о**вое местож**и**тельство мой приорит**е**т в том, чт**о**бы всё б**ы**ло уд**о**бно, интер**е**сно и заг**а**дочно. Все н**о**вые **о**пыты интерес**у**ют мен**я** – н**о**вое всегд**а** д**е**лает жизнь интер**е**сной!

GLOSSARY OF GRAMMATICAL TERMS

active voice When a verb is in the active voice, the subject of the sentence is doing the action: Максим купил мороженое. *Maksim **bought** an ice cream.*

adjectival pronoun A pronoun which changes based on gender, number and case. An example is мой, meaning *my.*

adjective A word that describes a noun and, in Russian, agrees with the noun in gender, number and case.

adverb A word that describes a verb, such as быстро (*quickly*).

agreement Words in Russian are said to agree if they change their endings to show the same gender, number and case. For example, in the phrase в интересном городе, the noun has a prepositional singular ending and the adjective agrees with this masculine noun as it has a masculine, prepositional singular ending.

animate An animate noun in Russian is a person or an animal. These nouns have a different ending in the accusative case in the masculine singular and masculine and feminine plural.

aspect In Russian, every verb belongs to either the imperfective or perfective aspect. Most verbs come in aspectual pairs, with the imperfective verb being used to describe process and/or habitual actions and the perfective verb being used to describe single and/or completed actions.

cardinal numeral This is the number form used for counting. For example: 3, 67 and 34,786.

case Russian nouns, adjectives and pronouns change their endings depending on which case they are in. There are six cases in Russian and each case fulfils a specific function. For example, the nominative case is used for the subject and the accusative case is used for the direct object.

comparative degree This is the comparative form of an adjective or adverb, such as интереснее (*more interesting*).

compound conjunctions These are short, set phrases that are used to link together parts of a sentence. For example: из-за того, что (*due to the fact that*).

conditional mood This is a form of the verb used to talk about hypothetical situations. In Russian, it is always formed with the past tense and the particle бы.

conjugation Every verb follows a certain pattern to form its different tenses, etc. and this is called its conjugation.

declension Every noun, adjective and pronoun follows a certain pattern to form its different endings (gender, case and number) and this pattern is called a declension.

demonstrative pronouns Words such as это (*this*) and то (*that*).

direct object In an active sentence, this is the person, animal or thing having something done to him, her or it, such as я купил машину. – *I bought a car.*

double negative In Russian, using a second negative does not cancel out the first negative. For example: Я ничего ей не подарил means *I **didn't** give her **anything**.*

gender Each noun in Russian is of one of three possible genders in Russian: masculine, feminine or neuter. This affects, for example, the endings of adjectives used to describe nouns: н**о**вый дом (*new house*), н**о**вая кварт**и**ра (*new flat*), н**о**вое зд**а**ние (*new building*).

gerunds These are adverbs that are formed from verbs: сл**у**шая р**а**дио, я улыб**а**лась (*listening to the radio, I smiled*).

hypothetical (impossible) conditions These are conditions that have not happened or are unlikely to happen: **Е**сли бы я съ**е**ла мн**о**го, у мен**я** забол**е**л бы жив**о**т. – *if I had eaten a lot, my stomach would have started hurting.*

imperative This is the command form of a verb.

inanimate An inanimate noun in Russian is any noun that is not a person or an animal.

indirect object In the sentence, Я подар**и**ла цвет**ы** м**а**ме (*I gave the flowers to my **mum***), м**а**ме (*mum*) is the indirect object and цвет**ы** (*flowers*) is the direct object.

indirect speech This is the same as reported speech and is when you say, for example, Он говор**и**л, что ем**у** гр**у**стно. (*He said that he felt sad.*)

indirect statements These are statements involving indirect speech.

infinitive This is the 'to (do)' form of the verb and is the form used in dictionaries. In Russian, the vast majority of infinitives end in -ть.

long form In Russian, adjectives are most commonly used in their long form, with the last two letters changing to agree with the noun that they are describing.

modal expressions These express ability, possibility, permission or obligation and in Russian are often expressed by words such as м**о**жно (*you can/it is possible*), н**а**до (*you must*) or нельз**я** (*you cannot/you must not*).

multidirectional A multidirectional verb of motion, such as ход**и**ть (*to go by foot*), is used if you are describing an action done on many occasions and/or in many directions.

noun This is a word that denotes a person, place, object or concept, such as студ**е**нт (*student*), дом (*house*), окн**о** (*window*) or своб**о**да (*freedom*).

number When discussing agreement in Russian grammar, there are two numbers: singular and plural.

ordinal numeral This is the number form used for showing order: п**е**рвый (*first*) or двадц**а**тый (20th).

passive voice When a verb is in the passive voice, the subject of the sentence is having an action done to them. A sentence where the verb is in the passive voice in English is often conveyed in Russian using a change in word order: Зубн**у**ю п**а**сту прода**ю**т в супермаркете. (*Toothpaste is sold in the supermarket.*)

personal pronoun Words such as я (*I*), он (*he*), с н**и**ми (*with them*).

positive degree the 'standard' adjective (or adverb), such as н**о**вый (*new*), rather than the comparative degree (б**о**лее н**о**вый/нов**е**е – *newer*) or superlative degree (с**а**мый н**о**вый – *newest*).

possessive pronoun A pronoun which indicates possession, such as the adjectival pronoun мой (*my*) or the personal pronoun ег**о** (*his*).

possible conditions These are conditions that could or will happen, such as **Е**сли я ем мн**о**го, у мен**я** бол**и**т жив**о**т. (*If I eat a lot, my stomach hurts.*)

prefix This is a letter or group of letters found at the beginning of words that help identify the meaning of the word. For example, п**е**ре- has the meaning of '*across*' in the nouns перех**о**д (*crossing*) and перев**о**д (*translation*).

preposition A word which shows location or some other relationship between a noun or **pronoun** and other parts of the sentence, such as в (*in/into/to*) or о (*about*).

pronoun A word used to replace a noun: **А**лисон живёт в Манч**е**стере. Он**а** англич**а**нка. (*Alison lives in Manchester. She is English.*)

reflexive pronouns A pronoun used to refer back to, or intensify the importance of, the subject of a sentence: Вад**и**м куп**и**л себ**е** н**о**вую футб**о**лку. (*Vadim bought himself a new T-shirt.*)

reflexive verb A verb which has the ending -ся or -сь and whose basic use is to describe an action where the subject of the verb is doing the action to themselves, such as одев**а**ться (*to dress oneself.*) Reflexive verbs are very common in Russian because they also have other uses.

relative pronoun In Russian, this is кот**о**рый, which is used to give additional information about a noun and is translated into English as *who, whom, which, that* or even omitted altogether.

reported speech See **indirect speech**

short form In Russian, some adjectives are used in certain circumstances in their short form, which agrees in number and gender but is only ever used in the nominative case.

spelling rules In Russian, there are two spelling rules which must always be applied:

> **Rule One:** after the letters ж, ч, ш, щ, г, к and х, the letter ы is never written but replaced by и, the letter я is replaced by а and the letter ю is replaced by у.

> **Rule Two:** о is replaced by е in an unstressed position after ж, ч, ш, щ and ц – for example, the genitive plural form of н**е**мец (*a German man*) is н**е**мцев.

stem This is the part of a word, such as a noun, adjective or verb, to which endings are added to create different forms. For example, the stem of the verb игр**а**ть (*to play*) is игр**а**-.

subject In an active sentence, this is the person, animal or thing doing the action of the verb: for example, солнце св**е**тит (*the sun is shining*).

subjunctive mood This is a form of the verb used to express concepts such as wishes, demands or requests. In Russian, it is always formed with the past tense and the particle бы.

suffix This is a letter or group of letters found at the end of words that help identify the meaning of the word. For example, the suffix -ость normally denotes a concept, such as ув**е**ренность (*confidence, certainty*).

superlative degree This is the superlative form of an adjective or adverb, such as с**а**мый интер**е**сный (*the most interesting*).

tense Unlike English, where there are many different tenses, verbs in Russian can be in one of only three tenses: the past, the present or the future. For example: я игр**а**л (*I played*), я игр**а**ю (*I play*), я б**у**ду игр**а**ть (*I will play*).

unidirectional a unidirectional verb of motion, such as идт**и** (*to go by foot*) is used to describe an action done on one occasion and in one direction.

verb a verb denotes an action or process, such as д**у**мать (*to think*) or существов**а**ть (*to exist*).

verbs of motion In Russian, verbs that denote motion, such as walking, climbing or carrying, have three closely linked infinitives: for example, 'to go by foot' can be expressed by a multidirectional imperfective verb (ход**и**ть), a unidirectional imperfective verb (идт**и**) and **a** perfective verb (пойт**и**). This is acknowledged as one of the hardest aspects of Russian grammar for non-native speakers of the language to grasp.

А

автобиогра́фия	*CV*
автостра́да	*motorway*

анги́на	*tonsillitis*

Б

ба́нка	*can, jar*
бе́гать/бежа́ть/ побежа́ть	*to run*
безогово́рочный	*unconditional*
бесповоро́тный	*irrevocable*
благодаря́ тому́, что	*thanks to*
богослуже́ние	*a church service*

бока́л шампа́нского	*a glass of champagne*
большинство́	*the majority of, most of*
боя́ться	*to fear, to be scared of*
буты́лка	*bottle*
буха́нка	*a loaf*
быть	*to be*

В

в де́тстве	*in childhood*
в мо́лодости	*in younger years*
в отноше́нии	*with regard to*
в ста́рости	*in old age*
в тече́ние	*during*
в то вре́мя как	*while*
ввиду́ того́, что	*in view of the fact that*
вводи́ть/ввести́ вакци́ну	*to administer a vaccine*
вели́кий пост	*Lent*
ве́чером	*in the evening*

ве́чная мерзлота́	*permafrost*
ве́чный ого́нь	*The Eternal Flame*
вме́сто того́, что́бы	*instead of*
води́ть/вести́/повести́	*to lead*
вози́ть/везти́/повезти́	*to carry (by transport)*
встреча́ться/ встре́титься	*to meet (by prearrangement)*
входи́ть/войти́	*to enter*
выходи́ть/вы́йти	*to exit*
вьетна́мки	*flip-flops*

Г

гото́вить/пригото́вить	*to cook*

грибо́к	*fungus*

Д

давно́	*a long time ago*
дальнобо́йщик	*long-distance lorry driver*
Да́льний восто́к	*Far East (of Russia)*
двою́родная сестра́	*cousin (female)*

днём	*during the afternoon*
до (+ gen.)	*before*
до того́, как	*before*
Добро́ пожа́ловать!	*Welcome!*

двою́родный брат	*cousin (male)*	доверя́ть (+ dat.)	*to trust*
де́верь	*husband's brother*	догова́риваться/ договори́ться	*to agree with/on*
демонстра́ция	*march, parade*	до́лжен/должна́	*must*
дерза́ть/дерзну́ть	*to dare*	доста́точно	*enough*
де́ятельность	*activity*	достиже́ние	*achievement*
диабе́т	*diabetes*	дух	*spirit*

Ж

жела́ть/пожела́ть	*to wish*	живопи́сный	*picturesque*
жена́	*wife*	жи́тель	*inhabitant*

З

за (+ асс.)	*(within)*	заседа́ние	*meeting*
заблуди́ться (perf.)	*to lose one's way*	засыпа́ть	*to fall asleep*
заведе́ние	*establishment*	зато́	*on the other hand*
завора́чивать/ заверну́ть пода́рок	*to wrap a present*	заходи́ть/зайти́	*to call in/pop in*
загора́ть (imperfective only)	*to sunbathe*	звони́ть/позвони́ть	*to phone*
зака́зывать/заказа́ть	*to order*	здра́вый смысл	*common sense*
закла́дка	*laying*	знако́миться/ познако́миться	*to get to know*
заключе́ние	*conclusion*	знамени́тость	*celebrity*
замести́тель(ница)	*deputy*	золо́вка	*husband's sister*
занима́ться	*to occupy oneself (with)*	зре́лище	*spectacle*
запреща́ть/запрети́ть	*to ban*	зять	*son-in-law*
зарпла́та	*salary*		

И

изде́лие	*product*	интересова́ться	*to be interested in*
из-за того́, что	*as a result of the fact that*	инфа́ркт	*heart attack*
иму́щество	*property*	иска́ть (imperfective only)	*to look for*
иногда́	*sometimes*	исто́чник	*source*

К

к сожал**е**нию	*unfortunately*
Кавк**аз**	*the Caucasus*
как б**у**дто	*as if*
как м**о**жно ч**а**ще	*as often as possible*
как т**о**лько	*as soon as*
канализ**а**ция	*sewerage*
к**о**е-что	*something*

кол**и**чество	*quantity*
к**о**локол	*a bell*
командир**о**вка	*business trip*
кошм**а**р	*nightmare*
куп**а**льник	*swimsuit*
куп**е**	*two- or four-berth sleeper compartment*
к**у**ртка	*short coat*

Л

л**а**зить/л**е**зть/пол**е**зть	*to climb*
л**е**дник	*iceberg*
лек**а**рство	*medicine*
лет**а**ть/лет**е**ть/ полет**е**ть	*to fly*

лож**и**ться	*to lie down*
лом**а**ться/слом**а**ться	*to break*
люб**о**й	*any*

М

магистр**а**ль	*mainline, highway*
м**а**ло	*not much of*
м**а**чеха	*stepmother*
мечт**а**	*dream*
микрорай**о**н	*(newly developed) area of town*

мне к**а**жется, что	*it seems to me that*
мн**о**го	*lots of, a lot of*
морос**и**ть	*to drizzle*
муж	*husband*

Н

на (+ асс.)	*for (followed by an amount of time in the future)*
на мой взгляд	*in my view*
на нед**е**ле	*in the week*
наводн**е**ние	*flood*
н**а**вык	*skill*
назнач**а**ть/назн**а**чить	*to arrange*
наним**а**ть/нан**я**ть	*to hire*
насто**я**щий	*real, genuine*

нев**е**стка/снох**а**	*daughter-in-law*
нед**а**вно	*recently*
немн**о**го	*few*
непреодол**и**мый	*insurmountable*
неприв**ы**чный	*unaccustomed*
н**е**сколько	*a few*
неуж**е**ли?	*really?*
неч**а**янный	*unintentional*

находить/найти	to find	носить/нести/понести	to carry (on foot)
начинаться	to start, be started	ночью	during the night

О

область	administrative region	осадки	precipitation
обнаруживать/ обнаружить	to discover	освобождаться/ освободиться от (+ gen.)	to free oneself from
обратно	back, return	осматривать/ осмотреть	to look round
обслуживание	service	основатель	founder
обсуждать/обсудить	to discuss	оставлять/оставить	to leave (behind)
обусловленный	conditional upon, dependent on	отдавать/отдать	to give sth. to sb.
обходить/обойти	to go round	отечественный	Russian ('of the Fatherland')
обычай	custom	отличаться	to differ
обычно	usually	отменять/отменить	to cancel
одеваться/одеться	to get dressed	отмечать/отметить	to mark, celebrate
оказываться/ оказаться	to turn out to be	отправляться/ отправиться	to set off
опираться/опереться на (+ acc.)	to lean on, rely on	отчёт	a report
оползень	landslip	отчим	stepfather

П

паводок	flooding	понос	diarrhoea
пасмурно	overcast	поскольку	inasmuch as
пачка	packet	после (+ gen.)	(after)
перед тем, как	just before	после того, как	after
переходить/перейти	to cross	последствие	consequence
питаться (imperfective only)	to eat	постепенно	gradually
плавать/плыть/ поплыть	to swim	потому что	because
платок	headscarf	пояс	belt

плацкартное место	reserved seat/bed in open carriage	предлагать/ предложить	to suggest
племянник	nephew	предприниматель	entrepreneur
племянница	niece	представлять/ представить	to represent
по (+ dat. pl.)	(on … days)	предубеждение	prejudice
по моему мнению	in my opinion	прививка	inoculation
по отношению к (+ dat.)	in relation to	прикладывать/ приложить	to attach sth. to sth.
по ошибке	by mistake	примета	sign, token, omen
по сравнению с (+ instr.)	compared with	приносить/принести	to bring
повседневный	daily	принимать/принять	to receive, accept
повышение	promotion	приходить/прийти	to arrive
подавать/подать заявление	to apply	приходить/прийти в гости	to visit (people)
подменять/подменить	to substitute	прихожая	hall, lobby
подозревать	to suspect	проводить/провести	to spend (time)
подписывать/ подписать	to sign	проводник	conductor
поздравлять/ поздравить	to congratulate/wish	производство	production
пока	while	проливной	torrential
пока не	until	промышленник	industrialist
показывать/показать	to show sth. to sb.	просыпаться/ проснуться	to wake up
ползать/ползти/ поползти	to crawl	проходить/пройти	to go through
полярный круг	Arctic Circle	пустыня	desert
по-моему	in my opinion		

Р

работать	to work (as)	распространённый	widespread
радовать/обрадовать	to please	расчёт	estimate
разве?	really?	регистрироваться/ зарегистрироваться	to register

раздавать/раздать	to give out, distribute	редко	rarely
разрабатывать/ разработать	to develop	рекомендовать	to recommend sth. to sb.
раскрашенное яйцо	a decorated/painted egg	рецепт	prescription
распределять/ распределить	to assign, to send; distribute	решение	decision

С

с (+ gen.) ... до (+ gen.) ...	(from ... until ...)	совладелец	co-owner
с Новым Годом!	Happy New Year!	сопротивляемость	resistance, opposition
с тех пор, как	since	соревнование	competition
садиться/сесть	to sit down	сосед	neighbour
садиться/сесть	to take a seat; to get on (transport)	соскальзывать/ соскользнуть	to slip off
санузел	bathroom/toilet	составлять/составить	to constitute
свёкор	husband's father	сосулька	icicle
свекровь	husband's mother	социальные сети	social networks
сверхъестественный	supernatural	спешить	to hurry
светофор	traffic lights	список	list
свидетель	witness	справляться/ справиться с (+ instr.)	to cope with
сводная сестра	half -/stepsister	спрашивать/спросить	to ask
сводный брат	half -/stepbrother	сразу	straight away
свояченица	wife's sister	сталкиваться/ столкнуться с (+ instr.)	to collide with, come up against
сейчас	(right) now	становиться/стать	to become
селёдка под шубой	'herring under a fur coat'	стараться/постараться	to try to
Сибирь	Siberia	статья	article
скачивать/скачать	to download	стопочка	a shot glass
сколько?	how many?	суеверие	superstition
скорая помощь	ambulance	супруга	spouse
скучать	to miss	сутки	24-hour period

словно	*just like*	сходить (perf.)	*to make a trip to (on foot)*
СМИ	*mass media*	счастливого пути!	*bon voyage!*
снежный покров	*blanket of snow*	считаться	*to be considered*
собственность	*property, ownership*	съезд	*(motorway) exit*
событие	*event*	съездить (perf.)	*to make a trip to (by transport)*

Т

так как	*as, since*	тогда, как	*whilst*
так что	*and so*	торговаться (imperfective only)	*to haggle*
таяние	*melting*	тормозить/ затормозить	*to brake*
телеведущий	*television presenter*	триктрак	*backgammon*
терять/потерять	*to lose*	туча	*raincloud*
тесть	*wife's father*	тяжёлый	*heavy*
тёща	*wife's mother*		

У

увлекаться	*to enjoy*	устанавливать/ установить	*to establish*
удивляться/удивиться	*to be surprised*	утром	*in the morning*
удобный	*convenient*	уходить/уйти	*to leave*
ураган	*hurricane*	участвовать	*to take part in sth.*
Урал	*the Urals*	ушиб	*a bruise, an injury*
успех	*success*		

Ф

фабрикант	*manufacturer*

Х

характеристика	*reference*	хотя бы	*at least*

Ц

целоваться	*to kiss each other*

ч

ча́сто	*often*	че́рез (+ acc.)	*(in/after a period of time)*
частушка	*chastushka (a four-line ditty)*	что каса́ется	*as far as … is concerned*
чепуха́	*nonsense*		

ш

шторм	*gale*	шу́рин	*wife's brother*

я

я ду́маю, что	*I think that*	явле́ние	*occurrence, phenomenon*
я счита́ю, что	*I consider that*	явля́ться	*to be*